The Promise of Friendship

SUNY series in Contemporary Continental Philosophy
―――――――
Dennis J. Schmidt, editor

The Promise of Friendship

Fidelity within Finitude

SARAH HORTON

Published by State University of New York Press, Albany

© 2023 State University of New York

All rights reserved

Printed in the United States of America

No part of this book may be used or reproduced in any manner whatsoever without written permission. No part of this book may be stored in a retrieval system or transmitted in any form or by any means including electronic, electrostatic, magnetic tape, mechanical, photocopying, recording, or otherwise without the prior permission in writing of the publisher.

For information, contact State University of New York Press, Albany, NY
www.sunypress.edu

Library of Congress Cataloging-in-Publication Data

Name: Horton, Sarah, 1992– author.
Title: The promise of friendship : fidelity within finitude / Sarah Horton.
Description: Albany : State University of New York Press, [2023] | Series: SUNY series in contemporary continental philosophy | Includes bibliographical references and index.
Identifiers: LCCN 2023002662 | ISBN 9781438495156 (hardcover : alk paper) | ISBN 9781438495170 (ebook) | ISBN 9781438495163 (pbk. : alk. paper)
Subjects: LCSH: Friendship.
Classification: LCC BF575.F66 H675 2023 | DDC 177/.62—dc23/eng/20230707
LC record available at https://lccn.loc.gov/2023002662

10 9 8 7 6 5 4 3 2 1

To my friends

Contents

Acknowledgments	ix
Abbreviations	xi
Introduction: Can One Write of Friendship?	1
Chapter 1 At the Origins of Friendship: Initial Displacements	7
Chapter 2 The Ethical Challenge of Friendship	31
Chapter 3 Within Finitude, Bearing the Infinite	63
Chapter 4 The Writing of Friendship: Reading Proust's *In Search of Lost Time*	89
Chapter 5 Fidelity in the Dark: On Presence and Knowledge	123
Chapter 6 The Creation of Impossible Friendship	141
Conclusion: Risking Friendship in the Twenty-First Century	167
Notes	173
Bibliography	197
Index	203

Acknowledgments

The act of writing, I will argue, is an act of friendship—and it does not arise ex nihilo but is summoned, unforeseeably, by the Other. Here, therefore, I wish to express my gratitude to all those who have shaped this book and supported me in completing it. I thank Richard Kearney for his mentorship, his comments on previous versions of this text, and the guidance he has provided since this project began. As one of his students, I have learned more than I can say from his approach to philosophy, and this book would not exist without him. I am grateful as well to Kevin Newmark for his comments and for our discussions of Derrida and of French literature, without which I could not have written the chapter on Proust or the material on Derrida; to Vanessa Rumble for her comments and for our discussions that informed my approach to Kierkegaard and thus also to the entire question of writing; and to Emmanuel Falque for his comments, for our discussions that led me to see the importance of finitude, and for welcoming me to Paris in 2019–2020. My thanks to Michael Rinella, SUNY's acquisitions editor in philosophy, and Dennis J. Schmidt, the series editor, for their support of this book, and to three anonymous reviewers for their comments. On July 26, 2021, I presented a version of chapter 2 at the 16th Annual International Conference of the North American Levinas Society, and I thank the participants for their comments. I thank my parents, Joseph and Joanna Horton, for actually encouraging me to go into philosophy, and I am also grateful for my mom's careful proofreading of every page of this text. I also thank Laura Booher Gearhart, Laura Burdick, Melissa Fitzpatrick, Jasmine Ho, Camille Kennedy, Katherine Manansala, Stephen Mendelsohn, Christine Rojcewicz, Michaela Sobrak-Seaton, Cathy Trammell, and Zachary Willcutt for many long discussions, on matters explicitly philosophical and otherwise. Melissa Fitzpatrick helped convince me that Levinasian ethics does not entail a rejection of friendship, and Michaela Sobrak-Seaton read and commented on my analysis of Edith Stein on empathy.

Thank you to all of you.

Abbreviations

Whenever I have referenced a text in both the original language and the English translation, the first page number refers to the original-language text, and the second to the English translation. When no translation is specified, the translation is my own.

All references not given here are found in the bibliography.

Aelred of Rievaulx

SF: *Spiritual Friendship*, edited by Marsha L. Dutton. Translated by Lawrence C. Braceland. Collegeville, MN: Liturgical Press, 2010.

Aristotle

EE: *Eudemian Ethics*. Translated and edited by Brad Inwood and Raphael Woolf. Cambridge: Cambridge University Press, 2013.

NE: *Nicomachean Ethics*. Translated by Robert C. Bartlett and Susan D. Collins. Chicago: University of Chicago Press, 2011.

Benjamin, Walter

TT: "Die Aufgabe der Übersetzers." In *Gesammelte Schriften*, vol. IV–1, 9–21. Frankfurt am Main: Suhrkamp, 1972. "The Task of the Translator." Translated by Harry Zohn. In *Selected Writings: 1913–1926*, vol. 1, edited by Marcus Bullock and Michael W. Jennings, 253–63. Cambridge: Belknap Press, 1996.

Benveniste, Émile

D: *Le vocabulaire des institutions européennes 1: Économie, parenté, société*. Paris: Les Éditions de Minuit, 1969. *Dictionary of Indo-European Concepts and Society*. Translated by Elizabeth Palmer. Chicago: HAU Books, 2016.

de Man, Paul

C: "'Conclusions': Walter Benjamin's 'The Task of the Translator.'" In *The Resistance to Theory*, 73–105. Minneapolis: University of Minnesota Press, 1989.

Derrida, Jacques

GD: *Donner la mort*. Paris: Galilée, 1999. *The Gift of Death and Literature in Secret*. Translated by David Wills. 2nd ed. Chicago: University of Chicago Press, 2008.

H: *De l'hospitalité: Anne Dufourmantelle invite Jacques Derrida à répondre*. Paris: Calmann-Lévy, 1997. *Of Hospitality: Anne Dufourmantelle Invites Jacques Derrida to Respond*. Translated by Rachel Bowlby. Stanford: Stanford University Press, 2000.

HE: "L'oreille de Heidegger: Philopolémologie (*Geschlecht* IV)." In *Politiques de l'amitié suivi de L'oreille de Heidegger*, 341–419. Paris: Galilée, 1994. "Heidegger's Ear: Philopolemology (*Geschlecht* IV). Translated by John P. Leavey, Jr. In *Reading Heidegger: Commemorations*, edited by John Sallis, 163–218. Bloomington: Indiana University Press, 1993.

PF: *Politique de l'amitié*. Paris: Galilée, 1994. *The Politics of Friendship*. Translated by George Collins. New York: Verso, 2005.

R: *Béliers: Le dialogue ininterrompu: entre deux infinis, le poème*. Paris: Galilée, 2003. "Rams: Uninterrupted Dialogue—Between Two Infinities, the Poem." In *Sovereignties in Question*, edited by Thomas Dutoit and Outi Pasanen, 135–63. New York: Fordham University Press, 2005.

Descartes, René

M: *Meditationes de prima philosophia.* In *Œuvres*, vol. VII, edited by Adam and Tannery. Paris: Cerf, 1904. *Meditations on First Philosophy.* In *The Philosophical Writings of Descartes.* Translated by John Cottingham, Robert Stoothoff, and Dugald Murdoch. Cambridge: Cambridge University Press, 1984.

Falque, Emmanuel

CRB: *Passer le Rubicon: Philosophie et théologie.* Brussels: Lessius, 2013. *Crossing the Rubicon: The Borderlands of Philosophy and Theology.* Translated by Reuben Shank. New York: Fordham University Press, 2016.

GG: *Le Passeur de Gethsémani.* 1999. Reprinted in *Triduum philosophique*, 17–163. Paris: Cerf, 2015. *The Guide to Gethsemane.* Translated by George Hughes. New York: Fordham University Press, 2019.

MF: *Métamorphose de la finitude.* 2004. Reprinted in *Triduum philosophique*, 165–363. Paris: Cerf, 2015. *The Metamorphosis of Finitude.* Translated by George Hughes. New York: Fordham University Press, 2012.

TE: "Éthique du corps épandu." *Revue d'éthique et de théologie morale* 1, no. 288 (2016): 53–82. "Toward an Ethics of the Spread Body." Translated by Christina Gschwandtner. In *Somatic Desire: Recovering Corporeality in Contemporary Thought*, edited by Sarah Horton, Stephen Mendelsohn, Christine Rojcewicz, and Richard Kearney, 91–116. Lanham, MD: Lexington Books, 2019.

Heidegger, Martin

GA 3: *Kant und das Problem der Metaphysik*, edited by Friedrich-Wilhelm von Herrmann. GA 3. Frankfurt am Main: Vittorio Klostermann, 1991. *Kant and the Problem of Metaphysics.* 5th ed., translated by Richard Taft. Bloomington: Indiana University Press, 1997.

GA 11: "Was ist das—die Philosophie?" In *GA 11, Identität und Differenz*, edited by Friedrich-Wilhelm von Herrmann, 3–26. Frankfurt am Main: Vittorio Klostermann, 2006. *What Is Philosophy?* Translated by William Kluback and Jean T. Wilde. New Haven: College & University Press, 1956.

GA 55: *Heraklit: 1. Der Anfang des abendländischen Denkens, 2. Logik. Heraklits Lehre vom Logos*, edited by Manfried S. Frings. GA 55. Frankfurt am Main: Vittorio Klostermann, 1979. *Heraclitus: The Inception of Occidental Thinking and Logic: Heraclitus' Doctrine of the Logos.* Translated by Julia Goesser Assaiante and S. Montgomery Ewegen. London: Bloomsbury, 2018.

Levinas, Emmanuel

EI: *Éthique et infini: Dialogues avec Philippe Nemo.* 1982. Reprint, Paris: Fayard, 2004. *Ethics and Infinity: Conversations with Philippe Nemo.* Translated by Richard A. Cohen. Pittsburgh: Duquesne University Press, 1989.

EN: *Entre nous: Essais sur le penser-à-l'autre.* 1991. Reprint, Paris: Grasset, 2016. *Entre nous: Thinking of the Other.* Translated by Michael B. Smith and Barbara Harshav. New York: Columbia University Press, 1998.

OB: *Autrement qu'être ou au-delà de l'essence.* 1978. Reprint, Paris: Kluwer Academic, 2011. *Otherwise than Being or Beyond Essence.* Translated by Alphonso Lingis. 1991. Reprint, Pittsburgh: Duquesne University Press, 2006.

TI: *Totalité et infini: Essai sur l'extériorité.* 1961. Reprint, Paris: Kluwer Academic, 2012. *Totality and Infinity.* Translated by Alphonso Lingis. Pittsburgh: Duquesne University Press, 1969.

Marcel, Gabriel

CF: "La Fidélité créatrice." In *Essai de philosophie concrète*, 220–59. Paris: Gallimard, 1940. "Creative Fidelity." In *Creative Fidelity*, 147–74. Translated by Robert Rosthal. New York: Fordham University Press, 2002.

TMF: "Le Mystère familial." In *Homo viator: Prolégomènes à une métaphysique de l'espérance*, 95–132. Aubier: Éditions Montaigne, 1944. "The Mystery of the Family." In *Homo Viator: Introduction to a Metaphysic of Hope*, 68–97. Translated by Emma Craufurd. 1951. Reprint, Gloucester, MA: Peter Smith, 1978.

Merleau-Ponty, Maurice

PP: *Phénoménologie de la perception*. Paris: Gallimard, 1945. *Phenomenology of Perception*. Translated by Donald A. Landes. New York: Routledge, 2012.

VI: Merleau-Ponty, Maurice. *Le Visible et l'Invisible*. Paris: Gallimard, 1964. *The Visible and the Invisible*. Translated by Alphonso Lingis. Evanston: Northwestern University Press, 1968.

Montaigne, Michel de

E: *Essais*. First published 1580. In *Œuvres complètes*, 1–1907. Edited by Maurice Rat and Albert Thibaudet. Paris: Pléiade, 1963. *Essays*. Translated by John M. Cohen. 1958. Reprint, London: Penguin Books, 1993.

Plato

L: *Lysis*. Translated by Stanley Lombardo. In *Plato: Complete Works*, edited by John M. Cooper, 687–707. Indianapolis: Hackett, 1997.

T: *Theaetetus*. Translated by Joe Sachs. Indianapolis: Hackett, 2004.

Proust, Marcel

S: *À la recherche du temps perdu*. Edited by Jean-Yves Tadié. 4 vols. 1913–1927. Reprint, Paris: Pléiade, 1987. *In Search of Lost Time*. Translated by C.K. Scott Moncrieff and Terence Kilmartin. Translation revised by D. J. Enright. 6 vols. 1981. Reprint, New York: Modern Library, 2003.

Ricœur, Paul

    CR: *Parcours de la reconnaissance*. Paris: Stock, 2004. *The Course of Recognition*. Translated by David Pellauer. Cambridge: Harvard University Press, 2005.

    OT: *Sur la traduction*. Paris: Bayard, 2004. *On Translation*. Translated by Eileen Brennan. New York: Routledge, 2006.

Stein, Edith

    PE: *Zum Problem der Einfühlung*. Halle: Buchdruckerei des Waisenhauses, 1917. *On the Problem of Empathy*. 3rd ed., translated by Waltraut Stein. First published 1964. Washington, DC: ICS Publications, 1989.

Thomas Aquinas

    ST: *Summa Theologica*. Translated by the Fathers of the English Dominican Province. Christian Classics Ethereal Library. https://www.ccel.org/ccel/aquinas/summa.i.html.s.

Introduction

Can One Write of Friendship?

The question "What is friendship?" is, to say the least, overdetermined. Behind the word "friendship" lies a host of cultural assumptions and debates. On the one hand, "friend" often seems, in common parlance, to mean little more than "acquaintance" or, at best, "person whose company I currently happen to find pleasant," with no deeper sense of commitment. On the other hand, the fears that twenty-first-century Americans in particular use the word "friend" far too readily and that social media is spreading a facile conception of friendship show that the notion of friends as deeply committed to each other, even for their entire lives, remains an ideal. The ease with which we can "friend" people on Facebook is alarming only if we suspect that the name of "friend" ought to mean something more profound—but criticizing shallow notions of friendship is far simpler than discovering whatever more profound sense it might have. Op-eds pointing out that Facebook "friends" are often not real friends and advising us not to mistake shallow social media relationships for genuine friendships are commonplace, almost to the point of being cliché, yet we still struggle to determine what, exactly, friendship might be. Might it be the case, however, that this struggle is not simply a product of twenty-first-century alienation and atomization but is essential to any attempt to speak of friendship? Might not wrestling with the question "What is friendship?" involve from the start a certain alienation insofar as friendship challenges the self's powers of knowledge and comprehension? For even those we dare to name "friends" are profoundly Other than ourselves, and we can never know precisely what will result from a long-lasting commitment.

Indeed, I can scarcely think of a better beginning for a discussion of friendship than a passage from Charles Baudelaire's prose poem "The Stranger" that calls into question our very ability to know what friends might be:

> Whom do you love best, enigmatic man, your father, your mother, your sister, or your brother?
> I have neither father, nor mother, nor sister, nor brother.
> Your friends?
> Now you are using a word whose sense has remained unknown to me unto this day.[1]

Significantly, Baudelaire's "enigmatic man" does not deny having friends; rather, he denies knowing the meaning of the word "friend." He implicitly claims to know what a father is, what a mother is, what a sister is, what a brother is, for he confidently asserts that he has none, but this confidence disappears when it comes to friendship. Perhaps he does have friends even though he does not know the sense of the word; in any case, we cannot exclude this possibility before considering what relation holds between knowing what "friend" means and actually having friends. Is it possible that having friends does not depend on knowing the definition of the word? Is it even possible, perhaps, that friendship is indefinable? Friendship, if it takes place at all, may take place beyond any possibility of definition.

This suggestion that friendship is beyond definition calls to mind the cry attributed to Aristotle, cited by Michel de Montaigne, who is in his turn cited by Jacques Derrida throughout his *Politics of Friendship*: "O my friends, there is no friend" (PF 17/1)—a paradoxical exclamation that calls out to *friends*, plural, while denying the *friend*, singular. The *singularity* of the friend thus seems at once essential to friendship—for how can there be friends if indeed there is no friend?—and yet forever unknowable, as the singular is precisely that which cannot be circumscribed within or referred to the general. And if it is true that friendship cannot be thought apart from singularity, investigating friendship cannot be a matter of giving a definition that would treat *friend* as the name of a genus. Furthermore, supposing that friendship does take place, or that it can meaningfully be said to take place, claiming the ability to define friendship would be incompatible with friendship insofar as such a claim would amount to an attempt to subsume the singular friend under a general category. Baudelaire's "enigmatic man" who confesses that he does not know what "friends" means, who does not even repeat this unknown word, may thus be closer to friendship than the questioner who takes knowledge of the word's meaning for granted.

In short, not only is it insufficient to simply ask what friendship is, but such a question already assumes that friendship is both possible and definable. This book seeks rather, therefore, to attend to this question and to the ways it must be complicated. Yet to circumscribe the discussion, and even to begin it at all, it is necessary to make certain assumptions about what sort of relationship is under investigation. Accordingly, let us suppose that this investigation concerns the character and possibility of a lasting, committed relation between two people—the sort of relation that might be named the most complete friendship—without, however, excluding the possibility of having multiple friends, including friends who are friends of each other, such that there may be a group of more than two people, all of whom are friends. In addition, it seems that friends know each other well, though it will be especially important to investigate the sense in which that is true. Friendship seems to entail a commitment to and love for the other that is not found in merely political relations; indeed, insofar as friendship is a deeper commitment than citizenship, friendship risks destabilizing the political realm. The complex place of friendship in relation to the political will require considerable examination: from Aristotle onward, friendship has often been taken as the foundation of civic life, yet it also seems to be a private relation that stands apart from the political. Friendship differs from familial relationships in that one cannot help being someone's relative, whereas one is not simply born into a friendship, though this is not to say that relatives cannot also be friends. At the same time, friendship is not merely arbitrary: it is not brought into existence by one person's sudden whim, nor does true friendship dissolve, as one must remain faithful to the friend even beyond the friend's death. Friendship differs from eros as well, for friendship contains no sexual element: friends qua friends neither become nor desire to become one flesh. It does not follow that people cannot both be friends and be in an erotic relationship, but even in that case, friendship and eros are different.[2] Friendship is, crucially, not a prelude to eros or otherwise a form of eros, nor is it in any way inferior to eros. Indeed, because it does not seek even a unity of the flesh, friendship stands as a unique sign of singularity and difference.

The preceding statements are preliminary remarks meant to open a way for further questioning. It bears noting that the initial problem this investigation of friendship faces—namely, that it must find some comparatively fixed starting point to begin yet thereby betrays, right from the start, the possibility that friendship cannot be thus fixed—is analogous to the problem of fidelity to the friend. For perfect fidelity would seem to require perfect understanding of the friend, yet claiming perfect understanding would itself be a betrayal of the friend's unknowability. Just as one who discourses on friendship betrays friendship, so too one always betrays the friend. Even if one cannot be perfectly faithful to the friend, however, refusing to attempt friendship is still further from fidelity than is attempting friendship imperfectly. Likewise, the only alternative to inadequate speech is total silence, and falling into absolute silence through an excessive fear of betrayal may be a greater betrayal of friendship than speaking of it. As Derrida observes in "Violence and Metaphysics," his response to Levinas's *Totality and Infinity*, "the philosopher (man) must speak and write within this war of light, a war in which he always already knows himself to be engaged; a war which he knows is inescapable, except by denying discourse, that is, by risking the worst violence" (173/117). This remark should be read not as a condemnation of philosophy but as an acknowledgment that there is no alternative to philosophizing within language. The self always already relates to the Other through language, and so, as dangerous as speaking and writing are, refusing to speak or write at all amounts to refusing any relation to the Other.

This book is a continuous wrestling with the joint dangers of, on the one hand, speaking too readily of friendship and the friend and, on the other, failing to speak at all for fear of speaking inadequately. Thus the interrelation of betrayal and fidelity is a crucial question throughout. Chapter 1 considers selected ancient and medieval examinations of friendship in order to clarify friendship's unstable place in the borderlands of hostility and hospitality and concludes that friendship, if it is to bind people into a community, must also shatter open any community in which they believe themselves to be comfortably at home. Chapter 2 further explores, in light of Emmanuel Levinas's ethics, the potential conflict between friendship and one's obligation to others. Investigating why friendship is good despite its dangers, chapter 3 then argues that friends translate the world for each other, and translation can never be perfectly faithful—but only within the finitude that renders perfect fidelity impossible can friendship take place at all. Chapter 4 takes up the suggestion, raised in Marcel Proust's *In Search of Lost Time*, that friendship is an illusion because, as the narrator of the *Search* claims, it pretends to offer knowledge of another even though such knowledge is impossible. Careful attention to the text of the *Search* reveals, however, that writing itself functions as an act of friendship and that true friendship is a relation across absence. Pursuing the notions of absence and presence, chapter 5 argues that one's knowledge of one's friend is always grounded in a deeper non-knowledge, for in the encounter with another, the self is called into question and dispossessed of itself. One never knows what will come of the promise. Finally, chapter 6 shows that the promise of friendship creates the self and the world that the self is called to translate for the friend. I conclude that although one can never achieve perfect fidelity to the friend, this is no reason to despair of fidelity: the very infidelity of the self's witness to the friend may still faithfully bear witness to the friend's irreplaceability. Certainly friendship remains a risk, but it is a risk to be undertaken in gratitude and joy, for friendship is a great good of our existence within finitude.

Over the course of these chapters, I seek to explore the productive tension between a phenomenological study of the conditions of possibility of friendship and a study of its impossibility—a study, that is, of the limits of any attempt to consider friendship as a phenomenon. I therefore consider how that which we call friendship emerges within human existence, while also highlighting the way it always exceeds and calls into question phenomenal expression. In other words, this analysis is focused on the hinge around which possibility and impossibility are articulated. Declaring that friendship is impossible might seem a natural response to the impossibility of perfect fidelity, yet such a claim would assume, just as much as the assertion that it is possible, that friendship is some definite *thing* of whose possibility we can speak, and we therefore can conclude neither that it is simply impossible nor that it is simply possible. Friendship is possible insofar as one admits that it is impossible: it is possible for those who love that the Other remains unknowable. Ultimately, inquiring into the character and possibility of friendship compels us to confront the limits of language and the horizons of human existence.

This book is thus inscribed on the one hand within the return to what one might call "human issues," to the study of self and other as *persons*, a return Paul Ricœur notably calls for in *Oneself as Another* when he deplores "the loss of [the] relation [of the problematic of the self] to the person who speaks, to the I-you [*Je-tu*] of interlocution, to the identity of a historical person, to the self of responsibility" (22/11)—a loss that began with the Cartesian cogito but that, Ricœur argues, the Nietzschean rejection of the cogito did not repair (see 11–38/1–26, "Introduction: The Question of Selfhood"). On the other hand, however, this study of friendship leads us beyond the sphere of the strictly human to that of language and languages. The impossible fidelity of friendship reveals itself also in the attempt to be faithful when translating, or even when writing in one's native tongue. Indeed, I argue that friendship is translation, and translation between languages is but one manifestation of translation. Friendship is thus essential to human life yet not exclusively human: translation between languages, and also writing within a single language, is an act of friendship.

As I seek to write of friendship, therefore, I also aim to bear in mind Maurice Blanchot's remark in *Friendship* that "friendship [. . .] passes by way of the recognition of the common strangeness that does not allow us to speak of our friends but only to speak to them, not to make them a topic of conversations (or essays), but the movement of understanding in which, speaking to us, they reserve, even on the most familiar terms, an infinite distance" (328/291). If what I have written may be a call and testimony to the friend, it will indeed be so only across "an infinite distance," the distance that marks the gift of a text that says at once less and more than I meant to say. For friendship always remains ultimately a secret, to some degree out of reach of the political, the general, the universal, and so this text, in seeking to write of friendship, falls short; yet insofar as it may be an act of friendship, this text is itself a secret that its author cannot comprehend wholly. This latter point is not an excuse for its failings, whatever they are; yet neither do its failings stand as a condemnation of its undertaking. I offer this text, without wholly knowing what I give or what will come of the gift, in the hope that its very failure to adequately testify to the friend may yet testify to the greatness of the secret.

1

At the Origins of Friendship

Initial Displacements

If indeed writing itself is or can be an act of friendship, then it does not suffice merely to ask what friendship is, for such a question deliberately seeks to stand outside its object rather than to enact it. Moreover, the question assumes that friendship can be taken as an object, yet the supposition that a relation between subjects can justly be regarded from an objective third-person standpoint is a dubious one. We can hardly assume that we know what a relation between subjects is—describing friendship in these enigmatic terms if anything makes further questioning all the more necessary—but we would do well to suspect that taking friendship as an object is in some way a violation. Thus if we claim to interrogate friendship, we face from the outset a difficulty like that Martin Heidegger describes in "What Is Philosophy?": "When we ask, 'What is philosophy?' then we are speaking *about* philosophy. By asking in this way we are obviously taking a stand above and, therefore, outside of philosophy. But the aim of our question is to enter *into* philosophy, to tarry in it, to conduct ourselves in its manner, that is, to 'philosophize'" (GA 11 7/21). So too if we wish to enter into friendship we have, if not to rephrase the question, then at least to think it otherwise. Let us turn, therefore, not to friendship itself but to its place, or rather to its way or path that displaces. Heidegger declares that "the Greek word *philosophia* is a way along which we are underway" (GA 11, 9/29, trans. mod.), and while we must bear in mind that *friendship* and *philosophia* are not simply synonymous—though it is ill-advised to discuss one without acknowledging the other—thinking friendship as a way along which we are always already displaced will compel us to bear certain key points in mind. First, friendship is not a mere object to be taken; if anything, it takes us. Second, and consequently, this investigation cannot properly be held at a distance from its subject matter. Finally, the place of friendship is rather a no-place: it cannot simply be localized and made present.

This exploration of the place or no-place of friendship begins with a return to certain ancient and medieval examinations of friendship to show that there is no point of origin at which friendship was simply present. The point is not to undertake a genealogical or historical analysis but rather to consider key moments that might each be taken as an attempt to assign friendship a definite place and of which any contemporary discussion of friendship must count itself an heir: the etymological origins of the word *philos*; Aristotle's treatment of *philia* in the *polis*; Thomas Aquinas's and Aelred's analyses of *amicitia* in the kingdom of God; and, finally, *philosophia* itself. Each time, it turns out that friendship is always already a danger and a displacing. Certainly the terms *philia*, *amicitia*, and *friendship* are not synonymous, but examining the particular sort of risk marked with the names *philia* or *amicitia* will reveal much about the risk marked with the name *friendship*—a risk that arises from friendship's place or no-place in the borderlands of hostility and hospitality. Friendship has often been valorized as the relation that upholds and even grounds the broader community: thus for Aristotle *philia* grounds the *polis*, and for Thomas Aquinas *amicitia* is the place where love becomes the *caritas* that extends to all of humanity. But grounding community and threatening community are not so easy to separate, for only the dispossession of ipseity can open it to alterity. The challenge is not only that friendship can in practice never be free of hostility but that if friendship is possible, it is possible only between strangers, not citizens secure in their ipseity—and so to bind people into a community it must also shatter open any community in which the so-called citizens believe themselves to be comfortably at home.

The Dangers of *Philotes*

Indeed, upon examining the term *philos*, we find not a stable origin in which *philia* can be safely grounded but rather an originary deferral. The bond between *philoi* is inscribed within the dangerous interplay between hospitality and hostility, which no law can fully tame. Consider Émile Benveniste's account of the word *philos* in the Homeric era, according to which *philos* initially referred to a binding, reciprocal commitment of hospitality: "the notion of *philos* expresses the behavior incumbent on a member of the community towards a *xenos*, the 'guest-stranger' [*l' 'hôte' étranger*]" (D 341/278).[1] Here we are far removed from the notion of a private emotional bond that characterizes contemporary understandings of friendship; neither, however, is this sense of *philos* that of Aristotle, who thinks it primarily in the context of fellow citizens of the *polis* and not in that of hospitality offered to the foreigner, the *xenos*. In the pre-Aristotelian, Homeric world, explains Benveniste, the bond between *philoi* is a legal relation established between a citizen who welcomes a stranger on the condition that this stranger submit himself to certain laws. Hence *philoi* are established as such by a particular sort of transaction—one that claims to preserve the boundaries of the community by obliging the stranger to prove that he is not a danger by submitting to the requirements of the bond. As this bond between *philoi* thus privileges the citizen's ipseity over the stranger's alterity, one can see how this understanding of the *philos* could eventually lead to Aristotle's account of *philia* in which the *xenos* no longer has an obvious place.

But of course things are not that simple. The citizen's ipseity is already conditioned by the other, after all, for what is a citizen if not one who exists within certain borders that exclude others? By their very attempt to secure ipseity, the borders of the *polis* testify that ipseity cannot be taken for granted. Benveniste writes that "[the *xénos*] finds no welcome, no lodging and no guarantee except in the house of the man with whom he is in a relation of *phílotēs*, a relation materially expressed in the *súmbolon*, the sign of recognition [*reconnaissance*], a broken ring whose matching halves were kept by the parties to the relationship. The pact concluded in the name of *phílotēs* makes the contracting parties *phíloi*: they are henceforth committed to a reciprocity of services which constitute 'hospitality'" (D 341/278, trans. mod.). From its very origins, the name of *philos* signs an attempt to demarcate the unstable boundary between hostility and hospitality by determining when each is a legitimate response to the stranger. *Philotes* is an explicitly legal and contractual relation that indicates that a particular stranger must be welcomed by a particular citizen and must himself serve as host should their positions be reversed. Others, who are not so bound, may and likely will be hostile to that stranger. Thus while alterity receives a certain recognition, citizens keep the upper hand because most of them remain free to reject or outright harm the stranger, even if he is in need. Significantly, however, this bond between *philoi* is symbolized by a rupture in the form of the breaking of the *sumbolon*:[2] although the rupture binds only two, the reciprocity inherent in their commitment serves as a reminder that each one is a potential stranger, that even someone who is now at home may yet become a *xenos*. The specter of strangeness, of foreignness, haunts each *philos*, and thereby alterity reappears at the heart of the very relation of *philotes* meant to domesticate it. The halves of the *sumbolon* mark an ipseity that was always already unstable, even to the point of breaking. No one, however secure in his citizenship he appears to be, can rest assured that he will never find himself a stranger.

At the same time, the broken *sumbolon* warns that hospitality too may break, that the limited hospitality offered to a *philos* is not so far removed from hostility as one might suppose. Because this hospitality is granted only to the one who bears the other half of the *sumbolon*, the Same, to borrow a Levinasian turn of phrase, remains hostile to the Other insofar as the Same decides which Others may be received. For that matter, the *philoi* bound by *philotes* may even be enemies: Benveniste points out that Ajax and Hector establish between themselves a bond of *philotes* to mark their "agreement to break off the combat for the time being by mutual consent and to resume it at a more favorable moment" (D 343/280, trans. mod.). Thus the hospitality required by *philotes* only limits, rather than ruling out, hostility between *philoi*—and even if the *philoi* are not enemies, the fact that they must explicitly pledge themselves to a certain hospitality suggests that hostility is normal and hospitality the exception. As Derrida explains, contrasting absolute hospitality with hospitality by right, "this right to hospitality offered to a foreigner 'as a family,' represented and protected by his or her family name, is at once what makes hospitality possible, or the hospitable relationship to the foreigner possible, but by the same token what limits and prohibits it" (H 27/23–25). The stranger has a right to hospitality only by virtue of a certain legal status that he is granted solely because his hosts recognize his family name and because he submits himself to the language and laws of the community. In contrast, a true stranger, one who is nameless, who cannot speak the language, who is ignorant of the laws, is "therefore treated not as a foreigner but as a barbarian other [*un autre barbare*]" (H 29/25, trans. mod.). Indeed, the *xenos* is not the *barbaros*, and the latter is excluded from the start. Hospitality by right, limited hospitality, is inseparable from that hostility from which the bond of *philotes* protects only the stranger who is not too strange. Hence it falls far short of the absolute hospitality that places no demand whatsoever on the other whose appeal comes in an unknown language, who gives no name, who is unrecognizable: "absolute hospitality requires that I open up my home [*chez-moi*] and that I give not only to the foreigner (equipped with a family name, with the social status of being a foreigner, etc.), but to the absolute, unknown, anonymous other [. . .] without asking of them either reciprocity (entering into a pact) or even their names. The law of absolute hospitality commands a break with hospitality by right, with law or justice as rights" (H 29/25). Absolute hospitality is a surrender of one's rights for the sake of another who may not be grateful, who may even be the very sort of outsider the laws were meant to keep out. It is the renunciation of ipseity's claims to priority. It is the refusal to prefer the recognizable stranger to the absolutely other. And it is most assuredly a risk. The request for reciprocity is an admission of one's own vulnerability, of one's own potential foreignness, and it is also an attempt to mitigate that vulnerability by asking for the other's protection. In contrast, absolute hospitality seeks no protection; to offer absolute hospitality would be to risk oneself absolutely. Indeed, it is a risk that we will never be able to fully take, for it is the justice that is always to come.

It would be a mistake, however, to suppose that *philotes* is simply opposed to absolute hospitality or that it is simply the exclusion of the other. Rather, bound by a break, *philoi* live in the unstable borderlands where hostility and hospitality intertwine, where the Same responds to the Other with neither pure welcome nor pure violence. In this risky territory, there are three dangers that demand particular emphasis, the first two of which are clear from the preceding analysis. First, in the name of the bond of *philotes* itself, the *philos* may well be hostile to the barbaric other or even to a non-barbaric *xenos* who exists outside that bond.[3] Second, if one does indeed place on the stranger the demands *philotes* calls for, one is thereby hostile to the very *philos* whom one also welcomes. The third danger is rather different, as it concerns hostility to one's fellow citizens—who, let us remember, are also Others to whom one has obligations. It is that one might, by receiving the *philos*, welcome someone who does in fact menace the *polis*. Critiquing Derrida's notion of absolute hospitality in *Strangers, Gods and Monsters*, Richard Kearney has warned that "in such non-discriminate openness to alterity we find ourselves unable to differentiate between good and evil" (72), and he proposes that we have a "legitimate duty to try to distinguish between benign and malign strangers, between saints and psychopaths" (70). It would be one thing, perhaps, if I and the stranger at my door were the only two in the world, but since we are not, must I not take care to avoid admitting someone who has come to kill those who dwell with me? Absolute hospitality risks not only the one who opens the door but others as well, and if a host binds himself to a betrayer who takes advantage of the security granted him to kill or otherwise harm others, the host is not a mere innocent bystander to his guest's crimes. Faced with potentially conflicting obligations to multiple Others, we live in the world of politics where hospitality to one may be hostility to another.

Thus the etymology of *philia*, which derives from *philos*, betrays a complex instability, a multifaceted wavering between and blending of hostility and hospitality. The bond between *philoi* bears within itself a potential threat to others—barbarians, *xenoi*, and citizens alike, and even the *philoi* themselves. Crucially, the preceding discussion raises questions not only about these ancient Greek concepts but also about friendship, for while friendship is understood, in the contemporary Anglophone world, as more personal and less formal and political than *philotes* and *philia*, it too entails certain obligations to the friend. Essentially, a friend is supposed to be someone on whom one can depend, and although for what and how much varies, is often unclear, and is not codified in law, the basic notion that friends depend on each other is well accepted. And how could one even be a friend to a wholly anonymous stranger? Thus we again face problems not unlike those raised with regard to *philotes*: it seems that friendship by its very nature excludes the anonymous, unrecognizable other, that friendship is hostile to the friend by demanding (and how can it not make such a demand?) that he give his name and a satisfactory account of himself, and that friendship threatens the community insofar as one might bind oneself to a friend who endangers it.

Philia and the *Polis*

At first, Aristotle's account of *philia*, in the *Nicomachean Ethics*, as the relation on which the *polis* depends even more than on justice itself, seems to avoid or at least ignore the dangers of *philotes*. *Philia*, for Aristotle, is rational and natural, and as such it is fundamentally safe in that the particular bond that holds between *philoi* poses no threat to the city as a whole or to virtue. In fact, it preserves and even grounds the city: Aristotle goes so far as to claim that "it seems too that *philia* holds cities together and that lawgivers are more serious about it than about justice" (NE 1155a24–25). Hence it would be misleading to say that the place of *philia* is within the *polis*; on the contrary, *philia* appears as the place within which the *polis* is sustained. *Philia* does not depend on the *polis* but vice versa. It is important to note from the outset that *philia*, for Aristotle, is broader than we generally take friendship to be, encompassing any relation in which people "have goodwill toward each other" and are aware of this mutual goodwill (NE 1156a3–4). Familial relations and the relation of ruler to ruled thus qualify as relationships of *philia*. The best, rarest, and most stable sort of *philia* is based on virtue, but other relations of mutual goodwill still benefit the *polis* by binding citizens together.

Crucially, Aristotle's account of *philia* derives from his understanding of nature. Humans are naturally communal; better, they naturally live in a *polis*—and it is in fact by virtue of *philia* that the *polis* exists as such rather than being a mere disconnected group of strangers who interact only in passing, without any deeper bond, however virtuous they may otherwise appear to be. As he explains, "no one would choose to have all good things by himself, since a human being is political and is disposed by nature [πεφυκός] to live with others. So this too belongs to the happy man, for he possesses the things good by nature [φύσει] and it is clear that it is better to pass the days together with friends and decent people than with strangers and people at random" (NE 1169b17–22). *Philia* is thus deliberate: it is not the result of chance and does not occur between mere passersby. In contrast, there is an unnamed virtue (sometimes identified as friendliness) that consists in treating everyone appropriately and being neither obsequious nor quarrelsome, and one who practices this virtue applies it in his interactions with everyone: "he will act similarly in the case of both those he does not know and those he does know [. . .]—except that he will also do what is suitable in each case" (NE 1126b25–27). Appropriate behavior toward strangers is virtuous, but it differs from appropriate behavior toward *philoi*, and one who encounters only strangers is missing something essential, no matter how virtuously he behaves in his dealings with them. In short, *philia* makes us more truly human, for it accords with our nature. One who lacks it is not only unhappy but is in some way unnatural, even against nature. Such a person is not truly a citizen of the *polis* but a drifter, a foreigner everywhere, a stranger to all. He is not, strictly speaking, an exile, since that designation would imply that he has a home from which he was cast out. For him, however, the *polis* is no home at all; he does not even belong to it as an exile belongs to his homeland. Only one who experiences the bond of *philia* can be at home in the *polis*. Moreover, one cannot be completely virtuous without *philia*: Aristotle asserts that "when people are friends, they have no need of justice, but when they are just, they do need friendship in addition; and in the realm of the just things, the most just seems [δοκεῖ] to be what involves friendship" (NE 1155a26–29). Because the friendless one lacks that whereby the *polis* is sustained, he cannot achieve the greatest justice. Thus he cannot attain the greatest heights of virtue, however admirable he may otherwise seem.

Not only is he seemingly at home in the *polis*, but one whose life involves *philia* is also apparently wholly at home in himself, never other than himself. Aristotle's account of *philia* seems to emphasize the self at the expense of the other, as he states that "a friend is an other [ἕτερος] self" (NE 1170b7, trans. mod.). On a first reading, ipseity appears to dominate alterity: the friend is other, it is true, but he is not absolutely other, for this otherness, this difference, emerges against the background of a fundamental sameness. Certainly one should aid one's friends and avoid selfishness: Aristotle maintains that although one should strive to avoid troubling one's *philoi* with one's own misfortunes, it is right to aid one's *philoi* in their misfortunes (NE 1171b15–26). Also, a proper regard for oneself entails seeking virtue rather than being greedy for wealth and honor: the true self-lover (φίλαυτος) pursues virtue and thereby "allots to himself the noblest things and the greatest goods" (NE 1168b30). The virtuous person does not, therefore, seek his own advantage at the expense of his *philoi*; on the contrary, he acts nobly and seeks to assist his *philoi* whenever they are in need. Still, ipseity and sameness seem to take precedence over alterity and difference in the Aristotelian narrative, as it is the self's flourishing, not the call of the other, that serves as a reason to seek virtue.

Here it bears noting that in this discussion, the male pronoun should not be taken as generic, as only men could fully participate in the life of the *polis* in the first place. Aristotle does consider the relation between husband and wife to be a kind of *philia*, but he explains that this *philia* "is based on superiority [ὑπεροχήν]"—specifically, the superiority of the husband over the wife (NE 1158b12). As a virtuous woman is still inferior to a virtuous man, the highest form of *philia* remains the province of virtuous men. Intriguingly, Julia Kristeva writes in *Strangers to Ourselves* that "the sexual difference, which has been in the course of time either erased or overemphasized in turn, is certainly not destined to be frozen into antagonism. The fact remains that in Greece the bride was thought of as a foreigner, a suppliant" (68–69/46). It was the bride's sexual difference from men that marked her as foreign, as one who was not truly a citizen, as a guest come to beg protection from the host. If, however, friendship disrupts ipseity and is possible only between strangers—contra this initial but dangerously incomplete reading of Aristotle—then Kristeva is entirely right to say that this difference need not "be frozen into antagonism." In that case, then insofar as the exclusion of women from friendship, or from the highest form of friendship, is a rejection of difference and an attempt to preserve ipseity, it is fundamentally contrary to friendship itself.

Thus far, however, it appears that we have a stable and orderly account of *philia* as the place that grounds the *polis* and in which sameness precedes difference. The fact that there is *philia* between husband and wife, even if it is not the highest form of *philia*, does indicate the possibility of difference within *philia*, as does the famous phrase "an other self," yet sameness still seems to triumph, with the husband superior to the wife and the self more fundamental than otherness. Yet if *philia* is the place within which the *polis* and self-identity are held, can we be sure that it is not also the place within which they collapse? At the very least it would be advisable to consider the stability of *philia* itself, lest it fall and take the safety of ipseity and of the *polis* with it. We must not, however, too readily maintain support and collapse in a naive opposition: what if indeed the drifters, the foreigners, the strangers—and not the citizens, not those who are safely at home, comfortable in their ipseity—are the only ones for whom *philia* is, in some sense of the word, possible?

Rereading Aristotle Otherwise

Although the danger of *philia* is not immediately apparent in Aristotle's *Nicomachean Ethics*, rereading the relevant passages reveals that *philia* is a greater risk than one might initially suppose. Let us return to the claim that "a friend is an other [ἕτερος] self": crucially, the very idea of an *other* self suggests a splitting or a doubling within ipseity. The reassuring sameness of the *philos* arises only along with a difference, an otherness that marks the self in the person of the *philos*. What is more, because *philia* is a reciprocal relation, each *philos* is the other's "other self." In *philia*, each *philos* encounters himself as other and finds the other's alterity reflected back onto himself. While the visible dividing of a ring symbolized *philotes*, Aristotelian *philia* is marked by an invisible dividing of the self—and because *philia* is necessary for happiness and makes us more truly human, we are most ourselves only when we are also other. Despite Aristotle's apparent privileging of the self, a certain alterity therefore proves essential to virtuous personhood. Thus *philia* is not, or not only, a privileging of the self at the other's expense. Here too we find a complex interplay of hostility and hospitality, an openness to alterity and also an expectation that one's *philos* will reciprocate one's love and will be able to offer a comprehensible account of himself. Hence we must ask, with regard to *philia* this time, a question previously raised about *philotes*: how can one respect the alterity of an other from whom one expects reciprocity and a certain comprehensibility? Recall also the three dangers to which *philotes* can lead: hostility to the barbaric other, hostility to the *philos* himself, and hostility to one's fellow citizens. Although *philia* is not the same as *philotes*, it too takes place within the borderlands of hostility and hospitality, and it is clear that a bond that holds, or purports to hold, the *polis* together could well lead to hostility to those who are obviously outsiders and so do not share in the bond. What of the city? If *philoi* are not wholly at home in themselves but are constituted in part by the alterity of the other, are they wholly at home in the *polis*? Again, Aristotle's account is more complex than it initially seems.

    The complexity of *philia*'s relation to the *polis* becomes increasingly apparent when we consider that *philia* may conflict with other obligations. Aristotle asks, for instance, "whether one must serve a friend [φίλῳ] more than a serious man, and whether one must repay a favor to a benefactor rather than give something away to a comrade [ἑταίρῳ], if both are not possible" (NE 1164b25–28). Although he sketches out an answer to the latter question—generally one should repay favors, unless "an act of giving outstrips in its nobility or necessity the repayment of a debt" (NE 1165a4)—he recognizes the difficulty of determining exactly what is owed to whom and which obligations outweigh others. Crucially, his conclusion that "one must not, on this account, give up the attempt but make the relevant distinctions, to the extent possible"

(NE 1165a36) suggests that there may not always be a way to determine which obligations are the most important. As valuable as *philia* is to the *polis*, then, other duties sometimes outweigh it—which means that if taken too far or valued too greatly, *philia* can undermine the *polis*. That *philia* is not always the most fundamental obligation also means that we cannot count on *philia* to guide us safely through the instability that the ultimate undecidability of certain ethical questions introduces at the heart of ethics itself.

What is more, *philoi* of virtue are in a sense strangers to the very *polis* of which they are citizens. Drawing a distinction between the *philia* of citizens, which one might call political *philia*, and the virtuous *philia* that is the best kind, Aristotle explains that "as fellow citizens [πολιτικῶς], it is possible to be a friend [φίλον] to many without being obsequious but as a truly decent person. Yet it is not possible to be a friend to many if the friendship is based on virtue and on what the people are in themselves, and it is desirable enough to find even a few friends of this sort" (NE 1171a19–21). That virtuous *philoi* share a dwelling already suggests that they stand at a certain distance from the rest of the *polis*, and this distinction between their relation to each other and their relation to other citizens underscores that distance. A community within a community, the virtuous *philoi* also stand apart from the wider community. Because Aristotle recognizes obligations that can outweigh *philia*, the *philoi* should not be wholly absent from the *polis*, yet neither are they wholly present to it. They are not only citizens and therefore are not wholly citizens: claimed by a bond other than that of citizenship, they are to some degree strangers to the *polis*. *Philia*, therefore, is no longer the place of the *polis* or a place within the *polis* but a place that intersects the *polis*, belonging neither to it nor outside it.

It does not follow, however, that *philia* simply undermines the *polis* rather than grounding it: the relation between *philia* and the *polis* is far too complex to reduce to one of two apparently opposed terms. Insofar as virtuous *philoi* spur each other on to greater virtue, and insofar as virtue involves good citizenship, they would support each other in fulfilling the obligations that outweigh *philia*. In addition, because of their virtue and their ability to correct each other, they would be better placed than others to act in the face of ethical undecidability. It is true, of course, that these summary remarks, far from neatly solving a problem, raise further questions about the relation between virtue and citizenship and about the extent of ethical undecidability that it will be necessary to take up again. Here, however, I do not aim to resolve these questions or, certainly, to suggest that any definitive resolution is possible; rather, the point is that *philia*, far from being a stable origin to which we can return to determine the nature of friendship, is from the start a perpetual displacing that no contemporary investigation of friendship can claim to have left behind. As different as popular contemporary conceptions of politics and friendship may be from Aristotle's, the interplays of hospitality and hostility, of citizenship and foreignness, and of same and other have not been tamed. Indeed, the only way to avoid these dangers would be to simply refuse *philia*. If friendship is possible, then it is most assuredly possible only for strangers and not for citizens comfortable in their ipseity, since ipseity is never stable, and the only way to seek to preserve ipseity would be to utterly reject the other with a hostility that would exclude friendship but would testify, against itself, to the inescapability of alterity. Investigating this *if* is precisely the task of this book.

Amicitia between Amor and Caritas

Because Western philosophy is the heir not only of Athens but also of Jerusalem, it is necessary to consider Christian interpretations of *philia* or *amicitia*. Let us turn, therefore, to Aelred and Thomas Aquinas,[4] whose work clearly illustrates that in God's kingdom as well as in the *polis*, friendship is a risk and a displacing and dispossession of the self. At first, one might expect to find that the Christian tradition, with its understanding of *agape* or *caritas* as godly love, dismisses *philia* or *amicitia* as simply human and therefore inferior. Notably, the Protestant theologian Anders Nygren's few references to friendship in his *Agape and Eros*, which emphasizes the superiority of God's agapic love over self-focused erotic love, are unfavorable: he asserts that "the love of friendship [. . .] is built in the last resort, according to Aristotle, on self-love" (186) and criticizes Thomas Aquinas for taking up this self-focused Aristotelian understanding of friendship (644–45).

Nygren's view is far from the only Christian theological or philosophical understanding of friendship, however, and just as the Aristotelian account of friendship is more complex than Nygren gives it credit for, so too is the Thomistic one. Consider Thomas's statement that "he who loves [*amat*] goes out from himself [*extra se exit*], in so far as he wills the good of his friend [*vult bona amici*] and works for it. Yet he does not will the good of his friend more than his own good: and so it does not follow that he loves another more than himself" (ST I–II q. 28 a. 3 ad 3). In light of this phrasing, Nygren's criticism is not altogether surprising, as it seems that love of self is more fundamental than love of the other. Thomas acknowledges alterity, however, with the phrase "goes out from himself": one who loves cannot simply remain within ipseity. And he affirms, with Aristotle, that "a friend [amicus] is called a man's 'other self' [alter ipse]" (ST—II q. 28 a. 1 resp.). This phrase remains as complex here as it was in Aristotle: at first glance, it seems to privilege ipseity, yet it also suggests that one is most oneself only through one's relation to the other. Loving the other is therefore good for the self. It is not that love of self takes precedence, as Nygren suggests, but that in *amicitia* the self and the other cannot be rightly thought or loved independently of each other.

In Thomas's view, in fact, all love is possible only because of God, which means that *amicitia* ultimately begins not with the self but with God. To properly grasp this point, we must first consider how Thomas relates *amor*, *amicitia*, and *caritas*. As James McEvoy insightfully observes, "Aquinas makes a link between *amor* and *amicitia*, and, following that, between *amicitia* and *caritas*, in such a way as to interrelate *amor* and *caritas* by the mediation of *amicitia*."[5] Employing the Greek terms, he adds that "between *eros* and *agape* we should interpose *philia*, as the concept which alone is capable of bringing an end to the *aporia*, or lack of passage, between the other two."[6] It is important to realize, however, that this translation into Greek is inexact, as McEvoy also recognizes,[7] because the etymological relation between *amor* and *amicitia* already indicates a closer relation between them than the Greek *eros* and *philia* imply. This is not to say that *eros* and *philia* were or should be considered as rigidly and wholly distinct but rather that the translation of these words into Latin shifts the terms of the discussion by suggesting from the outset that they are related. Indeed, Thomas distinguishes two forms of *amor*: *amor concupiscentiae*, translated as "love of concupiscence," which is love (*amor*) for the sake of someone or something other than what is loved, and *amor amicitiae*, translated as "love of friendship." "[T]hat which is loved with the love of friendship," he explains, "is loved simply and for itself" (ST I–II q. 26 a. 4 resp.).[8] Because it is directed toward ends rather than means, *amor amicitiae* is thus the higher form of *amor*, and Thomas connects *amor* and *caritas* by defining charity (*caritas*) as "the friendship [*amicitia*] of man for God" (ST II–II q. 23 a.1 resp.). It is in fact by *caritas*, or friendship for God, that we love our enemies and not only those whom we would naturally consider friends: "the friendship of charity [*amicitia caritatis*] extends even to our enemies [*ad inimicos*], whom we love out of charity [*diligimus ex caritate*] in relation to God, to Whom the friendship of charity [*amicitia caritatis*] is chiefly directed" (II–II q. 23 a. 1 ad 2). By becoming *amor amicitiae*, therefore, human *amor* transforms into the *caritas* that reaches God and, through God, the entire human race.[9] To say that *amicitia* is between *amor* and *caritas* is to identify *amicitia* as the place of this transformation—the place that, contra Nygren, connects man and God and that binds each person to every other.

Furthermore, it is only because God created us as beings who can love him that we are capable of directing our love to God in the first place. As Thomas Aquinas explains, "the fellowship of natural goods bestowed on us by God is the foundation of natural love [*amor*], in virtue of which not only man, so long as his nature remains unimpaired, loves God above all things and more than himself, but also every single creature, each in its own way [. . .]" (ST II–II q. 26 a. 3 resp.). In short, our capacity to love God and others is natural to us, and because it is God who gave us our nature, this capacity to love is a divine gift. By positing our ability to love as a gift from a divine Person, Thomas emphasizes that what comes first is not human self-love but rather God's love. The divine other takes priority over human ipseity.

Amicitia and the Kingdom of God

The role of the divine means that with Christianity, the apparent place of friendship shifts, becoming the kingdom of God and not, or at least not only, the geographically localizable *polis*. Certainly many Christian philosophers and theologians, including Thomas Aquinas, wrote about political life in this world, yet the idea that Christians belong to a community bound by neither time nor space could not but alter their understanding of human relations. Thomistic *amicitia*, like Aristotelian *philia*, is, therefore, essentially communal, though for Thomas, as Jean-Pierre Torrell puts it, "it is only then [in the communion of the saints] that friendship, already possible and real [. . .], can take on its ultimate dimension."[10] For true happiness is possible only in the next life (ST I–II q. 5 a. 3), and though God alone suffices for happiness, the next life is still a communal one in which there is *amicitia* (ST I–II q. 4 a. 8). Because the Church finds its end not in political life but in the enjoyment of God, *amicitia* in heaven is greater than *amicitia* in earthly civic society. Rather than being completed in this life, *amicitia* is directed toward an eschatological horizon. Moreover, whereas the *polis* depended on *philia*, *amicitia* and the entire communion of saints depend on God.

It is Aelred of Rievaulx, who lived roughly a century before Thomas Aquinas, whose *Spiritual Friendship* [*De Spirituali Amicitia*] most thoroughly examines *amicitia*'s place in God's kingdom, not only in heaven but also on earth. This is not to say that Aelred dismisses earthly political life as unimportant. On the contrary, he, like Aristotle, holds that certain civic obligations can outweigh friendship, and he goes so far as to state that if a friend poses a threat to "his country" or "his fellow citizens," one "must immediately sever the bonds of familiarity and not prefer the love [*amor*] of one person to the many" (SF 3.58). Civic life is not, however, central to Aelred's account of *amicitia*. He asserts rather that "friendship [*amicitia*] must begin in Christ, continue with Christ, and be perfected by Christ" (SF 1.10) and that *amicitia* will attain its fullest expression only in heaven, "when the friendship [*amicitia*] to which we on earth admit but few will pour out over all and flow back to God from all, for God will be *all in all*" (SF 3.134). Friendships on earth exist at a certain remove from their ultimate eschatological fullness—which means that friends in this world are *not yet* at home. Hence the privileging of the citizen over the stranger is not as secure as it seemed to be in Aristotle, or as one might have suspected it would be given Aelred's instruction to prefer the safety of fellow citizens to a single friend. Christians are citizens of earthly states, but at the same time they are on the way to their true home and so are, in a sense, strangers on earth.

Moreover, because *amicitia* must be referred to a third—Christ—it cannot be only the relation of a self to another self. Certainly it does intimately bind two people: distinguishing between *amicitia* and *caritas*, Aelred explains that we must have charity even for enemies, whereas "we call friends [*dicimus amicos*] only those to whom we have no qualm about entrusting our heart and all its contents, while these friends are bound to us in turn by the same inviolable law of loyalty and trustworthiness" (SF 1.32). He thus defines *amicitia* more narrowly than Aristotle defines *philia*: precisely because friendship is no longer thought chiefly in relation to the *polis*, it becomes possible to place greater emphasis on its personal nature.[11] And this intimacy does amount to a unity: Aelred affirms that "[f]riendship [*amicitia*] is that virtue, therefore, through which by a covenant of sweetest love [*dilectionis*] our very spirits are united, and *from many are made one*" (SF 1.21). Again, however, this unity is mediated by and grounded in Christ's alterity and therefore does not represent the triumph of ipseity. Further emphasizing this point, he states that the "one must lay solid foundation for spiritual love [*solidum quoddam ipsius spiritualis amoris*]"—a category that includes but is not limited to *amicitia*—and that this foundation "is the love of God, to which everything must be referred" (SF 3.5). The best unity, then, is one that is directed outside itself. It is significant that Aelred begins the dialogue—with an interlocutor to whom he calls himself "a friend"—with the words "You and I are here, and I hope that Christ is between us as a third." Two friends are joined in their love for God yet also remain separate in their love for God. As a friend, I must love my human friend, God, and the fact that my friend loves God more than he or she loves me—for God is the ultimate source of all that is good, and so it is always God that we must love most greatly. By loving God more than he or she loves me, the friend escapes me and remains other.[12] Christ marks the friend's alterity by standing *between* the self and the friend—not as a competitor or as an obstacle to their bond of *amicitia* but as its very condition. We love others most truly, according to Aelred, only when we love God above all else. Loving God first does not diminish friends' love for each other, for God is with them in their friendship; rather, it is by loving God first that friends love each other rightly.

The above usage of "he or she" is deliberate: Aelred considers that women are able to partake of friendship, even going so far as to argue that God made Eve from Adam's side "so that nature might teach that all are equal or, as it were, collateral, and that among human beings—and this is a property of friendship [*amicitiae*]—there exists neither superior nor inferior" (SF 1.57). Women may not be equal to men in civic life, but in Aelred's view at least, they are equal in the kingdom of God and may therefore participate in true friendship. On Aelred's analysis, the male/female difference is no longer a reason to regard women as inferior to men because both men and women were created and redeemed by God. By grounding friendship in God, the divine Other, Aelred opens friendship to human others more clearly than does Aristotle, both because he takes women as well as men to be capable of friendship and because his emphasis on the primacy of love for God decenters the ego and thereby highlights the friend's alterity.

For both Aelred and Thomas Aquinas, *amicitia* cannot be adequately thought in terms of presence, citizenship, and ipseity, both because friends are still waiting to enter their true home and because God's otherness is the source of their unity. Reading them makes particularly clear, therefore, that friendship secures the self only by destabilizing or displacing the self: the Christian friend is constituted by God and by the other person and is always on the way, within the world and yet also a stranger. Friendship itself is a way on which the self is displaced and that finds its completion only in the eschaton. Crucially, this eschatological horizon in which friendship would be made complete cannot be the annihilation or the sublimation of difference, as the friend will still escape me in his or her love for God. What is more, to love one's friend in heaven is to love that the friend is as God made him or her and thus to utterly surrender any claim to possessing the friend. The eschaton in which the self is brought home is also the dispossession of the self: the self surrenders to God all claim to itself and to the other.

Even so, hostility remains a danger for Thomistic or Aelredian *amicitia*, at least in this world, as it did for Aristotelian *philia*: any community risks becoming hostile to outsiders, even if the community is itself composed of outsiders and maintains universal love as an ideal, and the reciprocity of friendship still seems to contrast with absolute hospitality. Finally, let anyone who suspects that friendship to God is a safe and easy thing remember the name of Abraham, called a friend of God (II Chronicles 20:7, Isaiah 41:8, and James 2:23) and whom God commanded to sacrifice his son. Far from reducing the dangers of friendship, therefore, the introduction of the Christian God radically destabilizes the self by demanding an absolute fidelity that, if we take seriously the reading of it offered under the name Johannes de Silentio in *Fear and Trembling*, calls into question ethics itself. Indeed, it will be necessary to return to *Fear and Trembling* in the following chapter.

The Origin of *Philosophia*:
Heidegger on the Fall of *Philein to Sophon*

Thus far this investigation into the origins of friendship has primarily inquired into friendships among human beings, with some consideration of friendship with God, but the very word *philosophia* should serve as a reminder that *philia* can be understood still more broadly: philosophy itself is a kind of friendship. The moment has therefore come to return to the Greek language and also to Heidegger's "What Is Philosophy?" Once again, we turn to a decisive moment in the history of *philia* in the hopes of finding a stable origin: Heidegger writes that "the name 'philosophy' summons us, if we truly hear the word and think on what was heard, into the history of the Greek origin [*Herkunft*] of philosophy" (GA 11 10–11/35). And once again, the quest for an origin will find an originary displacement and deferral.

For Heraclitus and for Parmenides, writes Heidegger, there was as yet no *philosophia*; Heraclitus referred rather to the *aner philosophos*, who is "*hos philei to sophon*, he who loves the *sophon*" (GA 11 14/47)—or, to put it another way, he who is a friend to the *sophon*. Between the *aner philosophos* and the *sophon* there is, then, a common language and law. Having encountered such bonds before, we guess at once what we have found here—a relation of limited hospitality! We may hope that Heidegger will give the lie to this suspicion that the forgotten origin of philosophy is so apparently inglorious, but then we will be disappointed, for in a passage that it is worth quoting at length, Heidegger describes the relation of the *aner philosophos* and the *sophon* as a reciprocal arrangement that takes place within a shared language: "[P]*hilein*, to love, signifies here, in Heraclitus' sense, *homolegein*, to speak [*sprechen*] as the *Logos* speaks, to correspond [*entsprechen*] to the *Logos*. This correspondence stands in accord with the *sophon*. Accord is *harmonia*. That one being reciprocally unites itself with another, that both are originarily [*ursprünglich*] united to each other because they are at each other's disposal [*zueinander verfügt sind*]—this *harmonia* is the distinguishing mark [*das Auszeichnende*] of *philein*, of loving, thought Heracliteanly" (GA 11 14/47, trans. mod.). Speaking with, reciprocity, each one being at the disposal of the other—these are all notions we recognize from Benveniste and Derrida. But at the origin, at the moment before the question of Being was forgotten or covered over, should we not find something far grander—far more absolute—than a bond of limited hospitality? Does not limited hospitality fall short of everything we have been taught to aspire to in the pursuit of philosophy? Certainly we must examine more closely that which takes place in the event of *philein to sophon* rather than hastily applying Derrida's analysis of limited hospitality or Benveniste's treatment of *philotes*. In order that the conclusion of this examination might not be determined in advance, however, let us suspend the ideals about philosophy and about origins that might make us hesitate to associate *philein to sophon*—which in any case, insists Heidegger, is precisely not *philosophia*—with limited hospitality.

The first question that imposes itself is deceptively simple: Whose is the shared language? We are told that the *aner philosophos* "loves [*philei*] the *sophon*" and that *philein* means, "here" and for Heraclitus, "to speak as [*wie*] the *Logos* speaks." What is more, Heidegger writes later on, "to the Greeks the nature of language reveals itself as the *logos*" (GA 11 25/93, trans. mod.). Thus the *Logos*, in speaking Greek, does speak its own language—and the *aner philosophos* also speaks his own language. Between them, so it seems, there is no need for translation. They, unlike those bound by *philotes*, are not *xenoi* to each other. It is, however, the *aner philosophos* who "speak[s] as the *Logos* speaks"—that is, according to the *Logos* or after the fashion of the *Logos*—and not vice versa, though they share a tongue. With the phrase "*after* the fashion," I deliberately suggest the question of time. For if the *Logos* speaks first, who can say what might happen in the temporal gap between its words and those of the *aner philosophos*, what play of language might disrupt the very notion of a "nature of language" by separating sense and signifier? But Heidegger intervenes before this questioning can go too far: the *aner philosophos* and the *Logos* are, he states, "originarily united to each other." They speak together, in unison, from the beginning. Their bond, then, is not the bond of *philotes* that occurs within a preexisting system of laws and language, for in their correspondence they speak the system into being. If they are absolutely united from the outset, there is no gap between them, no interval during which meaning could be lost as words cross from one to the other. Thus is the purity of the origin preserved—except that there was a fall, and this must give us pause. What *philein* means "here" is not what it means always and everywhere. The language of the *Logos* and of the *aner philosophos* has already set off at a pace that neither nature nor man can follow. Time itself is the temporal gap in which anything might happen.

What apparently did happen, as any reader of Heidegger knows to expect, was a forgetting—yet not only a forgetting but also a combat. For Heraclitus, Heidegger explains, "the *sophon* says this: '*Hen Panta*,' 'One (is) All.' [. . .] The *sophon* says—all being [*Seiende*] is in Being [*Sein*]. Said more pointedly—Being *is* being. [. . .] Being gathers being together insofar as it is being. Being is the gathering together—*Logos*" (GA 11 14/49, trans. mod.). And for *philein to sophon* to become *philosophia*, this originary unity, this knowledge of the truth of Being, had to fall to "the attack of Sophist understanding" (GA 11 15/51, trans. mod.). The *aner philosophos* and the *Logos* could not vanquish, and *philein to sophon* fell and became only *philosophia*. Their loss indicates precisely that their supposedly originary unity was not perfect. It was rather, like *philotes* and even Aristotelian *philia*, a bond whose place was unstable. And that its place was unstable shows that they did not wholly control their bond—which means that they could not unreservedly and absolutely bind themselves to each other. The notion of limited hospitality thus illuminates anew the danger of *philein*. The bond between *philoi*—whether or not both are human—is always somewhat out of their control, vulnerable to time and to a language or languages that escape them, that escape even what we might have supposed to be language's nature. Their temporary unity was possible only because they spoke the same language, yet this very condition of their unity left it vulnerable to attack, for language is not static, and one whose name now seems to be known may yet become or prove to be an anonymous stranger. *Philein to sophon* was never stable, as it depended on a correspondence and was therefore too limited a hospitality to be safe from hostility. Or, to put it another way, there was no fall, for *philein to sophon* was falling from the start. What happened was in truth always already happening. The forgetting, or the covering over, is not something that happened or began to happen at a temporally or linguistically determinable moment, for it cannot be separated from the never fully determined movement of time and language themselves.

Philosophia, Eros, and Grace

In other words, *philein to sophon* was always already *philosophia*. But to fully grasp the implications of this claim, it is necessary to examine more closely Heidegger's analysis of the result of the combat against the Sophists. He reports that "[t]he saving [*Rettung*] of that which is most astonishing—being in Being [*Seiendes im Sein*]—came to pass through a few who set out on the way in the direction toward this that is most astonishing [*auf den Weg machten in der Richtung auf dieses Erstaunlichste*], that is, the *sophon*. By doing this they became those who *strove* for the *sophon* and who through their own striving awakened and kept alive the yearning for the *sophon*" (GA 11 15/51, trans. mod.). It is precisely because they strive for the *sophon*, however, that this saving is incomplete. The long string of prepositional phrases with which Heidegger describes this striving, *auf den Weg machten in der Richtung auf dieses Erstaunlichste*, underscores their distance from the *sophon*: what has been saved is not the truth of Being itself but rather a search that, for all it is "on the way in the direction toward" this truth, is only ever toward it, aimed in its direction, and on the way—or even, still more literally, *toward* or *onto* the way. Certainly there is danger in taking too literally set phrases such as *auf den Weg machen* and *in der Richtung auf* and thereby producing a translation that sounds more unnatural than the original—yet there is also danger in taking too casually normal, standard phrases that ought to startle us. For what occurs in this series of prepositions is not only a displacement—movement toward the *sophon*—nor the trace of a past displacement—the movement away from harmony with the *sophon*—that requires a new displacement back toward the *sophon*, but rather an endless displacing that cannot be reduced to a single moment. The striving never reaches its goal. These new thinkers "who *strive* for the *sophon*" will not attain harmony with the *sophon*, and because *philein* was that harmony, their manner of loving it cannot be called simply *philein*. As Heidegger explains, "because the *philein* is no longer an originary harmony with the *sophon* but is a particular striving *towards* the *sophon*, *philein to sophon* becomes '*philosophia*.' This striving is determined by Eros" (GA 11 15/51, trans. mod.). Eros, therefore, strives for the supposed harmony of *philein*—but this harmony never was and cannot be. Thus the consummation of eros is impossible, and there is no end to its striving.

By seeking this absolute unity, this totality, philosophy risks becoming egoism. It is true that Heidegger, by calling us to be attuned to Being, indicates that the self must set aside its conception of itself: Heideggerian eros is not simple egoism—but insofar as it is not egoism, that is not because it does not seek totality, the triumph of the Same over the Other, but rather because the totality it seeks is unattainable. Heidegger's 1943 seminar on Heraclitus, however, complicates the matter further: Heidegger describes "favor [*Gunst*]" as "the reciprocal essential relation that is here called by the name *philia/philein*" (GA 55 132/100); then, commenting on a fragment of Parmenides, he states that " 'eros,' thought essentially, is the poetic [*dichtende*] name for the thinking [*denkende*] word 'favor,' insofar as this word names the now dawning essence of *phusis*" (GA 55 132/101, trans. mod); and he goes on to state that "favor is the essential feature of *eris* (strife), provided that we think this inceptually and do not conceive of it only as quarreling and disputation based upon the contrariety of disfavor [*Ungunst*] and resentment [*Mißgunst*]" (GA 155 133/101, trans. mod.). Taking a cue from Derrida, who in his reading of this passage of Heidegger (translating *Gunst* as *grâce*, grace) suggests that "conflict and discord are neither strangers nor opposed to the grace of friendship" (HE 389/196, trans. mod.), I ask: what if the very impossibility of attaining the supposed, sought-after harmony is the favor, the grace? What if the grace of eros is that it cannot succeed and the grace of *philein* is that it was always already fallen? *Philosophia* is then a striving that does not seek to end itself in totality.

To be attuned to the *logos*, to strive for friendship with the *logos*, could then be to wrestle with it—as Jacob wrestled with God, a combat in the dark with an anonymous and name-giving stranger. "For I have seen God face to face," said Jacob/Israel afterward, "and yet my life has been delivered" (Genesis 32:30, ESV). "My life has been delivered": the self receives its life and its name from the other, and this gift comes, unexpectedly, through struggle. The other—be it God, a human, or *logos*—is not tame; friendship is not safe; and seeking a consummation that would be pure harmony, pure totality, amounts to refusing grace. Even the perfection of friendship in heaven to which Aelred and Thomas Aquinas look forward is not, let us recall, the end of difference, and for Aelred and Thomas, insisting on the totality of the ego would certainly be a rejection of divine grace. "One could say," writes Derrida, "that *Éris* is also the truth of *philia*, unless it be also the inverse" (HE 390/196). "One *could* say"—for the self cannot capture the event of friendship in language. Yet at the same time one must speak, if only to testify to the failure and thereby to open oneself to the other by acknowledging that one cannot control the narrative. Whatever Jacob or the philosopher may have initially intended in their combats, the struggle with the other must be or become, not the attempt to dominate the other, but the attempt to bear witness to the other. As Kearney has noted in *Anatheism* (20), it is significant that Jacob/Israel makes peace with his brother Esau after wrestling with the stranger. Struggle and surrender must go hand in hand: surrender to the other from and through whom the self receives itself, and struggle to bear witness to the inexpressibly other. Bearing witness is both a service to and a struggle with the other, for self and other always only meet at night. Put another way, fidelity to the other struggles with the other because fidelity always fails; the other always exceeds the self's testimony. At the touch of the stranger, philosophy itself limps, precisely because bearing witness to the stranger is impossible yet essential.

Philia, amicitia, philosophia: nowhere do we find a stable point that permits us to clearly demarcate the boundaries of friendship and make it safe for the community and the self. Yet how could the encounter with another ever be made safe? Even to one's fellow citizens or fellow believers, one may have conflicting obligations, and those fellows are not, in truth, a uniform and predictable class whose differences from each other and from oneself may be discounted. To encounter another, one must always risk oneself, for the other is never wholly knowable—yet to risk oneself may be the only way to receive oneself. If indeed friendship may ultimately be said to ground the self, this grounding can only be a radical displacement of the self, a summons outward toward the other that saves the one thus called from a solipsism devoid of grace.

2

The Ethical Challenge of Friendship

Ethics without Friendship?

Friendship, whatever else we may say of it, has been a radically destabilizing force from the beginning, which means that the relation between ethics and friendship has never been a straightforward one—and the question, or even the struggle, becomes still more complex when we turn to Emmanuel Levinas's ethics of absolute responsibility to and for the Other. Simply put, Levinas's ethics seems to discredit friendship because Levinas posits a self who is absolutely responsible for every Other according to a radically asymmetrical ethical relation, whereas friendship is generally thought as a mutual relation between oneself and a particular other person, to whom one is bound more closely than one is to those who are not one's friends. It is unclear, moreover, how this mutuality that we usually envision when we think of friendship might relate to the struggle in the dark and the radical displacement of the self proposed above. Because Levinas insists on the disruption of the ego by the call of the Other, to whom the self can never adequately testify, questioning friendship in light of Levinas's ethics will go some way toward clarifying these points as well.

If indeed Levinas is right to say that "[the Other] is the persecuted one for whom I am responsible to the point of being his hostage" (OB 98/59), how can I prefer one person—the friend—to any other, and what could possibly remain of the notion that friends return each other's love? The demands of the ethical relation to the Other thus seem to exclude all that characterizes friendship. While no one can serve all others equally, it does not follow that the self may choose whom to aid on the basis of those personal qualities by which, so it appears, friends are often drawn to one another. As Levinas asserts, "the best way of encountering the Other is not even to notice the color of his eyes!" (EI 79/85). Likewise, I should not notice his virtues, his interests, his personality: all these have nothing to do with the ethical relation to one who transcends me, for I am bound to serve the Other even if everything about him repulses me. It may be that I must oppose the Other, even unto violence, for the sake of the persecuted third who is also an Other, but then I am in the realm of politics, not of ethics—and though it is impossible to avoid the political, I must never confuse it with the ethical. For the demands of politics, while inescapable, arise only from the struggle to serve multiple Others who are at odds.[1] At once transcendent and destitute, the Other commands me and depends on me, and from "the Height and [. . .] the Humility of the Other" (TI 218/200) there comes no call to the closeness of friendship.

What is more, not only do I have no right to ask that the Other reciprocate my love, but when it comes to ethics, the very idea of reciprocity is incoherent. The relation to the Other, emphasizes Levinas, is nonreversible precisely because the Other transcends any system within which a common measure between self and other could be established. If the relation could be reversed, then "they would complete one another in a system visible from the outside" (TI 24/35). Asking that the Other be responsible to and for me as I am responsible to and for the Other is a denial of the Other's transcendence and as such is nonsensical. One might protest that within friendship reciprocity is freely given, not asked for. Yet the very fact that there is a word for "friendship," as if the relation could be encompassed and comprehended by a word, seems to suggest a totality, a system within which two (or perhaps more) are held and are equally named friends, as though each one could be substituted for the other.

Levinas appears to confirm such an association of friendship with totality when, laying out his differences with Martin Buber, he states that "the I-Thou is an event *(Geschehen)*, a shock, a comprehension—but does not permit us to account for (except as an aberration, a fall, or a sickness) a life other than friendship: economy, the search for happiness, the representational relation with things" (TI 64–65/68–69, trans. mod.). Thus friendship appears on the side of economy and happiness, not of the Desire of the Other that "is situated beyond satisfaction and nonsatisfaction" (TI 196/179). In friendship, implies Levinas, I take the Other as an object that is present to me. Although the coming of the friend may seem to disrupt my ipseity, it is not a genuine encounter with alterity.

As Alan Udoff points out in "Levinas and the Question of Friendship," considering why Levinas neglects friendship in his writings, conceptions of the good life in which friendship plays a key role have tended to emphasize the presence of the friend. Here one thinks, for example, of Aristotle's recommendation that "one ought to share in the friend's perception that he exists, and this would come to pass by living together and sharing in a community of speeches and thought" (NE 1170b11–14; quoted by Udoff in a different translation, 143). Yet this emphasis on presence is the mark of the Western philosophical tradition that Levinas condemns for its egoism. That Levinas has virtually nothing to say about friendship is thus no accident: Udoff argues that this omission is part and parcel of his insistence on the radical alterity of the unknowable Other (154–55). He observes that in Levinas's philosophy "the height that is infinite responsibility takes the place of the striving for the highest good. In the world that is burdened with suffering and fault, that good first came to light in the embodiment of the friend. Now absent, where is it to be found?" (155–56). It is not that ethics has nothing to do with goodness; on the contrary, Levinas writes that "goodness consists in placing oneself in being such that the Other counts more than myself" (TI 277/247, trans. mod.). But the locus of the good life is irrevocably displaced: no longer does it center on a shared life with one who is present to the self. The good is precisely *absent* because goodness means substituting oneself for the Other who is never wholly present, who transcends me in a way that classical understandings of friendship cannot account for. Levinasian ethics is therefore without friendship—unless it is possible to think friendship otherwise.

Levinas's ethics thus challenges the typical understanding of friendship on three grounds: friendship is based on presence rather than on transcendence and radical alterity, it implies an unjustifiable preference for one Other over everyone else, and it entails a totalizing reciprocity. Aristotle and Aelred both recognize that friendship may conflict with other ethical obligations; now, however, it appears that fidelity to the friend may conflict with ethics itself. At the very least, it may seem necessary to turn exclusively to the political realm if we are to justify something like friendship, as it is within the political realm that I may and even must, for the sake of the third, notice the Other's virtue or vice. Certain people will be more effective allies than others in the fight against injustice, and because I cannot, as a practical matter, serve all people, it is necessary to work with others to accomplish as much as possible for the cause of justice. The camaraderie that arises when one works with others to achieve a common goal is not only permissible but even advisable insofar as it is easier to work with comrades than with people who are effectively strangers. But this camaraderie is not an intrinsic good; rather, it is good only insofar as it is useful for the pursuit of justice. Thus it is not friendship, if by friendship we mean a relation that, although not asymmetrical, is not based solely on the friend's ability to be of use, even if that use is defined by a cause greater than myself. This distinction should not be drawn too harshly: one may be related by both friendship and camaraderie to the same person or people, and the one relation may develop from or within the other, even to the point that in a given case one cannot meaningfully distinguish what belongs to camaraderie and what to friendship, save perhaps by wresting the relation in question from the concrete situation in which alone it has its senses. Still, because friendship and camaraderie are not the same, it is necessary, in order to rethink friendship after or with Levinas, to go further than a study of camaraderie alone would permit.

Friendship after Levinas: Beyond Presence

Surprisingly enough, however, most of Levinas's few references to friendship are favorable. For instance, when he contrasts friendship (*amitié*) with love (*amour*), friendship no longer appears on the side of economy but rather is directed toward the Other: Levinas explains that "love and friendship are not only felt differently; their correlative differs: friendship goes unto the Other; love seeks what does not have the structure of a being, the infinitely future, what is to be engendered" (TI 298/266, trans. mod.). Erotic love operates on a different temporality than friendship, as the engendering of the child, who is both self and other, is a discontinuity within time itself that points to the always-future messianic time of forgiveness and triumph over evil (TI 299–302/267–69, 313–18/281–85). Friendship does not offer this discontinuous time that directs us to "the infinitely future"—but because it is aimed toward the Other, it does avoid the self-absorption of eros. As Levinas states, shortly after comparing love and friendship, "love does not transcend unequivocally—it is complacent, it is pleasure and dual egoism" (TI 298/266). This point is crucial, considering that one of the chief dangers of friendship would seem to be a neglect of one's ethical obligation in favor of a selfish devotion to the friend. Here Levinas appears utterly unconcerned with this danger, straightforwardly linking friendship with openness to the Other as if there were no reason to fear that the notion of friendship might be irredeemably associated with presence and ipseity.

In fact, in the closing section of *Totality and Infinity*, Levinas goes so far as to imply that "goodness" *is* "friendship and hospitality":

> To posit being as Desire and as goodness is not to isolate beforehand an I which would then tend toward a beyond. It is to affirm that to apprehend oneself from within—to produce oneself as I—is to grasp oneself with the same gesture that already turns toward the exterior to extra-vert and to manifest—to answer for what it grasps—to express; it is to affirm that the becoming-conscious is already language, that the essence of language is goodness, or again, that the essence of language is friendship and hospitality. (TI 341/305, trans. mod.)

The self is always already in relation to the Other: there is no preexisting, isolated I who only subsequently turns outward. Or, to put it more strongly, to be a self is to direct oneself toward the Other. Turning toward the Other does not mean turning from something, from some prior state of undisturbed ipseity; it is a turning from the no-place of "the impersonal *there is*" (TI 207/190) in which the self would be lost if not for the Other. And if language, this turning toward the Other that already comes from the Other,[2] is "friendship and hospitality," then friendship begins not with a lone self emerging from its solitude to seek a companion, nor even with the self's knowledge of the Other, but rather with the word that summons me. I am not master of my friendships but am called to them; indeed, I am already committed to them by the word that is not mine. The phrase "friendship and hospitality" implies that the two are not synonymous, but they have this at least in common: I may turn away neither friend nor guest, for I am promised to them. Should I speak to reject the promise, my tongue betrays me: language itself is the promise, and I cannot escape it—nor should I wish to, since it is by friendship and hospitality, by turning outward from myself toward the Other, that I am myself at all.

Yet are we not moving too quickly by repeating the word "friendship," as though its meaning were plain? In "Philosophy, Justice, and Love," Levinas states, after all, that "every 'other man' is a friend" (EN 127/117, trans. mod.); what then of friendships between two particular individuals? It remains that we have cause to suspect that Levinasian ethics forbids what still seems to be a privileged relationship with one person and not others. Although his positive uses of the words "friendship" and "friend" are striking, a resolution to the conflict between ethics and friendship will not come that easily. Still, as a preliminary indication that friendship and ethics need not be wholly at odds, consider an address to Levinas, or an invocation of his name, signed by Maurice Blanchot, published the year after Levinas's death, and written, as the title of the short work that these words conclude would have it, *Pour l'amitié* (for friendship):

> Greek *philia* is reciprocity, an exchange of the Same with the Same, but never an opening to the Other [*Autre*], discovering the Other [*Autrui*] as the one responsible for him, recognition of his pre-excellence, awakening and sobering by this Other [*Autrui*] who never leaves me in peace, enjoyment (without concupiscence, as Pascal says) of his Height, of what always makes him closer to the Good than "I" am.
>
> That is my salute to Emmanuel Levinas, the only friend—ah, faraway friend—whom I call *tu* [the French informal form of "you," in contrast to the formal *vous*] and who calls me *tu*, not because we were young but by a deliberate decision, a pact at which I hope never to fail. (35)

Aristotelian *philia* is not, I have argued, the straightforward valorization of ipseity that it initially appears to be, yet if we read Aristotle today looking for signs of alterity, this is in part thanks to Levinas. Significantly, it is immediately after invoking the radical alterity of the anonymous Other that Blanchot *names* Emmanuel Levinas and claims a relation of friendship with him. What is more, immediately after implicitly critiquing the notion of reciprocity, he notes that he and Levinas mutually address each other as *tu*. As Blanchot's friend, Levinas is at once close and faraway—faraway because he is Other, and all the more so because he is dead at the time this writing appears, yet close by virtue of "a deliberate decision, a pact." It bears noting that even the most deliberate of decisions can be recognized as such only retrospectively: only subsequent commitment reveals that the decision was indeed decisive, and as the commitment is never-ending, the decision must be continually reiterated. This closeness is itself a responsibility, less a refusal of distance than a vow to bear witness to one singular Other in his distance, even his absence. After Levinas, friendship must abide in the tension of an intimacy that does not demand presence but rather is radically open to the Height of the Other. Such an intimacy must itself be a responsibility, not a refusal of distance but a vow to bear witness to one singular Other in her distance, even absence. It is not that Blanchot's thought is the same as or an extension of Levinas's; rather, Blanchot's words offer an excellent expression of this tension that constitutes friendship.

The Singular Individual

To understand friendship as mutual intimacy and openness to the Other's radical alterity, let us consider the singularity of both self and Other. Singularity means that the human person is in no way assimilable to a totality. The Other does not call to me as a member of a species calling to a fellow representative of that species, for both self and Other would then be replaceable: in that case the Other might as well be anyone else, and anyone else could replace me in my responsibility. This claim is not, of course, a denial of the biological fact that human beings belong to the same species; the point is that the biological fact is not primordial. The call of the Other summons and commands me prior to any concept under which we could be subsumed. My responsibility to and for the Other derives not from anything we have in common but from the "primordial *expression*" in which the face of the Other calls to me, "Thou shalt not commit murder."[3] Levinas expresses the significance of singularity when he writes that "there exists a tyranny of the universal and of the impersonal, an order that is inhuman though distinct from the brutish. Against it man affirms himself as an irreducible singularity, exterior to the totality into which he enters, and aspiring to the religious order where the recognition of the individual concerns him in his singularity" (TI 271/242). It is because the Other does not belong to any totality that he or she is destitute and only I can come to his or her aid. The original command lies at the heart of ethics because it speaks both of the Other's sheer vulnerability and of my obligation to protect his or her life. Therefore that command, "Thou shalt not commit murder," orders me to recognize the Other as singular, for attempting to subsume the Other under a concept—that is, to assimilate him or her into a totality—is precisely attempting to deny the Other's radical alterity and my absolute responsibility. Moreover, because the responsibility falls to me and me alone, because I am irreplaceable, it falls to me as an "irreducible singularity." Indeed, only as an "irreducible singularity" can I serve the Other; otherwise my relation to the Other would itself come under a totality by virtue of my own part in that totality. Singularity is thus central to Levinas's thought.

The individuality of the Other is also important and in fact follows from singularity. The reference to "the recognition of the individual" already suggests that singularity and individuality—the fact of being unique such that no substitution is possible—cannot be separated. Indeed, Levinas insists on individuality as well as singularity, writing that "it is my responsibility before a face looking at me as absolutely foreign [. . .] that constitutes the original fact of fraternity" (TI 235/214) and soon afterward adding that "human fraternity [. . .] involves individualities whose logical status is not reducible to the status of ultimate differences in a genus, for their singularity consists in each referring to itself" (TI 236/214). Thus the self is human precisely as a singularity summoned irreplaceably—that is, as an individual—to the ethical responsibility. And, crucially, because no individual can be substituted for another, the Other must be an individual, or else another could substitute for him and he would thereby be subsumed under the universal. Singularity thus entails individuality, and to recognize the Other as utterly singular is to recognize him or her as an individual for whom no other can be substituted. In "Philosophy, Justice, and Love," Levinas explicitly affirms the Other's individuality with the words "every other is unique" (EN 114/104).[4] It is justice, not ethics, that must to a certain degree deny this uniqueness, this individuality, of every Other by making the "comparison of what is in principle incomparable" (EN 114/104)—that is, of different persons. The ethical relation necessarily occurs between one singular individual and an Other singular individual.[5]

Yet if it is true that the Other is a singular individual, what are we to make of Levinas's apparent insistence on stripping the Other of all individual qualities? Recall his infamous assertion, which earlier appeared as an indication of friendship's incompatibility with ethics, that "the best way of encountering the Other is not even to notice the color of his eyes!" (EI 79/85). If I am not to notice any of the Other's features, how can I notice his individuality? True, the color of his eyes does not suffice to identify him, but Levinas's statement surely does not apply to physical features alone, since none of the Other's characteristics have anything to do with my infinite responsibility. It is necessary, however, to bear in mind the context of this assertion: Levinas is arguing that phenomenology cannot provide an adequate account of the face because "phenomenology describes what appears. [. . .] The relation with the face can surely be dominated by perception, but what is specifically the face is what cannot be reduced to that" (EI 79–80/85–86). The injunction to not notice the color of the Other's eyes warns us, therefore, that the Other's individual singularity is not wholly given in perception. Levinas's primary point is that the Other's characteristics do not affect my ethical responsibility, but given the singularity, and hence the individuality, of the face, we can also conclude that what individuates the Other is irreducible to appearing phenomena. If it is true—and I argue that it is—that the friend cannot be reduced to appearing phenomena, then Levinas's claim that one should not notice the color of the Other's eyes ceases to be an obstacle to friendship.

In maintaining that individual singularity is not reducible to perception, Levinas is in accord with John Duns Scotus, for whom we cannot in this life know the haecceity—*thisness*, or the principle of individuation—of any thing or person, including ourselves, but only their appearances.[6] Yet although we cannot perceive that which individuates anything or anyone, Scotus argues that all that exists is individuated, not by virtue of *not* being anything else, but rather "through something positive intrinsic [*per aliquid positivum intrinsecum*] to" it.[7] The principle of individuation thus inheres in the person or thing, not in its differences from other things to which it might be compared. Furthermore, although it is not possible to comprehend any singularity, it is possible to recognize singularity non-intellectually. Emmanuel Falque, commenting on Scotus in *God, the Flesh, and the Other*, emphasizes the possibility of "knowing the singular *indirectly*" through the will: "what I do not know of singularity *intellectually* I experience by a pure motion of my will. The primacy of the will over the intellect, though subsuming it more than negating it, makes singularity for us here below the place of an *experience* or a *pleasure* [*jouissance*], rather than a knowledge [*connaissance*] or a vision of essence" (465–66/275). This movement of the will rejoices in what it does not and cannot know, and the experience of recognizing and responding to the singularity that remains unknowable in this world cannot be reduced to phenomena. While there are evident differences between Levinas's ethics and Scotus's ontology, it is unnecessary to investigate these differences further. Rather, based on this analysis of singularity, I propose two key claims: first, although the friend's singularity is not wholly given phenomenally, one does recognize the friend as a singularity; and second, this recognition does not involve comparing the friend to others.[8]

Encountering the Friend: Beyond Preference

To develop and defend these two claims, I begin by returning to Levinas's warning against noticing the Other's individual characteristics. Certainly, I must not refuse to aid the Other because, for example, she dislikes dogs—but if the Other's opinion of dogs is a matter of complete indifference to me, I am disregarding a facet of her self. It is common enough for people to say that they want to be seen for who they are, and by that statement they mean that they do not want to have to hide their personalities, their interests, even their virtues and vices, to be loved. Put more positively, they want someone to appreciate the assemblages of traits, however odd, by which they are given phenomenally; they do not, one hopes, want others to appreciate their vices, but they want friends who will help them combat those vices instead of turning away in disgust. Of course, the supposed ideal of simply being oneself—a cliché people often have in mind when they express the desire to be seen for who they are—is an impossible one. Interests and character traits are subject to change; one may misunderstand or actively deceive oneself about one's own character; and in any case the self is always other than itself. One can never just be who one is, much less be seen for who one is. Yet however clichéd and simplistic the formulation is, one who says, "I want to be seen, even appreciated, for who I am" is not merely talking nonsense. Even Sartre's waiter who can but play at being a waiter is more truthful if he says, "I am a waiter" than if he says, "I am a journalist"[9]—and if he had to keep his job a secret or face condemnation, he would quite reasonably be glad to encounter a person who accepted his occupation. This acceptance falls short of friendship, but the crucial point at this stage of the argument is that noticing details of the Other's life and character can be a way of caring for the Other.

Furthermore, even if one does not have to hide one's interests or beliefs, it is still a delight to discover someone who shares them. Upon meeting, for example, someone who reads the same books or works for the same causes, one thinks with joy, "I have found someone with whom to share what matters to me!"[10] This encounter is a genuine moment of recognition: each sees the other person and responds by rejoicing in some aspect of that person's self that others would pass by, not out of any moral failing but simply because no one is suited to pursuing all worthwhile interests or working for all good causes. Again, this falls short of friendship, but it provides an occasion for two people to be drawn to each other. Perceiving and welcoming another's interests, personality, and virtues is part of recognizing him or her as a specific individual whom one values. One's own pleasure in the activities one shares with another in no way diminishes the ethical value of that sharing; on the contrary, the self's pleasure adds to the Other's pleasure. If, for instance, Alice loves to play tennis, she does not want to play it with someone who is doing so only out of a sense of obligation; rather, she wants to encounter someone who also loves tennis, who will be glad that she loves it, and who will therefore enjoy playing it with her. What is more, because the pleasure people take in shared pursuits grows precisely through being shared, it is not the egoistic enjoyment of which Levinas writes. Each person delights in the other's pleasure in their shared activity at least as much as in his or her own.

The preceding analysis thus furnishes a preliminary reply to the question of whether ethics permits preferring one person to another. Because people have different interests and personalities, not all Others will even desire to share activities with a given self. In addition, as it is impossible to pursue shared interests with everyone, the only options are to do so with a few or with none, and it would be unreasonable to withhold the good of pursuing common interests together from everyone just because a single person can share it only with some. The above discussion fails, however, to adequately consider what friendship is. Imagining friendship today, we often think of a private sentimental relation in which people pursue shared interests and accurately recognize and appreciate each other's perceived characteristics. But this companionship, however pleasant and even beneficial it may be, is not the transformative, destabilizing relation that calls the self out of itself toward another.

While the ready companionship that arises between two or more people who enjoy sharing some activity need not exclude the struggle in the dark through which one strives to bear witness to another and through which one receives oneself, it is essential not to confuse the two. Seeing another's characteristics is not necessarily wrong and may indeed be part of caring for him or her, but seeing *only* another's characteristics is to create for oneself a simulacrum of him or her, and it therefore cannot suffice for friendship. To rightly consider the relation between ethics and friendship, we must reckon with the *unknowable* singularity of the Other. Thus far, too, this analysis has said nothing of fidelity, yet without an enduring commitment that binds them, two people with common interests are merely friendly acquaintances and will hardly be spoken of in the same breath as Orestes and Pylades, who wished to die for each other. Let us, therefore, reflect more deeply on what it means for two people to be drawn together in friendship.

Friendship, as it is commonly understood, seems to involve choice, unlike familial relations, into which one is born and which hold whether one likes it or not. Yet the language of preference and choice proves inadequate in the face of singularity. Stating that I prefer one brand of ketchup to others implies that all the brands are subsumed under the universal "ketchup," that I have compared them with each other, and that I have chosen one out of the totality of brands of ketchup. Choosing and preferring a friend, however, is not—must not be—selecting one person out of an ensemble, as though the chosen friend were an object that could be compared with other objects in a class and that had the good fortune of pleasing me more than the others. Such a selection would demean the friend and deny her singularity. What then occurs when one seems to choose a friend?

Confronted with the mystery of the supposed choice of or preference for the friend, one can hardly find a better starting point than Michel de Montaigne's famous remark concerning his friendship with Étienne de la Boétie: "If I were pressed to say why I loved him, I feel that it could be expressed only by replying: 'Because it was he, because it was I'" (E 186–87/97, trans. mod.). The point is not to describe or universalize one person's experience; rather, Montaigne's inability to adequately describe friendship testifies to a secret that underlies any conscious decision or experience. "'Because it was he,'" writes Montaigne, and not "'Because it was he, not they.'" For there is no *they*, no totality to which *he*, or for that matter *I*, could be said to belong. *He* is elected not out of many but precisely as a singularity, elected with a mysterious election that, in stark contrast to the preference for a brand of ketchup, admits of no comparison. Indeed, *I* too am elected, summoned to friendship without, in truth, the slightest notion why: Montaigne dares not claim that his reply explains anything but only that it expresses (*exprimer*). *Express*: to press out (the French and English verbs have, conveniently enough, the same root). He presses the secret that is his friendship, seeking its *why*, and finally wrests from it only two phrases that reveal the folly of the insistent "Why?" by not answering it. These phrases stand as dramatic flourishes that, pressed out of the overflowing of the secret, name two more secrets—two unknowable singularities, *he* and *I*—as a reproach to anyone who thought friendship required a reason. "The rose is without why / It blooms because it blooms";[11] so too with friendship. In the end Montaigne does know better than to try to unfold (explain, *expliquer*) his friendship for La Boétie, as though it could be laid out and displayed for the public. "There is, beyond all my reasoning [*discours*]," he admits, "and beyond all that I can specifically say, I know not what inexplicable power of destiny that brought about our union" (E 187/97, trans. mod.). He makes no appeal to any private sentiment, as if friendship could be brought into being and sustained by emotion; he says nothing, even, about any decision they made to befriend each other. Their friendship is less a secret that they share than a secret that shares them. He is, after all, writing of it insofar as he can; that it remains a secret is less his decision (though perhaps he would have decided thus, were it up to him) than a truth he cannot alter.

Commenting on the line "'Because it was he, because it was I,'" by which "[he has] always been less moved than offended," Blanchot is at once insightful and over-hasty: he writes that "it is later, when the same Montaigne gives up on introducing into his writings *Le Discours sur la servitude volontaire* [written by La Boétie] (which was supposed to be their central point) that he returns to juster, less exalted sentiments, giving us to understand the complexity of friendship and the discretion that it requires when one speaks of it."[12] The very grandeur of Montaigne's statement is, however, its discretion: by strikingly failing to explain anything at all, it proclaims the impossibility of adequately speaking of the friend. Who, indeed, are *he* and *I*? Montaigne does not even name La Boétie; a pronoun stands in for the proper name, as if to foreshadow his "giving up on" including La Boétie's work in his *Essays*. The famous line describes no sentiment, no experience, no decision; it expresses, rather, the impossibility of explaining friendship by reference to any sentiment, experience, or decision, and so it compels Montaigne, and us as well, to speak more discreetly than he, or we, might perhaps wish. Although he goes on to mention his first meeting with La Boétie, he has already admitted that nothing in this meeting or subsequent to it can explain their friendship. Levinas and Blanchot decided to call each other *tu*, the French informal form of *you*, and Montaigne decided to affirm, in writing, that he and La Boétie were friends—yet not only is the decision to befriend another recognizable as such only in retrospect, but it is impossible to give a full account of any such decision, precisely because the decision binds two unknowable singularities. The primordial inexplicability that Montaigne encounters when he tries to give an account of his friendship underlies and precedes any conscious decision.

To consider that friendship is primordially a preferential relation is to misunderstand its nature. Preference is never fundamental to friendship. It is not false to say that Montaigne preferred La Boétie to other people, but his account suggests the crucial point that friendship is not a matter of the self examining a group of people, deciding that it prefers one person to the others, and entering into a friendship with that person on the basis of that preference. In practice, one is friends with this person and not that person, but the comparison implied by "and not that person" does not ground the friendship. One can cite qualities that the friend has and that others lack, yet the friendship holds—if indeed it does—by virtue not of others' insufficiencies but of the friend's sufficiency. The question of whether ethics permits preference is thus in part a red herring: given that one does notice and appreciate the friend's characteristics, it is useful to see that this appreciation may be consistent with ethics, but friendship is not grounded in preference. Indeed, comparison and preference cannot possibly ground friendship, because if friendship were based in some comparison of the friend to others, the self and its capacity to know and judge others would be privileged over the friend and the promise that binds friends together. Yet in friendship I am promised without knowing exactly to whom or to what the promise commits me, for I can never wholly know either the friend or the others to whom I might later compare him or her. The promise precedes my knowledge and my judgment. I choose the friend—if I can be said to choose at all—not out of an ensemble but by responding to the call that, prior to any choice or decision on my part, prior even to the dichotomies between choice and necessity, action and passivity, reason and passion, awakens me to the possibility of friendship.

Indeed, to say only that I choose the friend places too much emphasis on my subjectivity and risks implying that I could simply choose to end the friendship if I no longer enjoyed the other person's company or ceased to share interests with him or her. Friendship is not fundamentally constituted by shared activities, pleasure in each other's company, and approval of each other's characteristics. While all these things may feature in friendship, they suffice only for what I have above called companionship, a relation that, like Aristotle's friendship of pleasure, is "easily dissolved" if one person changes (NE 1156a19), since "those who love on account of pleasure feel affection for the sake of their own pleasure" and not for the sake of the other (NE 1156a16–17). Those who take pleasure in each other's company only because they like those qualities by which the other person is given phenomenally are not truly committed to each other—which is not to say that such pleasure is necessarily wrong, only that it is not friendship. Even admiring another person's virtue does not in itself entail being bound and transformed by any lasting commitment to that person. And while the impulse to seek the company of one person rather than another may be selfish—though it may also be a legitimate expression of care for that person—that impulse is not friendship either. It is true that pleasure or admiration may lead me to desire friendship with another, but friendship so far surpasses this initial pleasure or admiration that I cannot explain the friendship by reference to them. If, upon concluding that another's company is pleasant, I declare, "I will befriend this person," then I do not and cannot fully know what I am saying. The promise that binds friends is both a choice that must be reiterated and a necessity that commits them to that continual reiteration of that choice, always before they can possibly realize to what they are committed.

Encountering the Friend: Beyond Ethics

The number of friends it is possible to have is limited, as Aristotle recognizes when he suggests that one cannot be friends with more people than can live together (NE 1171a1–2). If one is friends with some and not others, this is not because one devalues the others but because one's love for some exceeds what is commanded—and not simply by one's own decision, as though an explanation of friendship lay within the self, but by a blessing, a *something more* given to both self and Other. Given by whom, or by what? No sign tells. Those who believe that all that is good is from God will thank him, seeing a revelation of his existence in the astonishing truth that two can be elected for friendship without explanation. For one who holds this belief, it is not that God forces two people into friendship, thereby providing a comprehensible account of that friendship, but that he creates the conditions in which the mystery that is friendship can arise: friendship points the believer to God not as a logic puzzle points to its solution but as a gift points to its giver.

In any case, friendship implicates me in my individual singularity—in my haecceity—more profoundly than does ethics. I am the willing hostage of Levinas's Other, and, crucially, I come to the Other only as a hostage. That is, the Other summons me specifically because I have no right to hand my responsibility over to anyone else, but it is not the case that the Other rejoices in my singularity any more than in that of a third party. It is only because I cannot appeal to the third party, who for me is also an Other, that I cannot think the Other making such an appeal: if I imagine the Other calling someone else, I imagine myself evading my responsibility. The Other calls me *as* the singular individual that I am, but not *because* I am the singular individual that I am. This is a critical nuance, as it is here that the gap between ethics and friendship appears. For the friend does call me in particular because I am myself. Such a "because" does not attenuate the point that friendship arises beyond reason: Montaigne's "Because it was he; because it was I" does not in fact explain the friendship. The "because" marks a mystery, but the mystery is one that is essential to friendship. In friendship it is not only that I must not imagine the friend convoking anyone else in my place, but that the friend does not and would not do so. Every reader of Levinas reads him from the position of the self; Levinas himself wrote from the position of the self. But no reader of Montaigne reads him from the position of La Boétie—who died nearly a decade before Montaigne began writing the *Essays*. Levinas insists that none can substitute for me—but all the same Levinas's Other does not mourn the self's death.

It may seem ridiculous to suggest that my love for the friend exceeds my love for the Levinasian Other because the former gives the friend the possibility of mourning—the possibility, to borrow a phrase from Derrida (though he wrote rather of the self facing another's death), that with my death the world will end.[13] Yet this statement makes clear that the friend calls to me because I am myself, whereas the Other calls to me as the one who must aid him.[14] The friend desires not, or not only, aid but *my* world (which, it is true, I also receive from him or her). The Other makes an appeal that could have reached anyone—but I alone heard it, or at least I must act as if that were so. In contrast, the friend calls to me as if I were the only one there—since friendship is not grounded in comparisons of potential friends—but not because I am the only one there. In friendship, therefore, my irreplaceability is essential both to the friend and to myself. I give to the friend the occasion to rejoice in my singularity—and so, inevitably, to face the possibility that I will die first. Friendship is, surprisingly enough given Levinas's often extreme language, a greater self-giving than ethics precisely because there is more to give. It seems as if I must give the Other everything, but the Other does not ask for everything: he or she does not ask for the world that will end with my death. This I am not obliged to give to anyone who does not desire it. In fact I cannot give it to one who does not desire it, for I cannot force anyone to mourn.

A consideration of Levinas's account of dying for the Other illustrates at once the distance between and the closeness of ethics and friendship. Commenting on 2 Samuel 1:23, which proclaims of "King Saul and his son Jonathan" that "'in their death they were not divided,'" Levinas notes that it is "as if, contrary to the Heideggerian analysis, in death, all relationship to the other were not undone" (EN 212/215, trans. mod.). Crucially, dying-for follows living-for: if I die for the Other it is because I have lived for him or her, and, inversely, if I live for the Other it is because I will die for him or her. This dying-for may not be a literal saving of the Other's life, which saving would in any case grant the Other a temporary reprieve and not, as Heidegger emphasized, a permanent escape from death. Saul and Jonathan in fact died in the same battle. What Heidegger did not see, according to Levinas, is, first, that dying to save the Other's life is not reducible to the granting of a merely temporary reprieve and, second, that any death may be for the Other if it concludes a life offered as a sacrifice for the Other. Dying-for means that "worry over the death of the other comes before care for self" (EN 213/216). It means that there is more to human being than the animalistic drive to preserve oneself; it means that even in my death I am directed toward the Other. With this insight Levinas shatters the last refuge of egoism, namely the supposition that the self is alone for its death, its ownmost possibility, and is therefore primordially concerned with itself, only secondarily turning toward others. Indeed, since only the relation to the Other saves me from impersonal totality, it is care for the Other that grounds any possibility of care for myself.

The point that the self's bond to the Other does not end with the moment of death is essential to any analysis of friendship. What Levinas does not consider is that my death might, in some cases, bequeath to the Other a world whose trace remains, however imperfectly, only in the testimony of the Other should he or she outlive me. He does, it is true, take seriously the Biblical claim that Saul and Jonathan "were not separated in death." Here he comes closest to suggesting the possibility of friendship: perhaps self and Other are not separated even if the self dies and the Other lives, which would imply that the self leaves the Other some heritage, and not only vice versa. That he does not explicitly state this, let alone consider the notion of the Other bearing witness to the self, is likely because he would have suspected that such an idea was incompatible with the asymmetry of the ethical relation. To be clear, my aim is not to critique ethics in itself—one cannot be friends with everyone, and so ethics is essential—but rather to argue that friendship is not unethical and indeed is a great good. For the self, certainly, faithful witness is an obligation—yet not only an obligation, for the self would not deny the friend even were such a thing permissible. The friend, even after death, has given me a world that for my own sake as well as the friend's I do not desire to make over in my own image, lest I fall into a solitude that in the ennui of its oblivion would be more painful than the knowledge of loss. Though the ethical relation is also a barrier against solitude, friendship is a still greater one, precisely because it implicates me more profoundly. Likewise, in leaving to the friend the possibility of bearing witness to me I am not demanding reciprocity but am offering, as a final gesture, a safeguard against that solitude. The Other receives this safeguard only if he or she is my friend—that is, again, only if he or she desires it. For friendship may be said to be the desire to mourn another. I do not mean that one desires the friend's death but rather that one desires to be faithful unto mourning. Neither do I wish to paint a tragic picture of friendship; although we must for the moment dwell on this aspect of friendship, it is far from summing up all that friendship is. Mourning itself is not only tragic, for it signifies not being left to oneself. It is the friend's last gift to me and my last gift to the friend.

Mutual Friendship

That friendship is not a demand for reciprocity is an essential point. Indeed, although justifying the reciprocity of friendship does entail going beyond Levinas, who did not explicitly consider that such reciprocity might be good for both self and Other, the conflict between ethical asymmetry and reciprocal friendship is considerably less of a problem than it initially appears to be. Friendship in fact accords with ethics in forbidding any attempt to compel the Other to reciprocate. As Tomáš Tatranský puts it, "the loving response of the other is not enforceable, since it must remain free as my gift was";[15] and as Melissa Fitzpatrick pointedly observes, "if one is chiefly concerned about reciprocity, it is worth asking whether the friendship is in fact equal or based on the good."[16] Reciprocity must be freely given, not demanded as a right: friendship is not friendship if it is wrested from one party against his or her will.

What is more, one friend's love for another is not given in return for the other friend's love. It is a source of joy for friends that they both love each other, but imagining that one friend's love is meant to repay the other friend's love misunderstands the temporality of friendship. Historically, one friend may indeed be the first to love the other, but regardless of the historical sequence of events that can be considered as establishing the friendship, it is as if each friend is the first to love, for neither forces the other to respond. Yet it is also as if each friend is the second to love, responding to the other's love with a gratitude that does not insult by offering repayment. Each friend loves well enough the other's generosity in loving to know that no recompense is possible. The reciprocity of friendship is better understood as, to borrow a phrase from Paul Ricœur's *The Course of Recognition*, a mutual recognition or mutual gratefulness. The French *reconnaissance* means both "recognition" and "gratefulness," which allows Ricœur to point out with particular clarity that recognizing a giver means being grateful. He identifies gratitude [*gratitude*] as "the soul of the division between good and bad reciprocity. Gratitude [. . .] puts the pair *give/receive* on one side, and that of *receive/return* on the other. The gap that it opens between these two pairs is a gap of *inexactness*, in comparison to the equivalence of justice but also to that of buying and selling" (CR 352/243, trans. mod.). In other words, gratitude separates giving and receiving such that they have no common measure. Return, performed with gratitude, does not measure the gift and repay it; it is itself a gift. As Ricœur explains, "the values of exchanged presents are incommensurable in terms of market costs," and "the fitting time to return the gift" is also "without exact measure" (CR 352/243). Here he is not writing specifically about friendship; he explains that agape "is indifferent about getting something in return" (CR 352/243). The temporality of gratitude is, however, characteristic of friendship. One friend gives to the other not in response to a demand but out of love, and the other friend returns the gift not to avoid indebtedness but out of love. Ricœur identifies this exchange of gifts, which is not an exchange in the ordinary, economic sense of the word, as festive: they are acts of celebration that the regime of duty and obligation cannot comprehend (CR 353–54/244–45). This is not to say that it is ever possible, in practice, to avoid the economy of exchange; but if something is good, as this non-economic exchange of gifts is, its impossibility is no reason not to strive for it.

It is worth noting that the lack of any alternative verb to "love" marks a certain linguistic gap: there is no verb that is proper to a sustained friendship. French permits one to designate the love of friendship by writing *aimer d'amitié* ("to love with friendship," literally "to love of friendship") or romantic love by writing *aimer d'amour* ("to love with love," literally "to love of love"); *aimer* by itself, much like *love*, often refers to romantic love but can be used for other kinds of love, including friendship. English, though, has no equivalent to *aimer d'amitié*, and the one verb unique to friendship is "befriend," which refers to the beginning of a friendship rather than its continuation. By a happy linguistic coincidence, the temporality of "befriend" further reinforces that friendship is always to be reiterated or recommenced and is never a completed project. The promise binds for eternity and is also eternally new. There is no end to generosity.

Levinas did not write of the Other loving, caring for, or befriending the self. Despite his disagreements with Levinas, however, Ricœur explicitly states that, far from overturning asymmetry, mutuality needs it: "The avowal of dissymmetry [. . .] protects mutuality against the pitfalls of a fusional union" (CR 376/263, trans. mod.). The Other still transcends the self. Mutuality is not a demand that the Other be made present or comprehensible; an uncrossable distance between self and Other remains.[17] Moreover, when Ricœur writes of mutuality, it is not only the self's advantage that he has in mind. Far from it. Mutuality welcomes both self and Other to the festival that is the non-economic exchange of gifts, and this circulation of gifts multiplies rather than diminishes the love between self and Other. Each gift I give to the Other comes from my love for him or her while also returning to the Other his or her love for me, though not as repayment and in a way that does not lessen my debt. In this way the Other receives more from mutuality than from a strictly non-mutual ethical relation.[18]

Friendship without Ethics?

It is far too soon, however, to conclude that peace has been made between friendship and ethics. Where ethics meets justice, friendship poses a danger precisely because it implicates me in my singularity even more deeply than ethics. Levinas knows well that the interests of different Others do not always accord, but if I consider myself equally bound to them all, is there not less danger that my own preferences will lead me astray? If, in contrast, I am bound in fidelity to one friend more than to anyone else, will I sacrifice other Others on his or her altar? Worse, does friendship demand that I do so? Granted that friendship is not grounded in preference, we must still consider whether in practice it amounts to an unethical preference by requiring or at least inclining me to care about the friend's good to the detriment of others.

Commenting on an example from Roman history, Montaigne attempts to deny the threat friendship poses to others but instead proves that it is indeed a danger. He recounts that after the murder of Tiberius Gracchus by the Roman Senate, Gaius Laelius interrogated Gracchus's closest friend, Caius Blossius, and asked him "how much he would have been willing to do for [Gracchus]." Blossius having replied, "Everything," Laelius asked what he would have done "if [Gracchus] had ordered [him] to set fire to our temples." Blossius initially answered, "He would never have ordered me to do that," but when Laelius pressed the point, he simply said, "I would have obeyed" (E 187/98, trans. mod.). Montaigne hesitates before this declaration, asserting that Blossius ought to have repeated that Gracchus would never have given such a command. He then assures his readers that Blossius's answer, however "brazen" and unwise it was, was not "seditious," precisely because as Gracchus's friend he knew perfectly well that Gracchus would not have desired that he set the temples afire (E 188/98, trans. mod.). Thus Blossius knew that in reality there was no danger that he would have set the temples on fire, and he was not threatening Rome by stating what he *would* have done if an impossible condition were met. After all, Montaigne explains, if someone were to ask him, "If your will ordered you to kill your daughter, would you kill her?" he would have to reply that he would kill her even though, knowing how utterly such a crime repulses him, he also knows that he would never in fact will it. The cases are no different, he insists, because one knows one's friend's will as surely as one's own (E 188/98, trans. mod.). Yet in the midst of this attempt to prove that friendship is no threat, he lets slip a truth that undoes his argument: "[Gracchus and Blossius] were friends more than citizens: friends more than friends or enemies of their country" (E 188/98, trans. mod.). They did in fact place their friendship higher than the good of Rome and its citizens. I do not write "their fellow citizens" because they belonged to each other more than to Rome. The individual's will may bow to a higher authority, such as God or the state, and therefore turn away from a crime that it would otherwise have desired. A greater threat than the individual's will is the will of whomever the individual takes as the highest authority: what that authority commands, the individual will do, though it be a crime. One who is devoted to the friend will be deaf to the cries of the third, the other Other, should the friend demand it.

The friendship Montaigne envisions thus seems to exclude justice. Granted that preference does not ground friendship, does friendship not amount, in practice, to the choice to prefer the friend's good to that of others? Montaigne, for all his delicacy in this matter, cannot demonstrate otherwise. As Derrida observes, Montaigne can argue that friendship is not dangerous only by subordinating it to a "reason and virtue" that "could never be *private*. They cannot enter into conflict with the public realm" (PF 211/184). In short, friendship is not a threat only if it is fundamentally altered by becoming public—or, to put it another way, it is not a threat only if a third, in this case the Roman Republic itself, stands between the friends. "And yet," Derrida recognizes, "Montaigne seems to continue to dream of a fundamental apoliticism or transpoliticism, which would command secrecy, a secrecy that would also be unconditional" (PF 211/184, trans. mod.). If the friend were the only Other, this dream of a secret, apolitical relation that concerns only the two it binds would be more than legitimate; it would be the truth, for without the third there would be no need for politics, for justice. But the friend is not the only Other, and betraying another for the friend's sake is both unjust and unethical (since harming an Other is always unethical, even when justice compels it).

Note that if Gracchus and Blossius were not devoted citizens of Rome, it would mean nothing that they were "friends more than citizens." Consider Luke 14:26: Jesus states, "If anyone comes to me and does not hate his own father and mother and wife and children and brothers and sisters, yes, and even his own life, he cannot be my disciple" (ESV). As Søren Kierkegaard's Johannes de Silentio, the pseudonymous author of *Fear and Trembling*, comments, we must not imagine that Jesus meant for us to lessen our love for our families. No: "if this passage is to have any meaning it must be understood literally," for it does God no honor to pretend that for his sake we fail in our duties (165/73). As he explains,

> a man requires his wife to leave her father and mother, but if he considers it a demonstration of her extraordinary love to him that she for his sake became an indifferent and lax daughter etc., then he is far more stupid than the stupid. If he had any idea of what love [Kjærlighed] is, he would wish to discover that she was perfect in her love as a daughter and sister, and he would see therein that she would love him more than anyone in the kingdom. (165/73)

For her husband's sake, the wife leaves those whom she loves perfectly; it means nothing if to marry him she leaves a family that she likes only moderately. For God's sake also, we must give up what we love perfectly—and so too for the friend's sake. It is equally meaningless to love a friend more than the citizens of a state one loves but little. Fidelity is an altar on which one sacrifices what one loves most.

Thus we return to *Fear and Trembling* and to the story of a friend of God who obeyed when God commanded him to kill his beloved son as a sacrifice. We know how the story ends: Abraham also obeyed God when, after he had bound Isaac and raised the knife, God ordered him to sacrifice the ram instead. But de Silentio reminds us that the apparently reassuring ending does not in fact make Abraham's readiness to sacrifice his son less shocking, for "during the time before the result, either Abraham was a murderer every minute or we stand before a paradox that is higher than all mediations" (159/66). Thomas Aquinas maintained that friendship to God enables us to love all people in charity—yet it was also friendship to God that led Abraham to set forth to sacrifice his son. While the ethical, for Kierkegaard, is not ethics as Levinas understands it—the ethical is a universal system that has no room for the individual—it is clear enough why this teleological suspension of the ethical repels Levinas, for whom the highest command is "Thou shalt not murder." In Levinas's view, if justice requires the sacrifice of one for the sake of another, the one who makes the sacrifice, however necessary it may be, is not a knight of faith and does not merit the awe with which de Silentio regards Abraham.

In the teleological suspension of the ethical, we encounter once again the danger of friendship—and not only of friendship to God but also of friendship to a person. As Derrida points out, "everything happens as though one could not be responsible at the same time before the other and before others, before the others of the other. [. . .] [W]hat is said of Abraham's relation to God is said of my relation without relation to *every other (one) as every (bit) other [tout autre comme tout autre]*, in particular my relation to my neighbor or my loved ones who are as inaccessible to me, as secret, and as transcendent as Jahweh" (GD 109–10/78, trans. mod.). To be sure, Kierkegaard never stated, under the name of de Silentio or otherwise, that the ethical is suspended in fidelity to the human Other as in faith to God, and he would hardly consider fidelity to a person equally important as fidelity to God. Still, Derrida's remark is less out of keeping with Kierkegaard's thought than one might at first suppose. Two individuals cannot be related in the ethical precisely because the ethical is the universal; to relate to another as an individual to an individual therefore requires a suspension of the ethical. Moreover, the sheer profusion of analogies in Kierkegaard's works that clarify the relation to God by analogy to relations to others—including, for instance, the example of the woman who loves her parents perfectly but leaves them for her husband—indicates that the ethical is insufficient not only when it comes to the relation to God but with regard to human relations as well.

It turns out that rejecting the *suspension* of the ethical, as Derrida presents it, amounts to rejecting *ethics*. Because I am responsible for every other, Derrida explains, "at the instant of every decision and in the relation to *every other (one) as every (bit) other*, every other asks us at every moment to behave as a knight of faith" (GD 110–11/79, trans. mod.). And here we find ourselves again confronted with the now-familiar dilemma: fidelity is also betrayal. Fidelity to one Other sacrifices another Other, for I cannot protect everyone, cannot be absolutely faithful to everyone. Even Abraham's fidelity was sealed with blood, of the ram rather than of the son—the ram that, according to Christianity, foreshadows another Son, a betrayed God who died for those who needed to be saved from their own infidelity toward him. It is worth recalling that the Christian belief that all sins are ultimately against God and that God became man to bear our sins on the cross is one Levinas regarded with tactfully-stated concern, lest it be taken to diminish the self's responsibility.[19] And Derrida, commenting in "Literature in Secret" on de Silentio's suggestion that Abraham asked God's forgiveness for having meant to sacrifice Isaac, pointedly though briefly notes that "Abraham does not ask forgiveness of Isaac but of God, a bit like the French Conference of Bishops didn't ask forgiveness of the Jews but of God, even as they called upon the Jewish community to witness, in its own terms, the forgiveness asked of God. Here Abraham does not even call Isaac as a witness to the forgiveness that he, Abraham, asks of God for having wanted to put Isaac to death" (GD 169–70/127, trans. mod.). In any case, fidelity is indissolubly linked to sacrifice and to this question of forgiveness. If we hope that it is possible to avoid needing to ask forgiveness, we deceive ourselves. As long as there are multiple Others, and as long as I am responsible for every Other, I cannot avoid betraying one for the sake of another. It does not follow, however, that friendship is permissible, for friendship, so it seems, violates not only ethics but also justice. If I must need forgiveness, if I must sacrifice some Other, let it at least be in the name of justice and not friendship—is this the conclusion into which we are forced? I answer that it is not.

Friendship between Singularity and Universality

Once again, the role of singularity in friendship and in ethics proves crucial. Because the ethical relation is asymmetrical, the self's position with regard to the Other's singularity is not identical to the Other's position with regard to the self's singularity. Seeing the Other's individual singularity is impossible (at least in this life, if Scotus is right), but one must see the Other as a singular individual—must recognize, that is, that he or she is a singular individual. The self is called to respond to the Other *as* the singular individual that he or she is. In theory, the self is also called to respond to the Other *because* the Other is the singular individual that he or she is. I must obey the command "Thou shalt not commit murder" not because the Other belongs to the human race or to any other universal category but rather simply because the Other is the Other. In practice, however, the situation is more complicated: the moment the command enters into language, it risks entering into the universal. Levinas explains in *Totality and Infinity* that "the *relation* between the same and the other [. . .] is language" (TI 28/39)—but it is also the case that "the third party looks at me in the eyes of the Other—language is justice" (TI 234/213). Hence I do not respond to the Other only because of who he or she is but because he or she is the singular individual who in this moment stands before me (though never wholly present to me) on behalf of all Others.

In friendship, in contrast, I do love the friend simply because of who he or she is, regardless of any command that would relate us to the universal. At first glance, therefore, Aristotle's assertion that "when people are friends, they have no need of justice" (NE 1155a26–27) may seem to apply to friendship and ethics as well. We must be careful here, however, because it is impossible that there be no command. Aristotelian friends of virtue have no need of justice because they will treat each other rightly without needing to consult rules made for the *polis*, but because the ethical command is primordial and not made for political life, there is no question of needing or not needing it: it is the condition of any relation between self and Other. In arising without regard for the command *that relates one to the universal*—this clause is crucial—friendship in fact bears a striking resemblance to ethics as Levinas describes it in *Otherwise than Being*, where he distinguishes ethics from justice more strongly than he had in *Totality and Infinity*. In *Otherwise than Being*, he writes that "the third party introduces a contradiction in the saying whose signification before the other until then went in one direction" (OB 245/157). In the Saying that is beyond essence, the self is related only to the Other in his or her singularity: the Saying, "a foreword [*avant-propos*] preceding languages" (OB 17/5), is pre-universal and conditions the universal that inevitably arises from it. That said, friendship still differs from ethics for the reasons examined above: it is a mutual relation that implicates the self more deeply than ethics.

It is, however, impossible to avoid the universal. The Saying enters into language and becomes the Said—or, better, the pure Saying never was. And this falling that has always already begun should not be deemed a fall from grace, precisely because it is not a fall *from* anything: there never was a pure origin to fall from. It remains true that, as Levinas observed in *Totality and Infinity*, "the generality of the word [*mot*] institutes a common world. [. . .] Generalization is a universalization—[. . .] the offering of the world to the Other" (TI 189/174). Without universalization, without some sort of in-common, we could not share a world. Universalization is a double movement, both an attack on singularity and a gift of a world that is common enough for the singular self and the singular Other to meet there. Note also that language is not simply on the side of the universal but also resists it. Language is not a contamination of the pre-linguistic Saying; it is, to risk a tautology, the only way we can speak to and with each other. It is through language that the self in his or her singularity leaves solipsism, receives the world from the Other in his or her singularity, and gives the world to the Other.[20] There is no question of a Hegelian *Aufhebung* that takes up the singular into the universal while claiming to preserve it—the relation between the singular and the universal is rather less peaceful than that, as the former never ceases to resist the latter. Fidelity and betrayal go hand in hand: every testimony to singularity universalizes, and every universalization testifies to the singularity that resists it.

It is friendship, not passing interactions with people one may never see again, not casual acquaintanceships, that stands most strikingly at the articulation between the private and the political, between the singularity of the Other to whom one is devoted and the needs of all humans. Although this tension between the singular and the universal does structure every encounter with the Other, it is in friendship that my singularity is most deeply engaged. It is therefore in friendship that I am bound most strongly to the Other in his or her singularity—and in consequence it is in friendship that the impossibility of avoiding the universal is most shocking. When a casual encounter enters the universal, I may imagine that a more faithful relationship could have avoided the universal; in contrast, friendship demands a profound fidelity such that I am compelled to realize that if the universal cannot be avoided in friendship—and it cannot, or else I could not speak to the friend—it cannot be avoided anywhere.

Moreover, Derrida observes that although friendship clearly appears as a threat to the political, philosophers have not seen it primarily as a threat: on the contrary, "*the great philosophical and canonical discourses* on friendship will have explicitly tied the friend-brother to virtue and justice, to moral reason and political reason" (PF 308/277). In fact, I maintain, friendship upholds political life precisely by threatening it. Although the only justice that we can achieve in practice does universalize, it ceases altogether to be worthy of the name of justice if it forgets the singular. By insisting on the singular, the private, the secret, friendship reminds us that justice is meant to protect the singularity of each Other, even though it can never do so adequately. More casual relations than friendship accommodate the political too readily: a perfect Roman citizen might set fire to his city's temples for the sake of a friend, but never for an acquaintance. For an acquaintance, he might not (though he should) even pause to notice that in refusing, he was comparing the interests of the Other and the third. When the friend makes the request, even if he decides that the friend is so wrong that the best way to serve the friend is actually to oppose him in this matter, he remembers the importance of singularity. If we did not have friendship—this relation to an Other whom I do not wish to compare to anyone else—it would be easier to forget that comparison, while necessary for political justice, is always a betrayal.

The notion that friendship may serve as a corrective to political justice might call to mind Aristotle's acknowledgment of the importance of *epieikeia*, or decency, which he defines as "a correction of law in the respect in which it is deficient because of its being general" (NE 1137b27).[21] The key point is that the general or universal, though necessary—and Aristotle does insist on its necessity—will at some point encounter a case in which it fails. Levinas would reply that in truth the universal fails in all cases, although it is necessary and even useful, and although even our corrections to it remain within it. Friendship, then, stands as a reminder that the law is always and ever in need of correction.

But have we not seen that friendship too is a betrayal of the Others who are not the friend? I have no intention of suggesting that friendship is without danger or that it cannot become hostility. I argue rather that friendship does not permit an easy forgetting of those who are not the friend. Remember that devotion to the friend would be meaningless if one did not also love one's fellow citizens; even Abraham's fidelity to God retains something of the public because it depends on his love for Isaac. Recall also that "the third party looks at me in the eyes of the Other" (TI 234/213): all Others look at me in the gaze of any one Other, and therefore in the gaze of the friend. Others who are not the friend may, certainly, look directly at me; the point is that they look at me in the friend's look as well. Levinas's statement that "every other man is a friend"

(EN 127/117, trans. mod.) thus takes on a sense he did not anticipate: all are friends through the friend. Fidelity to the friend binds me also to all others. Responsibility to the friend thus becomes responsibility to all, and my responsibility to the friend includes a responsibility to not do wrong in his or her name.[22] This conclusion may seem simply to be a universalization, but the situation is more complicated than that: because I recognize the friend as absolutely singular, when the third looks at me through the eyes of the friend, I also recognize the third as absolutely singular. In practice, it is impossible to altogether avoid universalization, but all the same the friend stands before me as a singular individual who refers me to other singular individuals.

That all others look at me in the gaze of the friend makes possible a response to Kierkegaard's charge that friendship is a preferential love (*Forkjerlighed*, which may also be rendered as "taste" or "affinity") and that such a love is actually a preference for oneself—that is, self-love. In *Works of Love*, contrasting friendship with Christian self-denial and love (*Kjerlighed*) of the neighbor, he writes that "preferential love's most passionate boundlessness in excluding means to love only one single person; self-denial's boundlessness in giving itself means not to exclude a single one" (59/52). Then, arguing that preferential love ultimately proves to be self-love, he asks, "To be the one and only friend of this one and only admired person—would not this relation turn back in an alarming way into the I from which we proceeded?" (61/54). I have already argued that friendship is not grounded in preference or in those qualities that are given phenomenally and to which taste and affinity respond. Now we see more fully that friendship turns, not inward to the self, but outward to all others. Recall that the temporality of friendship is that of gratitude, not of exchange: giving and receiving have no common measure, and the gap opened by their non-alignment is the gap that enables friendship to open onto the world rather than collapsing into egoism and self-love. Because I neither demand repayment nor presume to attempt repayment myself, I am drawn outward from myself toward the friend, and by that outward movement, I am confronted with my responsibility to all. Although it is not only through friendship that I am faced with my responsibility to all others, friendship does direct me to that responsibility, and I can attempt to deny it only by rejecting the temporality of gratitude and therefore friendship as well. Again, it does not follow that friendship is without danger, that love for the friend will never conflict with love for others—but all the same, friendship does not permit me to cease loving others or to forget my responsibility to each and every Other.

Finally, opposing the friend for the sake of the third need not be a failure of fidelity. One does the friend no favors by allowing him or her to do wrong. Assuming that friendship and opposition are necessarily at odds is in any case too simplistic. Consider the words Nietzsche places in the mouth of Zarathustra in *Thus Spoke Zarathustra*: "In one's friend one should have one's best enemy. You should be closest to him in heart when you strive against him" (71–72/40, trans. mod.). The self and the friend/enemy pursue excellence precisely by resisting each other: they do not let each other stagnate or get away with weakness but sharpen each other. Zarathustra continues, "[Y]ou should be for [your friend] an arrow and a longing [*Sehnsucht*] for the overman" (72/41, trans. mod.). He is recommending not a destructive enmity but a creative one, a competitive relationship that drives the friends to greatness and strengthens them.[23] Fidelity to the friend is a struggle with the friend not only because one's witness is never adequate but also because one has the responsibility to be strengthened by the friend and to strengthen him or her. Spurring another onward to greater creativity or, to return to Levinasian language, greater justice will not always appear kind. It is, however, faithful because it is good for the Other himself or herself to become more just.

Levinas would surely warn that in struggling with the friend one risks imposing on him or her one's own selfish idea of what he or she ought to be. Nietzsche—and his Zarathustra, who sought "companions [*Gefährten*]" and not sheep in need of a shepherd (25–27/14–15)—would agree that one must not seek to create the friend in one's own image. He could add, however, as he writes in *The Gay Science*, that "the secret [*Geheimnis*] for harvesting from existence the greatest fruitfulness and the greatest enjoyment is—to live dangerously [*gefährlich*]!" (526/161). To live at all is to take risks; therefore to embrace life is to embrace risk. Friendship too cannot be made safe if it is to be worthwhile. I do not claim to wholly reconcile Levinas and Nietzsche; rather, one can read them as friends whose texts sharpen each other—and sharpen their readers, who must discern for themselves when to obey the Other and when to challenge him or her.[24] Neither do I claim to have removed the possibility of conflict between friendship and ethics or friendship and justice. Although one does not truly serve the friend by consenting when he or she acts unjustly, there is no guarantee that one will recognize the friend's injustice when one sees it, that one will know how to respond most effectively, or, for that matter, that there will be one most effective response. Nothing can alter the fact that the crossing of singularity and universality, where friendship stands, is dangerous: on the one hand, one may become absorbed in the friend's singularity to the exclusion of all else, and on the other hand, one may fall into the universal, which is only another way of forgetting both the Other and the third, who are absolutely singular. Even as friendship reminds us that we cannot avoid weighing and comparing different people's interests, it does stand outside of justice precisely because all human relations stand outside of justice: however necessary such comparisons are in practice, they never suffice to sum up one's relation with any Other. Yet because friendship confronts us with the singularity of the Other and because our friends may also spur us on in our pursuit of justice and of ethics (let us note that ethics itself both drives and questions our pursuit of justice), friendship at its best reinforces and strengthens our commitment to justice and to ethics.

Here one might protest that ethics alone should suffice, that we should not need another relation that points toward it. Indeed, one who is in the unfortunate situation of having no friends (understanding friendship as a relation of mutual fidelity rather than in the broader sense in which Levinas sometimes employs the word) does not thereby have an excuse to disregard ethics. Friendship cannot, however, be reduced to a signpost or a safeguard against our worst tendencies. Friendship is a surplus, a *something more* in which both self and Other receive beyond what ethics requires. That friendship can direct us toward true justice serves to defend it against the charge that it is fundamentally unjust, but while it is true that we should not need friendship to remind us of the Other's singularity, friendship does not arise because it is useful or even because it is necessary. It arises beyond any reason, and we should rejoice in it.

3

Within Finitude, Bearing the Infinite

When considering the goodness of friendship, it is all too easy to conclude, given the concrete ways that friendship benefits us—for instance, friends help us when we are in need, friends encourage us to pursue virtue, friends make our lives more interesting in the good sense of the word—that friendship exists simply to compensate for our insufficiencies. Even if any particular friendship is beyond explanation, it seems that friendship, as a general phenomenon, arises because individual humans lack certain things that their friends supply. Would it not be better, though, if we could rely wholly on ourselves, such that the benefits of friendship were superfluous? Any attempt to rigorously think friendship's goodness must also reckon with our limits as human beings. Only once we have developed an account of human finitude as a positive good, such that it would not in fact be better for us as human beings to be wholly self-reliant, can we fully appreciate friendship's goodness as well. Friendship, I argue, is not a compensation for unfortunate privations. Rather, friends translate the world for each other so that each one comes to experience the world not as the other does but in light of the other's always-unknowable experience.

Does Friendship Arise from Lack?

Aristotle wrestles with the relation between self-sufficiency, or our lack thereof, and friendship in the *Nicomachean Ethics*, observing that "people assert [. . .] that, since the happy are self-sufficient [αὐτάρκεσιν], they have no need of anyone in addition, whereas a friend, since he is another self, provides only what someone is unable to provide on his own" (NE 1169b4–8). According to this popular view that Aristotle cites, the ideal is a self-contained ipseity that has no need of the friend's alterity: to be truly happy is to be sufficient unto oneself, and therefore the only reason to have friends is that we fail to live up to this ideal. Friendship, to put it another way, derives its worth from our insufficiency, from our lack. Far from being a good in itself, friendship is good only in the way a bandage is good: that is, it is good only insofar as it is useful, and it would be better still to not need it at all. If one is wounded, it is certainly better to have a bandage than to not have one, but it would be better still to not be wounded in the first place. Hence the bandage is not an intrinsic good—a good that is good and desirable in and of itself, no matter what. The true good is not the bandage but rather health, and one desires the bandage only when one needs to use it to restore one's health. Likewise, if the popular opinion to which Aristotle refers is correct, friendship is not good in itself, and the true good is self-sufficiency. The self-sufficient person would have no more need of friends than the unwounded person has of a bandage. Because the friend is another self, friendship may permit the friends to reach a state that approximates self-sufficiency, but they would be happier still if they could be truly self-sufficient, with no need for each other. Friendship, then, seems to be a sort of bandage or crutch that allows people to compensate for their lack of self-sufficiency.

Aristotle rejects this view of friendship as a crutch that we ideally would not need and implicitly suggests that those who idealize self-sufficiency misunderstand the nature of human beings. As he explains, "no one would choose to have all good things by himself, since a human being is political [πολιτικὸν] and is disposed by nature [πεφυκός] to live with others. So this too belongs to the happy man, for he possesses the things good by nature [τῇ φύσει ἀγαθὰ]" (NE 1169b17–20). When people suppose that those who are happy are self-sufficient and need no friends, their definition of happiness is not suited to human beings. Humans cannot live well without others—which is another point that we must bear in mind when evaluating the place of alterity in Aristotle's thought. Certainly he is not a proto-Levinas, but here, again, his ethics proves not to be a simple triumph of the Same over the Other. It is true that he valorizes the contemplative life in part because it permits comparative self-sufficiency (see NE 1177a28–36), but complete self-sufficiency is neither possible nor—crucially—desirable for human beings. By virtue of his very nature as a human, even the contemplative philosopher desires companions. He is satisfied with those few with whom he can truly be friends, but he does not wish for solitude, nor should he.[1] And if humans should not aspire to complete self-sufficiency, then friendship is not a bandage compensating for an unfortunate lack, for our insufficiency is not a wound but is rather the condition that is proper to us.

This analysis does not go far enough, however, as it still offers a fundamentally negative picture of the human condition—that is, the human condition remains characterized by what it lacks. Having observed that humans naturally desire to live with others, Aristotle writes that "for the happy man, accordingly, there is need of friends [δεῖ ἄρα τῷ εὐδαίμονι φίλων]" (NE 1169b22). This phrasing underscores the notion of lack or insufficiency: the Greek δέω (here conjugated as δεῖ), like the English "need," conveys that the happy man would be lacking if he did not have friends. If, however, the condition we have until now been summing up under the name of "insufficiency" is in fact proper to human beings, it is worth asking whether we can describe it more positively rather than defining it only in terms of lack. It is true that humans are not self-sufficient. But focusing solely on this fact, however much one qualifies it by remarking that not being self-sufficient is good for us, still risks, by its emphasis on the *not*, giving the impression that the human condition is defined by falling short of an ideal. The focus, when one speaks of human insufficiency, remains too much on the self-sufficiency that we do not have. To understand friendship as a positive good, and not only or primarily as something that makes up for our lack of self-sufficiency, we must consider the human condition on its own terms.

Here Aristotle's *Eudemian Ethics* is clearer than the *Nicomachean Ethics*. It seems, admits Aristotle in the *Eudemian Ethics*, that the ideal life would not include friends. After all, gods do not need friends, or indeed anything at all, and "so too the man who is happiest will least of all need a friend, except to the extent that it is impossible for him to be self-sufficient" (EE 1244b10–12). On closer examination, however, it turns out that the "juxtaposed arguments"—that is, the conflation of the argument regarding what makes the gods happy and the argument regarding what makes humans happy—are the source of the confusion about whether friendship contributes to human happiness (EE 1244b23–24). In other words, if we find ourselves thinking that the best life for human beings would be a friendless one, that is because we have confused what is good for the gods with what is good for humans, thereby failing to consider human existence on its own terms. Human beings in fact derive pleasure from sharing their lives with others, and Aristotle concludes that "for us being in a good condition depends on something else, while, as for god, he is himself his own good condition" (EE 1245b18–20). This insight that a human being's good condition is different from, and not an inferior imitation of, a god's good condition is crucial. A god, or God, is greater than a human being, but it does not follow that it would be better *for a human being* to be in the same condition as a god, or as God. The point is a subtle one, but the crux of the matter is this: human existence is not best or most fundamentally defined by what it lacks in comparison to divine existence. And since the good condition of a human being is not fundamentally a matter of lack or insufficiency, and since friendship is an essential part of that good condition, it does not make sense to define friendship solely as compensation for human lacks.

To be clear, I do not deny—nor, certainly, does Aristotle—that friendship provides us with benefits that help compensate for our insufficiencies. Rather, I propose that understanding friendship as compensation for and a consequence of our lack of self-sufficiency is too limited a view of friendship and, indeed, of human existence. Consider an analogy: God has no need for beauty that lies outside himself because he is himself perfectly beautiful. Yet saying only that we as humans benefit from external sources of beauty because we are not perfectly beautiful reduces our desire for beauty to the result of an imperfection. And such a reduction is unwarranted: if one seeks to investigate the experience of being moved by the beauty of a cathedral or a symphony, it is nothing short of absurd to observe simply that if we were gods we would have no need for such experiences. Our capacity to rejoice in beauty is suited to human existence in the world and is not best or most fully described as a lack, for it is one of the joys of human existence. So too with friendship: although it does benefit us insofar as we are not self-sufficient beings, a purely negative analysis that reduces it to a compensation for our lack of self-sufficiency is so far from complete as to be utterly inadequate. Let us turn, therefore, to the notion of finitude, which will make it possible to understand friendship as a transformation of one's manner of existing in the world, not as compensation for regrettable insufficiencies.

Finitude as a Positive Good

Heidegger's distinction between finitude and the finite is crucial. The imperfect finite is opposed to the perfect infinite, but human finitude is more fundamental than human imperfection: as he writes, "in order to designate the finite [*Endliches*] in human beings it might suffice to cite any of our imperfections [*Unvollkommenheiten*]. In this way, we gain, at best, evidence for the fact that the human being is a finite essence [*endliches Wesen*]. However, we learn neither wherein the essence [*Wesen*] of his finitude [*Endlichkeit*] exists, nor even how this finitude completely determines the human being from the ground up as the being it is" (GA 3 219–20/154). We exist within finitude, that is, within limits marked by a birth we did not choose and by a death we cannot evade. Listing all our imperfections, all the powers that we lack, fails to express the essence of human being: we are not omniscient, not omnipotent, not infinite, not eternal, not omnipresent—and in all these "nots" we find no positive, concrete account of an existence marked by the horizons of birth and death. The temporal is not the mere negation of the eternal: to properly interrogate the phenomenon of our existence within time it would not do to develop an account of God's eternity and then negate that account without a word for what temporality *is*, as though the temporal and our experience thereof were merely derivative of an eternity we have never experienced. Likewise, finitude—which is essentially temporal—is not the mere negation of the infinite. To properly understand finitude—existence within limits—we must begin not with infinity but rather with an interrogation of how our limits shape our experience.

More recently, Emmanuel Falque has made finitude and its goodness a cornerstone of his thought, and he sharply distinguishes finitude from the finite. Taking his cue from Heidegger, he explains that finitude "transgresses [. . .] and does away with any mundane duality to indicate here the limited and contingent horizon of an existence 'on a human scale.' We must therefore be careful not to confuse the 'finite being' with one who 'lives in finitude'" (GG 41/16). The infinite and the finite refer to each other, and although, etymologically speaking, it is *in-finite* that is the negation of *finite* and not vice versa, the fact remains that the infinite seems to be on the side of perfection and the finite on the side of lack, incompleteness, and privation. Whereas a finite being stands at one pole of a dichotomy—in Falque's words, he or she "requires reference to another—the Infinite—of which he or she regrets being simply a limitation and desires afresh some kind of infinity"—finitude breaks free from this dichotomy because it "is happy simply with 'Being-there,' facing death and definitively anchored in an existence that is devoid, at least to begin with, of an elsewhere" (GG 41/16). Finitude, in other words, does not refer to anything beyond itself. Falque's distinction between limit and limitation proceeds along similar lines: "limit indicates simply the obstructed horizon of existence, following Heidegger, or yet the constitution of our created being, according to Aquinas. Limitation lays claim to the unlimited as if our condition were not the one in which we find ourselves as incarnate beings"—as if, that is, it would be better for us to be unlimited (CRB 157–58/127). In sum, *finitude* and *limit* refer to human existence considered in itself, unfolding within a horizon marked by birth and death and not defined with reference to an infinite, unlimited existence. *Finite* and *limitation*, in Falque's terminology, refer to human existence as contrasted with an infinite, unlimited existence. It is finitude and limit that are primordially constitutive of human existence.

At first glance these distinctions may seem merely semantic, but Falque employs them to insist on a positive account of human existence, meaning an account that describes it in terms of what it is, in contrast to a negative account that would describe it in terms of what it is not. Finitude, Falque emphasizes, is not a lack or an incompleteness but is a positive good that is suited to humans. As he insists, "only the *positiveness of finitude*, understood as realized within temporality by the future (death), and independent of all considerations of the finite (the insufficiency of man), or of the infinite (the plenitude of God), can tell us what the Being-there of man (*Dasein*) is" (MF 195/18, trans. mod.). Finitude is characterized by temporality and contingency, and saying that we are temporal and contingent is different from saying that we are not eternal and not necessary: the former statement describes actual human experience, whereas the latter defines human experience by referring to conditions no human has ever experienced. Of course, we are also finite: it is indisputable that we are neither eternal nor necessary, and eternity and necessity are only two of the many qualities that have often been attributed to God that we do not have. Describing human existence only in the negative terms of the finite is, however, like describing a sonnet by observing that it is not free verse, that it is not as long as a novel or a play, and that it does not have a plot. These statements are perfectly true, and it may be reasonable to compare the structure and effects of the sonnet to those of another literary form, but it is absurd to approach a sonnet as if it were a failed novel, play, or free verse poem. The rules that a writer must respect if she is to write a sonnet and not something else do prevent the sonnet from being a novel, a play, a villanelle, or anything other than a sonnet—but, crucially, they cause it to be a sonnet. In a sense the traditional sonnet does lack, for instance, a fifteenth line, but in a deeper sense it does not lack that fifteenth line because if it had one it would cease to be what it is. While it is easy to think human limits negatively, as mere constraints on our existence, we must rather think them as constitutive of our existence.

It does not follow that human beings are perfect or that our existence in the world leaves nothing to be desired. Certainly neither Falque nor I propose to consider such things as poverty and murder as goods that constitute us. But just as a sonnet may be flawed without thereby being a failed free verse poem, likewise our imperfections do not make us failed gods. Finitude is not defined by poverty and murder any more than the poetic form called a sonnet is defined by a poorly chosen rhyme. Human beings can, and all too often do, lack that which they ought to have, living without adequate food or without the kindness of their fellows. The absence of kindness or of sufficient food, to take only two examples, are genuine lacks: humans obviously live better when they have enough to eat and are treated with kindness and dignity. If, however, we were eternal and necessary beings, we would no longer be human. Regretting that one has insufficient food is regretting that one does not live as well as a human being ought; regretting that one is temporal and contingent, thrown into an unchosen existence, amounts to regretting one's humanity.

Finitude and Mutability

Living within finitude means existing as temporal beings, and that which exists within time is subject to change; hence humans are mutable. Humans do not only affect the world they inhabit but are also affected by it. What is more, as Maurice Merleau-Ponty makes clear in *The Visible and the Invisible*, to affect the world is to be affected by it, and vice versa—a point that demands closer examination, as it will prove crucial to our understanding of friendship. There is no neat division between subject and object such that the human being would either be wholly active, at a safe distance from that which she affects, or wholly passive, powerless in the grip of the world. When I touch a thing, Merleau-Ponty observes, I am at the same time touched, "such that the touch is formed in the midst of the world and as it were in the things" (VI 174/134). Neither I nor the world fully determines my experience of touch: the touch is constituted by the chiasm, the crossing-over, between my flesh and the flesh of the world. The notion of chiasm means that touching is not a one-way experience: if I can touch the world, that is only because I can be touched. It is not that I and the world are active and passive by turns, such that one moment I am touching, the next I am being touched, nor are touching and being touched one and the same; on the contrary, touching and being touched are intertwined throughout the touch, and this intertwining is more fundamental than the subject/object dichotomy. Neither touching nor being touched occurs without the other, but they are not the same. This inseparability of perceiving and being perceived is particularly clear with regard to touch—if I am in physical contact with a thing, then that thing is obviously in contact with me as well—but it is true of all other senses as well. I can see only because I touch the world with my gaze, yet what I see is not determined by my gaze alone: "finally one cannot say if it is the look or the things that command" (VI 173/133). I seek the things with my look, and they give themselves to me: sight requires activity and receptivity from myself and from the world. Whenever I am sensing, I go out to the world and receive from the world, not in turns but in a harmonious movement in which my perceiving and my perceptibility are intertwined. For that matter, the senses themselves are intertwined: sight is not touch and touch is not sight, but the senses all take place in and through "the same body" and "the same world" (VI 175/134).

Merleau-Ponty does not refer to finitude to explain intertwining and the chiasm, but what he describes is nonetheless constitutive of existence within finitude. To be thrown into the world is precisely to be in this chiastic relationship with the world. As a conscious being that did not choose to be conscious, a human being can never be a pure subject or a pure object. Because it did not constitute itself but was brought into existence without its consent, consciousness is never sheer subjectivity, yet consciousness is always actively interpreting the world and so is never mere objectivity either. It bears repeating that the chiasm does not conflate the self and the world: touch always occurs across gaps, a point Kearney has emphasized to defend Merleau-Ponty against Derrida's charge that the chiasm fuses self and other.[2] This point is particularly important because the world is never my world alone: the previous two chapters have emphasized that the human being is constituted through community with others. As Merleau-Ponty himself observes in *The Phenomenology of Perception*, "I am everything that I see and I am an intersubjective field" (PP 525/478). It is not that I become fused with others; rather, his point is that I am not split into two unrelated selves, one private and one public. And as his notion of the chiasm suggests, the encounter with others is mutually constitutive: both self and other are grounded in and shaped through their encounters, and neither has the power to reduce the other to an object. Even if one insists, with Levinas, on the transcendence of the Other, my ethical responsibility itself testifies that the Other is not a creature of solitude. There can be no question of reducing the Other to a present phenomenon—yet the Other's call is a call in part because it is heard. The call gives meaning to my freedom by summoning me to responsibility, and for this reason I am always already indebted to the Other who precedes me,[3] yet insofar as the call summons a subject, the Other too is constituted through intersubjectivity.

It is worth noting here that Merleau-Ponty's notion of the chiasm gives us another perspective on the reciprocity of friendship: there is a certain reciprocity to all our interactions with others because intersubjectivity is mutually constituting. It is true, of course, that I may desire a friendship with someone who does not wish to be friends with me: the reciprocity or mutuality of the chiasm does not mean that the other person will see me as I see her. For this reason, the previous chapter's arguments in support of mutual friendship remain necessary. The chiasm does, however, serve to reinforce the point that when I affect another it is not necessarily because I am demanding anything from her; to exist in the world is to mutually affect and be affected by others.

Friendship as Transformation within Finitude

In short, existing within finitude means being thrown into the world, which means being in relation to the world, and because there are other subjects in the world, it also means being in relation to others. Although friendship can never be fully explained, it remains that friendship can arise only because we are related to others. It is because we exist within finitude and because we share this finitude with others that we are shaped in and through our relations to others, so our experience of friendship can be properly understood only in the context of our finitude. The point here is not to demystify friendship's origins, as though we could discover some regulated process or method by which it arises, but rather to think its goodness more robustly. That friendship arises within the context of our finitude, understood as a positive good, serves to emphasize that it is inadequate to conceive of friendship as compensation for our insufficiency, as though human existence were fundamentally a matter of insufficiency. But what might this positive conception of friendship look like? In a word, I propose to understand friendship not as compensation but as transformation. Fundamentally, friendship, rather than compensating for our inadequacies, transforms our manner of existing in the world.

Once one partakes of friendship, one's entire experience of the world changes. Such changes may occur to greater or lesser degrees when one encounters another, but with the friendship that is a lasting commitment, the world, though never mine alone, now becomes the world that will end with the friend's death: thus the friend's death joins my own death as a horizon that bounds the world.[4] My friend's death is not my own: the friend and I are not fused into one being, and the horizons that are our deaths remain distinct. Yet I am not only in the condition of being-toward my own death but also find myself in the condition of being-toward-mourning, of being-toward the obligation to testify to the friend who has died. Mourning too is my own: none can bear witness to the friend in my place. Others may also mourn the friend—and if more than two may be friends, others can mourn as friends—but none of us can even attempt to fulfill another's obligation. Even—*especially*—as friends of the one who has died, we cannot substitute for each other, precisely because friendship profoundly implicates each one of us in his or her singularity.

Moreover, this transformation is not only a matter of a new and different future horizon bounding my existence—better, this new horizon transforms the existence that unfolds within it. Henceforth the friend is with me, whether present or not, at every moment. It is not a question of a codependency that demands the friend's physical presence at all times; rather, all my experiences are colored by the friendship. Derrida writes of "treating things as things of friendship" (PF 37/19). It is not only or primarily that things are transformed by a sentimental association with the friend; certainly such associations are possible—for instance,

Alice may always think of Laura when she sees kiwi fruit because kiwi is Laura's favorite food—but the transformation of the world and of the things in it is broader and deeper than that. Because friendship, as we have seen, implicates me in my singularity even more deeply than does the ethical relation, friendship renders particularly profound the realization that the world is not mine alone. My experience of the world intersects with the friend's at every turn.

It is true that I never stand alone as the sole judge of the world: I can never escape the gaze of strangers who also assign value to things. Yet I am more intimately bound to the friend than I am to the stranger because friendship is a lasting bond. Although the ethical obligation never ends, in practice it generally is not a lifelong commitment to any particular stranger. The Good Samaritan, having taken the injured man to an inn and paid the man's expenses, promises to pay any additional debt when he returns, but there is no reason to suppose the man will still need his assistance in a year. Friendship, in contrast, binds me to a specific person for my entire life, beyond any aid the friend requires from me. Thus in friendship even objects as banal as forks or sidewalks become, whether or not I consciously think of my friend in connection with them, part of the world that is not only my own, nor even mine and that of innumerable others whom I am bound to aid (though I can never wholly fulfill that obligation), but mine and that of the friend. This intersection of worlds is not limited to the world's end with the friend's death. When, for example, I receive good news from the friend—perhaps she has just gotten a new puppy or a good job—the world becomes brighter for me as well. Alice, unlike her friend, may hate kiwi, but kiwi will always be the fruit that she hates and that her friend loves. Or she may not know what her friend would think of, say, a particular building whose architectural style she appreciates, but everything she encounters is a thing to which the friend could assign some value. My friend's actual or possible valuation of things always touches my own. This is not only a matter of my consciously caring about what my friend thinks; as the earlier reference to the chiasm indicates, it is a transformation of my enfleshed orientation within the world.

Indeed, friendship is distinct from acquaintanceship in that the friend is never wholly absent: friends' care for each other is such that each one's experience of the world is always shaping the other's, at a level deeper than conscious thought. Compare embarking on a journey with a friend to doing so alone. The friend's companionship affects the entire experience of the journey, not only the moments at which one stops and consciously thinks about her presence. If they must choose between two paths, they will consult each other; if one is injured she will turn to the other for aid; if one encounters good fortune the other will also be glad: at such moments the friends are directly aware that the other's presence affects the experience of the journey. Still more fundamental, however, is the fact that such moments are possible and would not be if one had set out on the journey alone. Their very possibility suffices to shape the journey. One may not be consciously aware of a background noise until it stops; similarly, one may not realize that one's companion or one's solitude is shaping one's experience until some event brings this fact to one's attention. The lone voyager and the one with a friend face different sets of possibilities. Likewise, those who exist in the world with and without friends face different sets of possibilities—or, to put it another way, encountering a friend transforms the world in which one exists.

The human experience of friendship is defined by this transformation of one's world through the friend.[5] Through friendship, the self experiences the world otherwise. Gaining a new horizon, marked out by the friend's having been flung into existence toward his or her death, enriches one's life. In a sense, it is true that we have friends because we are not self-sufficient: if we were sufficient unto ourselves, we would not gain in joy, wisdom, or virtue from experiencing the world otherwise. Saying that friendship compensates for a lack fails, however, to describe the most fundamental structure of friendship precisely because friendship is a turning outward toward another. When Aristotle writes that "a certain training [ἄσκησίς] in virtue would arise from living with those who are good" (NE 1170a12), he is not regretting our inability to develop virtue on our own but is acknowledging that virtue is communal. Indeed, because virtue is practiced in community and involves care for others, why would we expect or wish to develop it in solitude? Beyond friendship's value for the development of virtue and the pursuit of justice, how could we expect or wish to find in ourselves the joy friendship brings when its joy is the gift of *an other* experience of the world? Being limited, we must go out of ourselves to find our greatest joys—better, it is because we are limited that we can go out of ourselves to find our greatest joys. Because friendship enriches the lives of the limited beings that we are, friendship is suited to our finitude—and as finitude is not a privation, so too friendship, being suited to it, is not a mere compensation for a lack but rather is a positive good.

Self-Sufficiency and Friendship in Plato's *Lysis*

Here it is illuminating to examine the aporetic ending of Plato's *Lysis*, a dialogue that asks what a friend is. Socrates and his young interlocutors, Lysis and Menexenus, conclude that the good cannot be friends to each other because the good are self-sufficient: "they don't yearn for one another when apart, because even then they suffice [ἱκανοὶ] unto themselves, and when together they have no need [χρείαν] of one another" (L 215b4–7, trans. mod.). Further discussion leads them back to the view that "the good [is] a friend only to the good" (L 222d6)—but as they have already rejected this idea, the dialogue ends with no answer to the question of what a friend is. Their error lies in the implicit assumption that one desires friends only when she lacks something that she ideally would have or be able to obtain on her own. Existing within finitude, however, entails existing in relation to others. Thus the good person does not seek solitude, for human life is inescapably communal. And thus the good person is not self-sufficient, nor is self-sufficiency an ideal for human beings. Friendship is good for me because I never could have transformed my world as the friend does, no matter how good a person I am, since the friend is Other. The transformation of my world through and by the friend is necessarily an event that cannot happen by my own doing but that comes to me from outside—and as finitude is suited to human beings, so too is this transformation within finitude.

Let us not move on from the *Lysis* too hastily, though: its aporetic ending is as significant as anything the interlocutors might have said. It also bears noting that before they fail, again, to see how the good could be friends to each other, Socrates does make the crucial suggestion that, whatever sense belonging to one another takes on in friendship, it may not mean being alike. Because he and the boys have concluded that "like is useless to like insofar as they are alike," he asks, "Why don't we agree to say that what belongs (οἰκεῖον) is something different from what is like (ὁμοίου)?" (L 222b10, 222c3–4). This insight is essential, since the greatness of friendship is precisely that the friend is not like me and is therefore able to transform the world as I could not. But it should hardly surprise us that Socrates and his companions are still unable to give an account of friendship, even after they take up this suggestion, for in truth it is no easy matter to define what a friend is. As Lysis and Menexenus depart, their guardians having arrived to take them home, Socrates speaks the last words of the dialogue: "Now we've done it, Lysis and Menexenus—made ourselves ridiculous, I, an old man, and you as well. These people here will go away saying that we suppose ourselves to be friends of one another—for I count [τίθημι] myself in with you—but what a friend is we have not yet been able to find out" (L 223b3–7, trans. mod.). He is careful not to say that they are friends, or even that they do believe they are friends; he says only that others will say that they "suppose [them]selves to be friends" and that he "counts [him]self in with" Lysis and Menexenus. At the same time, he does not deny that they are friends or even imply that others are unreasonable to think they believe they are friends. The question of their friendship remains suspended—suspended, what is more, by the appearance of the boys' guardians, who, according to Socrates (the narrator of this dialogue as well as a participant), arrive "like some kind of daimons" (L 223a2, trans. mod.). Interestingly, these daimonic-seeming guardians—who, in contrast to the deus ex machina of Greek theater, enter not to bring resolution but to foreclose any possibility of resolution—turn out to be foreigners, and barbaric foreigners at that: "At first our group tried to drive them off," remembers Socrates, "but they didn't pay any attention to us and just got riled up and went on calling in their barbaric accents [ὑποβαρβαρίζοντες]" (L 223a4–6, trans. mod.). Perhaps Socrates, Lysis, and Menexenus could have retraced their logic, found their error, returned to Socrates's insight that belonging is not the same as being like, and come to an agreement, were it not for this sudden irruption of the foreign. Perhaps, though, that agreement would have been a deceptive appearance. Indeed, if friendship is a struggle in the dark, then the foreign, the interruption, the barbaric accent that does not accord with the accepted *logos*, is always inseparable from the question of friendship. And so the guardians enter "like some kind of daimons" not in spite of their foreignness but rather because of it. They seem divine precisely because their arrival compels Socrates, Lysis, and Menexenus to leave open the question of what a friend is.

Interestingly, Socrates's narration of the dialogue is not addressed to anyone—or at least not to anyone who is named. No framing story explains to whom he is speaking. Let us suppose that he, Lysis, and Menexenus had concluded, as Aristotle later would, that the good are friends to the good: would they have thereby answered the question of *who* the friend is? No, for knowing, abstractly, that the good are friends to each other does not amount to knowing who it is that I dare to call friend. That Socrates's listener is unknown already hints at the unknowability of the friend. Furthermore, Derrida points out that the *Lysis* begins with a scene in which Socrates asks Hippothales to reveal the name of the one with whom he is in love; Hippothales refuses, embarrassed, and it falls to his companions to reveal that he is in love with Lysis (L 204b3–d1). Derrida comments, "Let us not forget that *Lysis* begins with the scene of a proper name that at first is unpronounceable: who is the loved one [*l'aimé*]? [. . .] Everything in the political question of friendship seems to be suspended on the secret of a name. Will this name be *published*? Will the tongue [*la langue*] be untied, and will the name be delivered over to a public space?" (PF 95–96/77, trans. mod.). Bound up with the question of *who* is the question of fidelity: *to whom* am I faithful when I am faithful to the friend? For I never know the friend fully, and let us not forget this point in the midst of the argument that the friend's experience of the world shapes my own. I experience the world not as the friend does but in light of her experience. No tongue, no language is ever adequate to the name of the friend. The aporia in which Socrates, Lysis, and Menexenus find themselves is thus better suited to friendship than any definite answer to their question—but what does it mean to address an unknowable friend? Thus far we have asked what it means to be faithful to the friend given the difficult relation between friendship and the political, and Derrida's remarks remind us that this question must continue to accompany us as we pose another, related question: what does it mean to be faithful to the friend when the friend must always remain unknowable and foreign to the self? And what if it is our very finitude that prevents us from knowing the friend more fully?

Friendship's Infinity: The Challenge of Impossible Fidelity

To wrestle as best we can with the meaning of fidelity to the unknowable friend, it is necessary to examine what I call friendship's infinity: friendship demands that one be infinitely (that is, perfectly) faithful to the friend. In friendship there is no limitation on fidelity, no point at which one has a right to say to the other, "Thus far I care about you, but no farther." What is more, death itself, the horizon that bounds each human life, does not limit friendship. Although we are creatures who dwell within finitude, within limits, fidelity to the friend is unlimited. To be clear, fidelity does not mean having no boundaries in the colloquial sense of the word—that is, fidelity does not mean doing everything the friend wants or having no secrets. The latter is impossible in any case, since no one can ever know another fully. Rather, one's care for the friend is unlimited, and caring for another entails neither complying with all of his or her wishes nor attempting, futilely, to reveal everything about oneself. Here one might suggest that virtue limits fidelity, but it would be better to say that fidelity requires that I be virtuous for the friend's sake. Fidelity itself may require that one oppose the friend, should the friend form some unjust design, but there is still no excuse for ceasing to be faithful. The possibility that fidelity may at times entail opposition renders fidelity more complex but does not make it limited. Friendship demands a fidelity that always remains dangerous precisely because it knows no bounds.

The demand that fidelity to the friend extend beyond death, unto infinity, is in fact inscribed into friendship from the start. Derrida emphasizes that "*philia* begins with the possibility of survival. [. . .O]ne does not survive without mourning [*porter le deuil*]" (PF 31/13). Right from the beginning, one knows that the friend might die first and that one will then mourn. This mourning amounts to a testimony: one bears witness to the friend, preserving the memory of the friend and "carry[ing]," as Derrida puts it in "Rams," written in honor of his dead friend Hans-Georg Gadamer, "the world of the other [. . .]. The world after the end of the world" (R 22–23/140). One can state the problem almost too easily: how can I—how could anyone—carry that which is gone forever? Am I not bearing only a false image of the friend's world? And do I not thereby betray her? Even in life I do not experience the world as she does—or, to put it more strongly, I do not live in her world. Her world transforms mine but does not become mine: there is always a gap between us. Little enough is said of the body in friendship, possibly because corporeality seems to play a far more significant role in erotic love, but in all our relationships with others we remain embodied. The very fact that friends qua friends do not seek to become one flesh means that our separate bodies testify to the difference that separates us. The embrace of friendship, because it does not seek oneness with the friend, reminds me that the friend's bodily existence in the world is not my own. Thus after the friend's death I find myself called to the witness stand to testify to a world that is gone and that I never directly experienced in the first place—and whose end is also the end of my world. Since the friend's death is a horizon of my world, for me it ends the world, yet somehow I remain, that I might seek to testify. I am caught in an impossible situation: to avoid being guilty of infidelity, I must bear witness, after the world's end, to a world I never saw, and any attempt I make to fulfill this responsibility only proves my guilt precisely because my very attempt at bearing witness denies the difference that separates me from my friend. To put it another way, either I am guilty of refusing the required testimony or I am guilty of false witness. One might seek to escape this dilemma by proposing that silence is itself a witness, and so it may be—but never a wholly adequate one, never one that tells the full truth of who the friend is and was. Silence may speak volumes—but, like words, it never speaks enough.

Fidelity in Translation

Derrida is, of course, all too aware of this problem. He observes that "*I must* translate, transfer, transport (*übertragen*) the untranslatable in another turn precisely there where, translated, it remains untranslatable" (R 77/161, trans. mod.). Indeed: and I add that the translation of the untranslatable also belongs to friendship in life. Friends mutually transform the world for each other, and this transformation is a translation: the transformation creatively renders each friend's world in new terms. Translation is not a matter of stripping meaning from the language that expresses it and then copying that meaning in a new language, for we have no access to language-free meaning. Nor is translation a matter of one language receiving passively from another, as though the so-called original text dictated a one-to-one correspondence between its words and the words of the translation. Translation arises in the gap between languages as a creative crossing between them, a polyvalent conversation that never does close the gap. Likewise, my world does not become a copy of my friend's, or vice versa, and neither of us is a passive recipient on whom the other imposes her world. We do receive from each other, it is true, but this reception is chiastic, not passive: to live in a transformed world is to creatively take up that transformation, thereby bearing witness to the friend in another movement of transformation. That is, I must actively orient myself in the world in light of the always-unknowable world of the friend. I must embrace the transformation of my world in order to live in that transformed world. If I do not respond to the call of friendship, I am certainly not a friend, and there is no formula for living out friendship any more than there is a formula for translating between languages.

Translation is not a mere analogy for friendship. The fundamental act of friendship is translation. The translator hesitates over possible words, not taking dictation from the text she translates, as if that text could identify one word as the correct one, but rather responding to the call to translate with a creative work that operates a double transformation. The original is transformed in the translation, yet the language of the translated text is also transformed: the call to translate summons the language of the translation to a movement it would not have made of itself. The translation exists thanks to both languages. Thus the act of translating is indeed chiastic: activity and receptivity are inseparably intertwined. Each friend translates the world for the other, who by taking up that translated world testifies to the friend in another movement of translation.

Furthermore, Derrida observes in "Des tours de Babel" that "the original is the first debtor, the first petitioner; it begins by lacking [*manquer*]—and by pleading for [*pleurer après*] translation" (218/207). The original pleads for translation because it is in truth not an original but a translation: there is always already a gap between it and itself, for its words never have a univocal meaning. Let us be clear: the lack of which Derrida speaks is not a lack that ever was or ever could be satisfied. It is not that the original fell from some prior state of perfection or sufficiency but that language itself is a falling, never self-identical. This falling is best understood not as an imperfection, an insufficiency, or a privation but as the condition of language itself. It is this very gap between sign and sense that makes translation possible—indeed, that summons translation—for without that gap each word would simply mean what it says, and the original text would be locked in a self-identity that would close it off from the other that is the language of the translation. Language is that which calls for translation. If sign and sense were identical, the result would be like nothing we know as language: stripped of metaphor and play, it would be not perfect but frozen.

The self too is other than itself, and it is only because of this alterity at its heart that the self is open to the other person. If I were purely self-identical, no other could disrupt me by transforming my world. To be human is precisely to call out, whether one realizes it or not, for transformation by and through the Other. And the struggle to be faithful to the friend is precisely the struggle of the translator. The singularity of a language and the singularity of a human friend resist the translation that would testify to them. In this connection it is important to note that testimony implies a certain public, a certain universalization. And thus we return, as ever, to the problem of the singular and the universal, the private and the political. Friendship is a secret that resists the political and can never be brought forth into the universal—yet it is a secret that calls forth testimony. The friends are not the only two in the world; the political inevitably exists. But the political exists to be resisted in the name of singularity, in the name of ethics, in the name of the true justice that is always higher than legal justice—in the name, precisely, of that whose name is a secret that cannot be disclosed. To be a friend is to testify to and for the singular against the universal that would crush it—and yet to testify is to enter into the universal. Once again we find that fidelity and betrayal go hand in hand. We are summoned to translate, yet translations are always unfaithful.

Infinity at the Heart of Finitude

This inevitable infidelity marks an originary crack in finitude, not a fall from a prior, perfect state of origin but an originary falling that has always already begun. To grasp this point, we must return to Falque's idea that finitude has no contrary. Recall that the finite is one pole of a dichotomy, with infinity as the other pole, whereas finitude is defined on its own terms and without reference to a privileged opposite. But we must be careful here. There is a difference between refusing to define finitude as the negation or privation of the infinite and claiming that finitude is self-identical, untouched by difference and wholly on the side of the Same. Falque argues for the former, not the latter, though he does not address the question of an originary difference. He emphasizes that our primordial experience of the world is one of finitude and that God transforms our finitude rather than removing us from it. These points are central to his thought because they mean that our finitude does not result from a fall from a prior, better state and that there is no philosophical or theological reason to wish we existed outside the limits of finitude.[6] Yet the very notion of infinite fidelity to the friend—that is, perfect fidelity, extending infinitely beyond death—suggests a haunting of finitude by its other. That other is not a contrary, for finitude and its contrary would simply be two poles of a system of opposites—that is, of a totality that explains and encompasses both. Rather, the other haunts finitude as its originary difference from itself. Infinity emerges at the heart of finitude not because finitude lacks anything it ought to have or because it would be better for us to become infinite but because finitude calls into question the fidelity whose horizon it is. That is, our very limits prevent us from knowing the other perfectly and thereby establish a distance between self and other. Infinite fidelity is demanded precisely because it is impossible: if there were no distance between self and other, the call for infinite fidelity would be superfluous since there could be no infidelity. The call for infinite fidelity arises from the very distance that makes infidelity possible.

Derrida also emphasizes finitude, though without drawing the distinction between finitude and the finite that Falque does.[7] Notably, in *The Problem of Genesis in Husserl's Philosophy*, he criticizes Husserl for "remain[ing] the prisoner of a great classical tradition: the one that reduces human finitude to an accident of history, to an 'essence of man' that understands temporality against a background of possible or actual eternity in which it has or could have participated" (41/5).[8] It is a mistake, Derrida insists, to seek a pure origin, free from the limits within which we now exist, from which we could suppose we fell. A phenomenology that preserves the dichotomies of the finite and the infinite, the temporal and the eternal, as well as the traditional privilege accorded to the infinite and the eternal, in fact fails as a phenomenology because it treats our existence within finitude as secondary.

Indeed, Derrida also affirms that if we were not thrown into a temporal existence, there could be no friendship. Thus Derrida writes, commenting on Aristotle's *Eudemian Ethics*, that "there is no friend without time (*oud' áneu khrónou phílos*)—that is, without that which puts confidence to the test. [. . .] The fidelity, faith, 'fidence' [*fiance*], credence, the *credit* of this engagement could not possibly be a-chronic" (PF 31–32/14).[9] By testing fidelity, time makes fidelity meaningful. Promising fidelity is pledging oneself to another for all time; thus the promise of fidelity makes sense only within time. To put it another way, fidelity is fundamentally temporal. Stepping beyond the horizon marked by finitude would not lead to better friendships but would put an end to friendship. The horizon that makes perfect fidelity impossible is also the horizon that constitutes friendship.

Fidelity at the Heart of Failure

The notion of translation should already have suggested to us that the same finitude that places a distance between friends and prevents perfect fidelity is in fact the very condition of friendship. Translation is possible precisely insofar as it is unfaithful: the gap between sign and sense that bounds translations and prevents them from ever being perfectly faithful is the condition of possibility for translation. Addressing, as well as testifying to and for, the unknowable friend is translating with no access to the original—and as we have seen, there never is a true original. This is not to deny that the friend exists, but one never knows even oneself fully. The friend too is always other than herself, never fully coinciding with herself, and thus translating herself. What, though, if we could leave finitude, close the distance between us, and know each other with no need for translation? Abolishing translation would be the death of language; would it truly be the death of friendship?

I reply that it would indeed be the death of friendship. Recall the reading of Heidegger's *What Is Philosophy?* advanced in the first chapter. If it is not to become an egoism, *philosophia* must strive with the *logos* without seeking a totalizing union with the *logos*. It is that struggle in the dark that shows us what friendship must be: not a striving for union in the manner of the Eros Heidegger portrays, but love across the gap between us. In truth, full knowledge of the friend would be the greatest betrayal: knowing the friend perfectly would amount either to absorbing him into myself (the egoistic union that *philosophia* must reject) or to having for myself a copy of the friend. "Thou shalt make no graven image": the resulting *eidolon* of the friend would be an offense not only against God but against the friend as well.[10] The stammering, limping (to recall another image from the discussion of *philosophia*), and even failing fidelity that is the best we can ever manage remains a truer fidelity than the supposedly perfect knowledge we might wrongly desire. Friendship lives from the distance between us.

To express the idea that friendship is constituted by the very distance that separates us, there are no better words than those of Simone Weil, written in a letter to her friend Gustave Thibon in 1942: "Soon there will be distance between us. Let us love this distance which is wholly woven of friendship, for those who do not love each other are not separated."[11] It is true that she was writing of a literal distance, having left France for New York, and Thibon comments that she wrote "with a presentiment that we should not see each other again."[12] Indeed, she died a year later in England, and if they met again it was not in this world. But the phrase "this distance which is wholly woven of friendship" describes perfectly the gap that is always between friends, whether or not they are separated geographically and while both are yet alive. The gap constitutes and is constituted by the friendship. As soon as one addresses or invokes the friend, one is always writing, communicating across distance, and never addressing one who is or could be wholly present. Between any two people there is distance, of course: one never knows another fully. But the bond of friendship, because it transforms one's world and implicates one's singularity more deeply than ethics (as the last chapter showed), entails that one knows the unknowability of a friend more intimately than that of a stranger—and for this very reason the distance reveals itself more clearly in friendship than in the relation to a stranger. One may therefore say, following Weil, "There is distance between us. Let us love this distance which is wholly woven of friendship, for those who do not love each other are not separated thus."

In Aristotle also we find a confirmation that we should not regret our finitude or desire to leave it behind:

> [T]he perplexity arises as to whether friends perhaps never wish for the greatest goods for their friends—for example, for them to be gods—since then they will no longer be friends to them, and neither will they therefore be goods, for friends are goods. So if it has been nobly said that a friend wishes for the good things for the friend for his friend's sake, the friend would need to remain as whatever sort he is. For the one friend will wish for the greatest goods for the other *as a human being*. (NE 1159a6–12, emphasis added)

At first it might appear that it is for one's own sake that one does not wish for the friend to become a god: selfishly, I refuse to wish him this greatest good because I am unwilling to lose the friendship. On closer examination, however, it becomes clear that the apparent greatest good—being a god—is in fact not a good at all *for a human being* precisely because becoming a god would mean ceasing to be a human being. I cannot wish that *my friend* become a god because he or she would thereby cease to be the one who is my friend; more bluntly, my friend cannot become a god because in becoming a god he or she ceases to exist. Thus if Alice wishes that Bob become a god, she is in fact wishing that Bob no longer exist. And ceasing to exist is certainly not a good.

Here one might press the point and insist that surely the being who was the friend would continue to exist in some sense of the word: neither the friendship nor the humanity of that being would survive the transition to godhood, but would there not be some continuity of consciousness between the human and the god? Perhaps it is only a philosophical sleight of hand that lets us say that becoming a god is not good for a human being: very well, becoming a god is not good for Bob qua human being, but surely it is good for Bob qua Bob, and for that reason Alice should wish it for him, and he in turn should wish it for her. Yet this argument supposes that being human is inessential to who Alice and Bob are, that they can exchange their finitude for the total self-sufficiency of godhood while still remaining themselves, much as they might change jobs, acquire new interests, and develop new virtues or vices without thereby ceasing to be Alice and Bob. To argue thus is to forget that finitude, as constitutive of human being in general, is also constitutive of each particular human being. Leaving behind finitude amounts to leaving behind that which constitutes oneself. My aim here is not to propound a theory of the continuity of self over time or to identify the essence of selfhood but only to point out that human selfhood, whatever it may consist in, is conditioned by finitude. For that matter, it is unnecessary, for this argument, to assume continuity of the self over time: let us suppose that Alice in 2003 is in some meaningful sense not the same person as Alice in 2019, or even that Alice on Monday is not the same person as Alice on Tuesday. Each of us is constantly changing, let us suppose for the moment, such that there is no continuous self. Nevertheless, these transformations still occur within finitude and are thus qualitatively different from the transformation into a god. And although I can never fully know who the friend is—the name of the friend always remains secret—the possibility of mourning that conditions the friendship tells me that the friend exists within finitude and would therefore cease to be by becoming a god.

Falque's observation that "nothing guarantees in fact that the best *in itself* would have to be, or would describe, the best *for us*" (GG 35–36/15) recalls Aristotle's claim that we do not wish for our friends to be gods. In itself, it is better to be God than to be a human, but it does not follow that it would be better *for us* to be God. And it certainly does not follow that it would be better for us to not exist, for God to never have created. If God created the world and found his creation good, then rejecting one's own existence out of dissatisfaction with the limits of finitude is an act of supreme ingratitude and arrogance. Even leaving aside the reference to God as creator, regretting finitude to the point of wishing humans did not exist amounts to an ontological suicidal and homicidal ideation that is utterly contrary to friendship. The limits within which human existence unfolds do not deprive us but constitute us and therefore are not to be regretted.

Let us return here to the concluding words of Blanchot's *Pour l'amitié*: "That is my salute to Emmanuel Levinas, the only friend—ah, faraway friend—whom I call *tu* and who calls me *tu*, not because we were young but by a deliberate decision, a pact at which I hope never to fail [*un pacte auquel j'espère ne jamais manquer*]" (35). That Blanchot concludes with the word *manquer*, here best rendered as "to fail," reminds us that friendship is always haunted by failure. Yet it is through the repeated failing that one keeps the pact. To be a friend is to struggle again and again, beyond the friend's death, to bear witness to the one who transforms my world. Failing is inevitable—but one keeps the pact in the repeated failing, or, better, the *repeated* or iterated failing is the keeping. Caught between the singular and the universal, I still continue to testify to my friend, for remaining mute and refusing to bear witness would be a worse betrayal. As Jean-Louis Chrétien aptly observes, writing of the secret and the promise in friendship,

> the gaze toward the friend is turned toward his being by welcoming, in his very gaze, the secret. In returning him his gaze, we return him his secret, but behold: from the one to the other, it is transfigured, it is made a promise. This secret that comes to us is returned to him as if to come [*à venir*]. We could not keep it otherwise. From this silence, a muffled word [*parole sourde*] that does not break it. For, as the poet [Paul Claudel] says, "To keep the secret that we know, it is not enough to keep silent!"[13]

Indeed. For the secret of friendship is one that can be kept only by testifying that it is a secret, and absolute silence does not testify to the secret but represses it. The "muffled word" testifies to the secret by speaking the promise to keep it—and the promise is never kept once and for all, is never fully realized, just as the secret is never made known even to its bearers, whose singularity always remains a mystery. The promise is ever and always *to be kept*. And the futurity of the promise is a blessing, since it means that the repeated failures do not end friendship: friends always take up the promise again, and the mutual translation of the world is never complete.

We must not, therefore, reject language as inadequate and refuse to speak of friendship, for language, with all its limits, is proper to our finitude. Language always does enter into the universal, it is true, but it always also bears the trace of the singular. Refusing language and falling into stubborn mutism would only be a mark of pride, of being too arrogant to fail for the sake of the friend. To be friends is precisely to live in the tension of wanting to be ever more faithful to our friends and embracing the finitude within which alone friendship is possible. This tension is more fruitful than any overcoming of it could be, for the overcoming would take us outside the limits that are proper to humanity, and it is as humans that we love each other in friendship.

4

The Writing of Friendship
Reading Proust's *In Search of Lost Time*

So far, we still have not fully reckoned with the potential impossibility of friendship: what does it really mean for one's world to be transformed by another who always remains in some sense a stranger? Might not the supposed transformation be the product of one's own imagination? Given these questions, the moment has come to turn to the challenge that Marcel Proust's *In Search of Lost Time* poses to friendship: in short, the narrator maintains that friendship [*amitié*] is an illusion precisely because it pretends to offer knowledge of another even though such knowledge is impossible. Worse still, friendship serves only to distract the artist from his task of creation. Erotic love proves useful because it inspires jealousy—which the narrator experiences first in his relationship with Gilberte and later, still more strongly, in his relationship with Albertine—yet jealous possessiveness inevitably fails to satisfy desire, for one desires precisely the other's Otherness that cannot be assimilated into the Same. This failure forces the lover to confront the impossibility of truly knowing another, whereas friendship not only permits but also encourages the friends to continue believing that they do know each other. Because erotic love thus plunges the artist into an awareness of his fundamental solitude, it favors the profound reflection that artistic creation demands. Friendship, in contrast, hovers at the surface of things, content with a mere semblance of both self-knowledge and knowledge of others, and so it is utterly contrary to the artist's search for truth. Its superficiality is damning.

The *Search* thus offers a blunt rejection of friendship unmatched by any traditionally philosophical work, and for this alone it would merit thorough consideration. Yet it is not only a matter of responding to this rejection, as if the *Search* simply posited an argument that one could reject independently of the narrative that both gives it its force and calls it into question. The *Search*'s critique of friendship can be understood only in the context of its portrayals of writing and of identity. Ultimately, careful attention to the text of the *Search* reveals that writing itself may be an act of friendship. This conclusion in turn makes it possible to understand translation not only as an inevitable betrayal but as the greatest possible fidelity to the Other, for to translate is to love that the Other is Other.

The crucial question of how we can know others is inscribed even in the narrator's giving of his pseudonymous name. He is often called "Marcel," and for ease of reference I follow this convention, but it is important to note that "Marcel" is not simply identified as his real name: he states, "[Albertine] would find her tongue, would say: 'My—' or 'My darling—' followed by my Christian name, which, giving the narrator the same name as the author of this book, *would have been* [*eût fait*] 'My Marcel,' 'My darling Marcel'" (S III.583/V.91, trans. mod., emphasis added).[1] He does not say that it is his name or that he, the narrator, is also the author; rather, he offers "Marcel" as a placeholder to illustrate how Albertine addressed him. That we know him only by a name that he gives us in the French pluperfect subjunctive, a literary mood that here functions as (and is therefore rendered in English as) a conditional, underscores the impossibility of knowing the other: his very name is a fiction—or if it is not, if he did give his true name, we have no way of knowing that. His true name is unknowable not because we can be sure it is not Marcel—even that is more knowledge than we can have—but because the name he gives appears as fictional whether or not it is his so-called "true name." That the name is the same as Proust's tempts us to suppose that we can identify an authorial reality behind the name and thereby know something of its bearer directly, while at the same time the fact that we can know the name only as a fiction (even if it is the narrator's "real name") warns us against any such over-hasty claim to knowledge. At first glance, this implicit warning might seem to confirm the narrator's dismissal of friendship as illusory: the *Search*'s value lies in its nature as a work of art, and if we seek to appreciate it as such, then trying to know who the narrator really is, beyond what is given in the work, would be at best irrelevant and at worst distracting. Seeking complete knowledge of the narrator, as though writing were supposed to conjure a faithful imitation of some higher reality, would be going down a false trail—but recall that a "perfect imitation" is not in fact faithful but is a false *eidolon*. All names are pseudonymous insofar as they do not and must not give access to the supposedly "perfect" knowledge of another that, as the previous chapter argued, would be the death of friendship. The question of the narrator's name does warn us, once again, of the ultimate impossibility of answering the question "Who is the friend?" That this impossibility in no way implies that friendship is an illusion is, however, the main argument of this chapter. Indeed, I contend that writing, precisely because it destabilizes the self and undoes the self's claim to be able to answer such questions, can be understood both as friendship to language itself and as friendship to the reader who will receive and interpret the text.

Friendship versus Art

Marcel's claim that friendship is an illusion is inseparable from the vision of artistic creation that gradually unfolds over the course of the *Search*. The immediate occasion of his critique of friendship is his relation with Robert de Saint-Loup, whom he meets in the novel's second volume and who delights in regarding Marcel as his close friend. Finding himself unable to return the sentiment, however much he desires to when he observes Saint-Loup's devotion to him, Marcel comes to see friendship as an illusion whose deceptive appeal the artist must resist if he is to create a great work. It is no coincidence that only after Saint-Loup's death in World War I does Marcel at last resolve to realize the artistic vocation to which he had aspired but of which he had come to think himself incapable. Saint-Loup's death and Marcel's discovery of his vocation are separated by a number of years, it is true, and Marcel himself does not connect the two events, but the arrangement of his narration is telling: his account of his travel to the party at which the latter occurs immediately follows the passage devoted to the former. The friend—or a certain image of friendship—must die for the possibility of literary creation to emerge.

Indeed, Marcel's conduct over the course of the friendship prefigures his friend's death, as he insists on the necessity of sacrificing friendship for the sake of art. Though Marcel initially desired a friendship with Saint-Loup, the friendship, once established, proves disappointing, and Marcel writes to him to ask him to not visit, claiming to be busy with other obligations. In reality he is spending his time with a band of six girls that includes his future mistress, Albertine. Defending this choice to "sacrific[e] the pleasures not only of society [*la mondanité*] but of friendship to that of spending the whole day in this garden" with the girls, he maintains that "the beings who have the possibility of doing so—it is true that they are the artists, and I had long been convinced that I should never be that—also have a duty to live for themselves; and friendship is for them a dispensation from this duty, an abdication of self" (S, II.260/II.664, trans. mod.). A deferral of the artistic vocation accompanies this assertion that artists must "live for themselves": Marcel appeals to the duties of the artist to justify his resistance to friendship, yet when the particular resistance of which he speaks took place he believed that he could not be an artist. Moreover, Marcel never definitively states whether he is the *Search*'s author, and the *Search* ends before he begins to write his novel. Consequently, we know neither whether he wrote a novel at all nor, if he did, to what extent that novel met the criteria he laid out—just as we know neither that his name is Marcel nor that it is not. Friendship cannot be assigned any fixed place but is rather a displacing, and this resistance to friendship, suspended as it is in the wait for its future justification, is no more stable. Marcel resists friendship before realizing that it is art that justifies that resistance, and looking back he defends his actions in the name of art even as we do not know whether he truly does become an artist—nor will we ever know this, as he has no extra-textual existence. Only the novel that he finally resolves to write can give his resistance to friendship the sense that he desires to give it, yet as that novel remains always future, so too does the signification of that resistance.

Because all Others look at me in the gaze of the friend, it is unsurprising that the rejection of friendship should prove as potentially threatening to the broader community as friendship itself. The very meaning of selfhood is in fact at stake here: is the self communal or solitary? Even though friendship may endanger the community, it is also true that the self who refuses friendship defines itself as solitary. Thus as Marcel immediately elaborates on the claim that artists must "live for themselves," he makes it clear that what initially seems to be pure egoism is an acknowledgment of the truth that each person is inevitably alone. He explains that

> the march of thought in the solitary work of artistic creation proceeds in depth, the only direction that is not closed to us, along which we can progress—with more effort, it is true—for a result of truth. And friendship is not merely devoid of virtue, like conversation, it is also fatal [*funeste*]. [. . .] By these young girls, on the other hand, if the pleasure I tasted was egoistic, at least it was not based on the lie which seeks to make us believe that we are not irremediably alone and prevents us, when we chat with another, from admitting to ourselves that it is no longer we who speak, that we are fashioning ourselves then in the likeness of strangers and not of a self that differs from them. (S II.260–61/II.665, trans. mod.)

Here we find an image of friendship that serves as a reproach to the Aristotelian notion that the friend is "an other self," or at least to the simplest reading of Aristotle. In reality the friend is utterly *other*, to the extent that no true communication is possible between those who call themselves friends. Marcel reproaches friendship for emphasizing similarity and concealing difference: in his view, friends seek to become mere likenesses of each other, disregarding their singularity and refusing to learn from their differences. Transforming oneself "in the likeness of strangers" disrespects their foreignness by claiming it as one's own: it amounts to a denial of difference, a determination to conceal difference with a superficial resemblance. And Marcel holds out no hope for a friendship that would be based on difference: in truth, he insists, the self is irrevocably and wholly isolated. The meaning of the refusal of friendship must be deferred precisely because that refusal calls into question the possibility of any communication among human beings. Even the Levinasian relation between the self and the transcendent Other finds itself called into question, for according to Levinas the self and Other do communicate. How indeed could we fix the meaning of a refusal that grounds itself in the impossibility of communication? What might still surprise is that the self's solitude is not to be regretted, for it is the very condition of artistic creation. No longer can the pursuit of truth be thought in terms of *philia*; rather, insists Marcel, it demands solitude, and the artist is the one who willingly receives this demand.

The Force of Eros

This conclusion raises more questions than it answers, however. What becomes of language if the self is irrevocably alone? Is art only the self speaking to the self? What then occurs in the reading of the *Search*? And why, if the pursuit of truth is such a lonely endeavor, should Marcel take an interest in the girls, even going so far as to fall in love with Albertine? Let us for the moment hold the first three questions in suspense; they are both complex and essential, and a response to them will unfold only gradually. It is necessary first to consider the fourth question, which requires a digression on eros in the *Search*. What Marcel loves in Albertine is, as Miguel de Beistegui observes, precisely "her ability to inhabit a world that's different from his."[2] Before he knows her name, he is already filled with a desire for her absolute otherness, for "[her], with her desires, her sympathies, her revulsions, her obscure and incessant will" (S II.152/II.511). In truth the name *Albertine* is as pseudonymous as the name *Marcel*: it stands for an alien world, a world that he—and we—cannot enter.

Marcel's desire for Albertine manifests as a jealous possessiveness that serves to confirm that she is absolutely other. In the fifth volume, *The Prisoner*, she has agreed to live with him, and he desperately surveils her, fearing that she is cheating on him with the female friends he lets her go out to see. Yet his surveillance only redoubles his jealousy because surveillance by its very nature must approach its object from the outside. Marcel becomes an obsessive reader of signs but cannot enter into the world marked *Albertine*. Even if he had, *per impossibile*, received an absolute proof that Albertine had always been and would ever be faithful, Marcel would have remained unsatisfied, for what he truly desires is not Albertine's fidelity but Albertine herself, in all the glory of her alterity. To put it another way, he does not desire that Albertine choose to be faithful to him; rather, he desires her very power of choice, and not only that but all that reveals her as other than himself. That her fidelity would be a choice already offends his jealousy because he wants to absorb her into himself. Could he thus absorb her, however, even that would not satisfy him: transmuting her alterity into his ipseity would not grant him a gateway into her world but would simply destroy that which he desires. Hence he repeatedly tires of Albertine when he feels most confident of possessing her, and he returns to her only when such possession once more seems impossible. In *Sodom and Gomorrah*, he decides that he does not wish to marry her and resolves to break up with her to establish a relationship with the absent Andrée, only to return to Albertine when the discovery that she is close friends with two women whom he knows to be in a lesbian relationship reawakens his jealousy and inspires him to ask her to live with him in Paris: "at all costs it was necessary to prevent her from being alone, at least for a few days, to keep her close to me so as to be certain that she could not see Mlle Vinteuil's friend" (S III.506/IV.711, trans. mod.). Hardly has her captivity begun than he starts to tire of her presence: "I would wonder whether marrying Albertine might not spoil my life, not only by making me assume the task, too arduous for me, of devoting myself to another, but by forcing me to live absent from myself because of her continual presence and depriving me forever of the joys of solitude" (S III.537/V.25–26, trans. mod.). The more familiar she seems, the less he loves her, and only jealousy still binds him to her: "Of Albertine [. . .] I had nothing more to learn. Each day she seemed to me less pretty. Only the desire that she aroused in others, when, on learning of it, I began to suffer again and wanted to challenge them over her, raised her in my eyes to a lofty pinnacle" (S III.537–38/V.27, trans. mod.). Later, he is on the verge of finally breaking up with Albertine when her escape from captivity reawakens his jealousy: "what I had believed to be nothing to me," decides Marcel, "was simply my entire life" (S IV.419/V.563). Later still, after her death in a riding accident, when he misreads a telegram and wrongly thinks that she is still alive and wishes to marry him, he finds himself utterly indifferent, even revolted by the prospect of such a marriage (trying to remember her, he sees her as "an already very stout girl, mannish-looking" [S IV.222/V.872, trans. mod.]), and he reflects, "Yes, now that knowing she was alive and being able to be reunited with her made her suddenly cease to be so precious to me, I wondered whether Françoise's insinuations, our rupture itself, and even her death (imaginary, but believed to be real) had not prolonged my love" (S IV.222/V.872, trans. mod.). Because he desires her alterity, he loves her most precisely when she is most distant, most obviously Other.

Note that Albertine's alterity is embodied and is not only a matter of her soul or mind. Eros holds out the promise that the lovers shall become one flesh, but Albertine in her embodiment proves recalcitrant to Marcel's desires. When he watches her sleep, he has the impression that she is delivered into his possession, but a careful examination of the passage reveals that he is deceiving himself. In her sleep, Marcel reports, "she had taken refuge, enclosed herself, summed herself up in her body. In keeping her under my gaze, in my hands, I had that impression of possessing her entirely which I never had when she was awake" (S III.578/V.84–85, trans. mod.). The very fact that she is "enclosed in her body" reveals that he does not possess her: in her sleep she has become her own refuge from his insatiable jealousy. "Her life was submitted to me, exhaling towards me its gentle breath," claims Marcel—but at once he adds, "I listened to this murmuring, mysterious emanation, soft as a sea breeze, magical as a gleam of moonlight, that was her sleep. As long as it persisted, I could dream over her, and yet look at her, and, when that sleep grew deeper, touch her, kiss her" (S III.578/V.85, trans. mod.). She is no more submitted to him than the sea or the moon; if anything, it is she who unwittingly carries him off into a dreamworld.[3] He touches and kisses her sleeping body, but far from giving itself to him, that body remains distant, separated from him by an impossible gap. He recalls, "Whenever she moved her head, she created a new woman, often one I had never suspected. I seemed to possess not one but innumerable girls" (S III.580/V.87, trans. mod.). This bold claim implicitly admits that his apparent possession is and can be only a mere semblance. How could he possess Albertine when she is not even bound by number? All he possesses is a phantasm; his touch on the sleeping Albertine is not even skin-deep.

 Crucially, the novel's first-person narration serves to implicate the reader in Marcel's possessive jealousy: to guess at Albertine's doings, the reader is likewise compelled to interpret signs, and it is natural enough to hope, with Marcel, that the truth will be revealed—but the truth is precisely that no revelation is possible. Or, better, the true revelation is precisely that the other will remain eternally mysterious, eternally alien, a point the narrative further confirms by revealing nothing of Albertine's interiority. Marcel tries to determine what she does in his absence, but he hardly considers what she thinks or feels. That he does not attempt to reconstruct her experience is not simply a consequence of his limited perspective as the first-person narrator; after all, he famously recounts Swann's jealous love for Odette, imagining Swann's perspective in considerable detail. At first glance, therefore, the narrative's refusal to imagine Albertine's inner life seems only to reflect Marcel's selfishness: he wants to control her, and because he does not care what she thinks or how she feels about his jealousy, it does not occur to him to consider how she must have suffered from it, even after she escapes. That he imagines only Swann's story, not Odette's, may seem to reinforce the idea that the narrative reflects his selfishness: because he is himself a jealous man, in his account of events only jealous men get to speak, while the women whom they try to possess remain silent. More profoundly, however, Albertine's and Odette's silence functions in the text as a mark of respect for their otherness: I do not claim that Marcel himself intends to respect Albertine or Odette by refraining from imagining their thoughts (indeed, such a supposition seems unlikely), but even if Marcel did not intend it as such, their silence is the ultimate acknowledgment that his jealousy and Swann's were doomed to failure from the start.

Indeed, it is precisely because love excites this desperate jealousy that cannot but fail that Marcel finds value in it: jealousy brings about the confrontation with alterity that reveals the impossibility of knowing the Other and thereby forces the self to confront its fundamental solitude. What is more, encountering alterity leads the self to recognize that it too is other than itself. Thus Marcel thinks after receiving the news of Albertine's death, "It was not Albertine alone who was a succession of moments, it was also myself. [. . .] I was not one man only, but the march-past of a composite army in which there were, depending on the moment, passionate men, indifferent men, jealous men—jealous men of whom not one was jealous of the same woman" (S IV.71/V.660, trans. mod.). The self's inescapable solitude is not, it turns out, a solitude of self-identity but rather a still more profound solitude in which the self is cut off even from itself. Over the course of time many selves die even before death comes to put an end to all the self's manifold possibilities. Memory remains to bear witness to these past selves, but witnessing is decidedly not possessing.

In light of the self's multiplicity, the desire of the Other reveals itself not only as the desire to possess the other person but also as the desire to master one's own otherness. Even while he is still holding Albertine prisoner, in fact, it occurs to Marcel that "as there is no knowledge, one might almost say there is no jealousy, except of oneself" (S III.887/V.519.). Albertine comes to stand for the irreparable crack in the self, for the self's difference from itself, because it is in her multiplicity that Marcel finds his own reflected. The only possible union between Marcel and Albertine is this: for him, and without his fully realizing it, she represents the alien and uncanny self that he wishes to possess. It is significant that he suspects her of lesbian desires, not heterosexual ones: as Leo Bersani aptly remarks in "Death and Literary Authority," "Albertine's lesbianism represents a nearly inconceivable yet inescapable identity of sameness and otherness in Marcel's desires; lesbianism is a relation of sameness that Marcel is condemned to see as an irreducibly unknowable otherness" (239). Of course, Albertine and her presumed female lovers are not actually the same, and lesbianism, like any erotic relationship, whether heterosexual or homosexual, does not make it possible for one lover to actually absorb the other into herself. Nevertheless, lesbianism appears to Marcel as a union of the Same with the Same that he can never attain or understand. He does find evidence that Albertine is cheating on him with other women, though never absolute proof—a crucial point since, as noted, the truth about Albertine is precisely that she is unknowable. But the true cause of his misery is less the always-ambiguous evidence, which he can call into question, than his own desperate wish, which he ultimately knows is unfulfillable, to achieve this perfect union that he imagines Albertine experiences apart from him. Having observed the Baron de Charlus's jealous possessiveness of his male lover Morel, Marcel knows that male homosexuality is no solution to the problem of the divided self, since physical union does not amount to absolute union with or possession of the Other, but women remain sufficiently Other that he can fear they have found a solution from which he is cut off.[4] With a lover of the same sex, Albertine can, he imagines, know herself perfectly in and through another who is not truly Other, thereby ceasing to be a stranger to herself. His jealous anguish arises from the thought that she has found a way to heal the originary wound that divides the self from itself and that the path to this healing is forever closed to him. Ultimately, then, the name *Albertine* stands both for a world other than his own and for the otherness inherent in his own divided self—a shifting double meaning that is possible because the self does not rest securely in a stable world. Albertine's world is alien to him; so too is his own.

Eros, then, is valuable not because it offers unity but because the unity it seems to offer is impossible: thus eros forces the unwilling self to face its own uncanniness, its own foreignness, its own alterity. As I have already noted, the fulfillment of desire would destroy the Other that is its object; moreover, because the self is primordially Other than itself—it exists only as its own Other—absolute ipseity would amount to the death of the self. Thus erotic desire must not and cannot be satisfied, but its very unfulfillment may purge the artist of the illusion that one can ever comprehend the Other or achieve self-identity. As Marcel reflects, "I sensed clearly that the disappointment of travel and the disappointment of love were not different disappointments but the varied aspects which are assumed, according to the fact it applies to, by our inherent powerlessness to realise ourselves in material enjoyment [*jouissance*] or in effective action" (S IV.456/VI.271–72, trans. mod.). When we think of real life, we tend to think in terms of presence: we imagine that a place to which we have traveled or a person whom we love is given as present to us, with no need for interpretation, yet the actual presence of the place or person turns out to be disappointing compared to what one had imagined. The artist understands that in truth real life is never immediately given in presence but rather must be actively created through the interpretation of signs: "true life [*la vraie vie*], life finally discovered and illuminated—in consequence the only life really lived—is literature" (S IV.474/VI.298, trans. mod.). At this point we can see more clearly why artistic creation requires solitude or, more accurately, requires that the artist recognize his solitude: it is not that the artist is an egoist but rather that the artist must free himself from the illusions of so-called real life, including the illusion that union with others is possible, and he must create his own world by interpreting it. Thus Marcel realizes that "as for the inner book of unknown signs [. . .], for the reading of which no one could help me with any rule, this reading consisted in an act of creation in which no one can stand in for us or even collaborate with us" (S IV.458/VI.274, trans. mod.). Eros reveals that fundamental solitude, showing that there is no way to escape from the interpretation of signs into a world where the beloved, or anything or anyone else, would be immediately present to the lover. We should not imagine, however, that the artist, by turning inward, turns away from alterity: as we have seen, within the self is a multiplicity of selves. Furthermore, the self is marked by its encounters with other people. The very impossibility of knowing others affects the self to the core of its divided being. Marcel cannot know Albertine, for instance, and yet their relation marks him profoundly. The artist's solitude is always haunted by the unknowable Other.

Friendship versus Eros

Why, though, could friendship not reveal the illusion of presence and the unknowability of the Other? Eros is not the only experience through which one can discover that the notion of immediate presence is an illusion: in the above-quoted passage, Marcel himself cites his disappointment with travel as another such experience. More importantly, he does realize that he does not truly know Saint-Loup; why could this realization not provide the confrontation with alterity that is necessary for art? I reply that his recognition of the friend's alterity does fuel his art, and it in fact does so to a greater degree than Marcel himself realizes, precisely insofar as it leads him to resist friendship. In a novel where questions of reading, writing, and interpreting take center stage, Marcel's resistance to friendship amounts to a stunning refusal to read: his interpretation of friendship is summed up in his repeated insistence that friendship is too shallow to solicit interpretation. This resistance or refusal is fundamental to the text because, as we will see, it lets us glimpse the limits of interpretation in the face of absolute alterity.

We have already seen that Marcel recognizes that the friend is absolutely Other while indicating that friendship disregards the friend's alterity. It is worth examining another passage in which he returns to these themes, as his manner of restating them recalls the first chapter's analysis of the dangers of hospitality. He maintains that

> the whole effort of [friendship] is directed towards making us sacrifice the only part of ourselves that is real [*réelle*] and incommunicable (otherwise than by the means of art) to a superficial self which does not, like the other, find joy in itself, but rather a vague, sentimental glow at feeling itself supported by external props, hospitalised [*hospitalisé*] in a foreign [*étrangère*] individuality, where, happy in the protection that one gives it, it radiates its well-being in approval and marvels at qualities that it would call failings and seek to correct in itself. (S II.689/III.540–41, trans. mod.)

Initially, it appears that he is preferring a turn inward toward the self over an outward movement that welcomes and is welcomed by the Other. It is, however, the inward turn that actually recognizes the other as Other, for the outward movement is an attempt at abolishing difference by disregarding the unknowable singularity of each person. Friendship is open only to that which can be known and communicated with certainty—that is, the superficial, the meaningless—and it refuses to acknowledge that what is essential is unknowable. Considering the friend as an "other self," according to the most simplistic interpretation of the phrase that emphasizes *self* and not *other*, harms both self and other by preserving only that which is most superficial. In short, that which is communicated to "a foreign individuality" is meaningless, and the hospitality of friendship is in truth a hostility that rejects difference. Far from the absolute hospitality that welcomes the unknown Other who does not speak the language of the *polis*, friendship permits only the empty chatter of a self-congratulatory egoism. Once again, therefore, what may at first seem to be a statement of rank egoism on Marcel's part appears, on subsequent examination, to reveal a regard for alterity, and his analysis here is fully in keeping with his earlier description of friendship as "a sentiment which, instead of increasing the differences that there were between my soul and those of others—as there are between the souls of each of us—would efface them" (S II.96/II.431, trans. mod.). It is unsurprising, then, that he prefers eros to friendship: even before he definitively chooses Albertine as the one girl he desires above the others, when he spends time with the girls he finds himself confronted with a strangeness that does not seek to pass itself off as familiarity, an Otherness that does not pretend to be the Same.

This resistance to friendship on Marcel's part cannot be fully understood apart from Saint-Loup's own interpretation of friendship, which Marcel sums up as follows: "It was promptly settled between [Saint-Loup] and myself that we had become great friends forever, and he would say 'our friendship' as if he were speaking of some important and delightful thing that existed outside of ourselves, and which he soon called—apart from his love for his mistress—the greatest joy of his life" (S II.95/II.430, trans. mod.). Thus Saint-Loup views friendship as an entity that can be abstracted from the friends themselves. Far from rejoicing in the singular individual whom he can never fully know, he reifies what he calls their friendship, taking it as a thing separate from themselves, and rejoices in that abstract thing. Ultimately, therefore, he finds pleasure in a relation that binds nothing and no one, for he has separated the relation from the people who supposedly constitute it. He loves not Marcel nor even his experience of loving Marcel and being loved by him but rather his abstract conception of the love between them, such that he and Marcel become purely incidental. He does, it is true, enjoy this particular friendship so much only because he regards himself as a participant in it; it is what he calls "our friendship" and not, say, the friendship of Orestes and Pylades that he considers his "greatest joy." Yet by treating that friendship as an external thing, he inadvertently makes himself inessential to it all the same. Here we are far from Socrates's caution in the *Lysis*, where he dares not go so far as to say that he, Lysis, and Menexenus are friends; Robert de Saint-Loup, in a striking contrast, does not hesitate to speak aloud the name of friendship. We must dare to speak in order to bear witness to the friend—yet we must also beware of empty chatter that rashly claims more knowledge than we can have. Saint-Loup's conception of friendship is indeed one that turns away from both self and Other and that, as a result, becomes lost in abstraction.

Though Marcel recognizes that friendship, as imagined by Saint-Loup, is empty and superficial, he is unable to imagine it otherwise.[5] There is nothing worth interpreting in friendship, as far as he is concerned, because friendship is itself the refusal to interpret: it is a turn away from the night in which we encounter only obscure signs to the illusion of day that lets us rest in placid self-satisfaction, content to suppose that we know everything worth knowing. As Gilles Deleuze observes in *Proust and Signs*, "according to Proust, friends are like minds of good will that are explicitly in agreement as to the signification of things, words, and ideas" (41/30, trans. mod.). They are of one mind, which is to say they are hardly of any mind at all; they have no interest in interpreting signs because they find their perfect but shallow accord sufficient. In a world filled with signs, friendship emerges as an obstacle to interpretation that itself signifies nothing, that is unreadable simply because it offers nothing to read: it is a blank page that only covers over and distracts from a page of hieroglyphs that may well be equally unreadable but that assuredly do solicit the creative yet careful reading that is interpretation.

Here, however, we must proceed cautiously. Let us bear in mind the Latin roots of *solicit*: *sollicitare* means to disturb or, as Derrida emphasizes in "Differance," "to shake as a whole, to make tremble in entirety" (22/21). In this light, does not the *nothing* of friendship solicit interpretation at least as much as the visible signs?[6] For friendship shakes or disturbs interpretation precisely by blocking it. Faced with a blank book, one may naturally toss it aside in favor of one that clearly provides reading material, but the very absence of text, if one attends to it rather than retreating to signs that one recognizes as such, calls us to ask what it means to recognize signs as such in the first place. Why indeed should we take it for granted that signs will appear to us as signs? Labeling something as a sign or a non-sign is already an act of interpretation: assuming that the signs to be interpreted are directly given as signs repeats at a higher level the error of supposing that one can access pure, unmediated meaning. Certainly eros shakes interpretation by revealing that it is impossible to discover the truth of the Other, yet friendship may hint at a deeper disturbance still, one that is not the night of obscure signs but the night in which signs themselves seem to disappear, refusing themselves to the would-be interpreter.

Marcel's final dismissal of friendship, in the novel's last volume, confirms the suspicion that friendship solicits interpretation, in the sense of *sollicitare*. Returning to his repeated claim that friendship wrongly claims to offer knowledge of another even though such knowledge is impossible, Marcel describes it as "a simulation [*simulation*]" and as "madness [*folie*]":

> friendship [. . .] is a simulation since, for whatever moral reasons he may do it, the artist who renounces an hour of work for an hour of conversation with a friend knows that he is sacrificing a reality for something that does not exist (friends being friends only in that sweet madness that we have in the course of our lives, to which we readily accommodate ourselves but that in the depths of our intelligence we know to be the error of a madman who believes the furniture is alive and converses with it). (S IV.454/VI.269, trans. mod.)

Given his reification of friendship, it is little wonder that Marcel should compare the would-be friend to a lunatic who speaks to the furniture: one who believes he is speaking to his friend is speaking to someone who is not there because friendship, as Marcel understands it, is addressed not to the singular individual but to a false image, such that the one named the friend is in truth absent from the friendship. Is not madness, however, a matter of the interpretation of signs? In the madman who speaks to the furniture one may justly see an echo of the madmen whose delusions led Descartes to ask how he could know that he was not like them, deceived about the nature of the world and of his own body (M 18–19/12–13): in the *Search* as in the *Meditations*, the madman, given over to pathetic illusions, appears as a figure whose possibility threatens the narrator's search for truth, whether that search is a matter of philosophy or of art.

Yet caught as we are in a whirl of signs, apparent and otherwise, that solicit and resist interpretation—for to shake interpretation is to resist it—we should be at least as wary of sanity as of madness. The Cartesian ego that confines itself to what it can know with certainty may in truth be no saner than the madmen, and the *Search*'s madman who cannot distinguish between people and furniture should also call to mind Descartes's thinking thing that sees only clothing, never men. As Descartes reflects, "What else do I see other than hats and coats which could conceal automatons? I *judge* [*judico*] that they are men" (M 32/21, trans. mod.). The Cartesian sane ego is as distant from other people as the Proustian madman: neither can recognize the Other directly. One might object that the Cartesian ego, unlike the madman, has judged correctly—yet the force of this passage of the *Meditations* is precisely that Descartes does *not* yet know whether his judgments are any more accurate than the madman's. What he learns in the second *Meditation* concerns not the Other but himself: because what he thinks he knows about the external world comes to him by his judgment and not by his senses, "[he] can achieve an easier and more evident perception of [his] own mind than of anything else" (M 34/22–23). He has immediate access to himself alone; therefore in himself alone he must seek the ground of all his knowledge. With this conclusion, he resembles Proust's narrator, who, desiring to avoid madness, finds it more valuable to descend into the labyrinths of his own mind than to seek out friendship. Friendship, by revealing the threat of madness that haunts us, warns us that it is far from certain that we can rely on our interpretations of the world even enough to recognize the Other as Other. Eros still lets us imagine ourselves as connected to the world insofar as the lover at least knows, or thinks he knows, that the beloved is recognizable as Other; friendship shakes interpretation by revealing the world to me as a chaos in which I seek the Other but see only specters, automata, or even furniture. In this chaos the self finds itself unable to answer not only the question "Who is Albertine?" but also the more fundamental question "Am I addressing a *who* at all?"

Must the self then be content with the lonely certainty of a merely human *I am*? One cannot dodge the question by refusing to reify friendship as Marcel does. If he did not regard friendship as a thing, perhaps it would not have occurred to him to compare the would-be friend to a madman, but in any case he is right to glimpse the possibility of such an extreme isolation of the self. For it remains, even if one avoids the error of reifying friendship, that the friend is a stranger, and if one takes the isolated ego as one's point of departure and proceeds to rely solely on the ego's powers of interpretation, it is difficult indeed to see how any recognition of the absolutely Other as Other could be possible. The Other is, after all, that which does not fit the self's interpretive categories. Seeking to avoid the madness of thinking that he knows more than he truly does know—seeking, that is, only to guarantee the reliability of the ego's interpretations while disregarding that which challenges interpretation itself—the Cartesian ego is no closer to recognizing the Other than is the Proustian madman. The *Search* proposes, however, a path forward that Descartes does not mention: art. Recall Marcel's claim that friendship "mak[es] us sacrifice the only part of ourselves that is real [*réelle*] and incommunicable (*otherwise than by the means of art*)" (S II.689/III.540, emphasis added): though not exactly a way to avoid madness, and certainly not a way out of interpretation, art, including writing, does free the self from this extreme isolation. It is therefore to the theme of writing that I now turn.

The Dangerous Friendship of Writing

If friendship is madness, what then? Entertaining this notion may at first seem to blatantly contradict the principal thesis of chapter 3: that friendship is good because it operates a genuine transformation of my world such that I experience the world in light of the friend's experience. The friend's experience is, however, always unknowable, and might it not be a sort of madness to commit oneself to a transformative relation with an unknown Other? The question then becomes one of discernment, which is a matter less of avoiding madness and more of distinguishing between a destructive madness and a creative one that might, perhaps, even be called holy. The destructive and the creative will not always be as distinguishable as one would hope, but insofar as such a differentiation is possible, it permits us to recognize the dangers Marcel identifies in friendship without rejecting friendship categorically, as he does. There is no way to eliminate the dangers of friendship—yet a careful analysis of the *Search*'s presentation of writing will show that the danger here is not simply that friendship will distract from art, as though friendship and art were distinct, but rather that a shallow imitation of friendship will distract from creative friendship. For art itself turns out to be an act of friendship. As Marcel concludes, it is through art that his internal world can encounter the internal worlds of others: "By art alone are we able to emerge from ourselves, to know what another sees of that universe that is not the same as our own and of which the landscapes would have remained as unknown to us as those that may exist on the moon. Thanks to art, instead of seeing one world only, our own, we see it multiply itself, and we have at our disposal as many worlds as there are original artists" (S IV.474/VI.299, trans. mod.). Art is not an egoistical act of self-absorption in one's own interiority, as one might initially have suspected from the emphasis on solitude. Far from being an act of the self speaking to itself, art is the only way for the self to be free of solipsism and to truly communicate with others. Thus art, including writing, is a "dangerous supplement"[7] to the inadequacy of supposedly direct human relations. And dangerous it is, for writing about others involves portraying them as they appear to oneself and thus always carries the risk of betrayal—yet even so, the *Search* does bear witness to the unknowability of the Other.

At this point, we may finally take up the question of what happens in the writing and reading of the *Search*, or of any text. Crucially, every text is always a translation, for it is precisely by virtue of the gap between the text and itself that the text bears witness to the Other. What a text says is never simply what it means to say: as Derrida writes in his "Letter to a Japanese Friend" (and perhaps it is not merely a coincidence that this short essay on the translation of *déconstruction* is explicitly addressed to a friend), "There is already in 'my' language, a dark [*sombre*] problem of translation between what one can aim at, here or there, in this word [*sous ce mot*], and the usage itself, the resource of this word" (387/1, trans. mod.). That *dog* and *chien* do not have the same meaning is relatively straightforward. The English word and the French one have different histories and different cultural contexts, and even their different sounds give them different associations: they could not, for instance, play the same role in poetry because they would not have the same effect on the sound of a line. Yet *dog* also carries within itself a history and a host of possible contexts and resonances that exceed any meaning I could wish to give it when I use it. Even a single word cannot be contained within a lone desired signification; still less can a text be thus controlled. Because a text never manages to coincide with its own meaning such that it has one and only one utterly univocal sense or set of senses, it calls out for interpretation—calls out, that is, to the Other that already haunts it. Recall Derrida's observation in "Des tours de Babel" that "the original is the first debtor, the first petitioner; it begins by lacking—and by pleading for translation" (218/207). It is indebted to the Other because it exists only thanks to the Other: recall also that a language that was not already translation would be frozen in death. This primordial indebtedness testifies to the Other whether or not the text's author desired to make such a testimony: the text cries out that it exists only by virtue of an alterity that no comprehension can ever bring to heel. The author's solitude is not, therefore, solipsism: it is a retreat from the pretense of knowing others that points to the self's dependence on that absolute alterity. The solitude that points to the truth of alterity is a better friendship than the relation that goes by the name of friendship yet that claims to know all that is worth knowing about the other person.

Bearing witness to the Other cannot, however, be a matter of bearing witness to some generic alterity—as though it were even possible for the Other to be thought as a member of a genus—but must testify to the Other's singularity. We have already encountered the question "Who is the friend?" and have seen that the friend's name always remains secret, for no public name can encompass his or her singularity. Yet when all means of identification fall short, how does one speak of *the* singular other? What does it mean to bear witness to a *specific* unknowable one? These, too, are familiar questions that cannot be answered with any predetermined, universal plan. This reading of the *Search* does, however, make it possible to clarify the difficult, even impossible, fidelity to a singular Other by revisiting it through the lens of the fidelity that writing demands of the writer. A key passage occurs when the narrator finally realizes the sort of book he wants to write and seeks points of comparison for the task of writing that now faces him. One of the comparisons he draws is to friendship, which appears, moreover, as an art:

> How happy would he be, I thought, the man who had the power to write such a book! What a labor before him! To give some idea of it one would have to borrow comparisons from *the loftiest and the most varied arts*; for this writer [. . .] would have to prepare his book meticulously, perpetually regrouping his forces, like an offensive, endure it like a fatigue, accept

it like a discipline, construct it like a church, follow it like a medical regime, vanquish it like an obstacle, *conquer it like a friendship*, overfeed it like a child, create it like a world without leaving aside those mysteries that probably have their explanation only in other worlds and the presentiment of which is the thing that moves us most deeply in life and in art. (S IV.609–10/VI.507–08, trans. mod., emphasis added.)

This remark is, of course, far from the claim that writing is friendship, or vice versa. Indeed, if writing is *like* a friendship, does it not follow that writing is *not* friendship? If the artist must pursue writing as others pursue friendship, then perhaps Marcel is only subtly reiterating their opposition once more. Alternately, however, if he can state only that the book he desires to write would have to be conquered *"like a friendship,"* and not simply that writing *is* friendship, might this be because friendship, which shakes interpretation, cannot be rendered wholly present and comprehensible to observers? Given his repeated rejection of friendship, it is striking that he should invoke it here at all, and although friendship appears as only one element in a list of analogies, it is worth considering writing in more detail to see what force, unsuspected perhaps by author or narrator,[8] may lie behind this particular analogy. The comparison suggests that writing, though it does seem very different from friendship as we ordinarily think of it, can be conceived of not only as an act of friendship to others, but as an act of friendship to language itself, since it is from the writer's relation to language that the text arises. The previous chapter proposed that friendship is translation, understood as translation between my world and the friend's world—a chiastic movement in which friends transform each other's worlds and testify to each other according to the temporality of mutual giving and not of economic exchange. And if friendship is translation, then it is not surprising that translation between languages—the usual, more restricted sense of the word—or translation within one language—that is, writing—should be instances of friendship. In translation, in writing, we encounter again the impossible struggle to be faithful to one that is absolutely singular: here, the language in which one writes. In the case of translation between languages, it is a matter of fidelity to two that are absolutely singular: the language from which one translates and that language in which one writes the new text. When one speaks, one enters into the universal, it is true; yet each language is itself singular, for no language can be substituted for another, and there exists no totality that could subsume all languages and serve as an authoritative reference for the translator.

Crucially, the lack of any authoritative reference point means that the writer/translator cannot take up the position of an objective ego who, from the standpoint of a detached superior, passes judgment on the work. The writer is implicated from the start. Some translations are better than others: though *chien* does not simply and univocally mean *dog*, it does not follow that one could legitimately translate it as, say, *fiery* or *swim*. The point is that the process of writing, and indeed every consideration of whether one word is better than another, demands a certain submission to the language or languages involved: in fact, one who is considered to have mastered a language is precisely one who is most sensitive to its myriad nuances. Such a person may realize hitherto unimagined possibilities, to the point of seeming to do violence to the language: one may think here of James Joyce's *Finnegans Wake*, which begins midsentence and becomes still stranger from there, or, to take an example whose radical nature is not obvious to today's readers, of Victor Hugo's *Hernani*, which breaks with certain linguistic conventions of classical French theater.[9] To be sure, it often will not be evident whether a writer has done violence to the language or rather discovered new possibilities within it. Still, despite the uncertainty that dogs our judgments of literary merit, it remains that the great writer does not do violence to the language because she does not take it as an object upon which to act: she works with the language and is worked on by the language, for her creation exceeds even her own attempts to define it. The writer is not in control of her own work. "I judge that they are men," writes Descartes, and he does not ask whether the figures passing before his window judge *him* to be a man. They are passive objects, he an impassive observer. One who would write well cannot afford a Cartesianism that gives her a point on which to stand from which she may, herself unjudged, judge all. On the contrary, she must let the work call her into question: she must let it signify more than she herself can know. As Blanchot suggests in *The Writing of the Disaster*, "Would writing be to become, in the book, legible for everyone, and for oneself indecipherable?" (8/2, trans. mod.). Indeed, writing is recognizing the stranger in oneself, recognizing one's own indecipherability and offering it to the Other as a gift to be read.

Writing and Linguistic Hospitality

In writing, therefore, it is always a matter of what Ricœur names "the ordeal of the stranger" or "the test of the stranger" (*l'épreuve de l'étranger*) (OT 7/3).[10] Citing Franz Rosenzweig, Ricœur states that "to translate [. . .] is to serve two masters, the foreigner [*étranger*] with his work, the reader with his desire for appropriation, foreign author, reader dwelling in the same language as the translator" (OT 9/4). Indeed, to write is always to serve the stranger, for the language one calls one's own is never one's possession, is never the same as itself, and is never a strictly private affair. To write is to give one's text to an Other who, no matter how faithful a reader she is, may not read it as one had imagined. To write is therefore to open oneself to interpretation by the Other—which, again, is not to say that all interpretations the reader may offer are equally valid. The gift of the text is the opening of a dialogue: as Ricœur concludes, "by admitting and assuming the irreducibility of the pair of the own and the foreign, the translator finds his reward in the recognition [*reconnaissance*] of the impassable status of the dialogicality of the act of translating as the reasonable horizon of the desire to translate" (OT 19/10, trans. mod.). What Ricœur here says of the translator between languages applies also to the writer within one language: it is only when one surrenders the desire for total control of "one's own" language and "one's own" work and realizes that perfect fidelity is impossible that one can communicate with others. The desire for mastery and possession forecloses the possibility of communication by denying the Other in favor of the ego. In contrast, the friendship to language that writing demands dispossesses the ego and thereby opens the way to dialogue with the Other—which may become friendship with the Other. And this dialogue cannot be reduced to an economy of exchange that would only be another way of assimilating the Other: recall Ricœur's notion of mutual recognition, according to which the return is not a repayment but a new gift. To communicate is to enter into this mutual recognition—to recognize the Other and, crucially, to let oneself be recognized by the Other. What is more, these two elements of communication are inseparable because recognizing the Other as Other means recognizing him or her as one who can recognize the self.[11]

The Other recognizes and interprets me; things, such as furniture, do not. Thus friendship solicits interpretation, in the sense of *sollicitare*, by decentering the interpretive ego and subjecting the self to the Other's interpretation. To use language, furthermore, is already to open oneself to interpretation precisely because language can never be private. To say that language interprets me may still seem odd, even after the preceding analysis; the point, however, is not to anthropomorphize language by turning it into a knowing subject but to remove the knowing subject from its egoistic pedestal. The self is never given, even to itself, independently of language or of *a* language. The self arises within language, and not even within language in the abstract, as if there were such a thing, but within the specific language or languages in which it speaks and is spoken. Hence the self is subject to interpretation from the start, and its own self-interpretation is never simply its own but always occurs within the interpretive framework of a language or of multiple languages. It is not that the self is a mere object of language, devoid of creative power; rather, the point is that the self's creative power has its source in the self's relation to the language or languages in which it speaks and writes. To say that language interprets me is to say that I am not my own ground, that my own narrative escapes my control—which, far from being a denial of my ethical responsibility, emphasizes it by making clear that I cannot evade my relation to the Other.

At this point we can see more fully the impact of the claim that friendship is translation: friendship demands that I not only recognize but that I love the fact that my world and my self are always already given over to the interpretation of the Other. The madness of false friendship treats the friend as furniture by seeking only the Same that will not call the ego into question. Though I am chiefly focusing on writing, all art strips the self of this desire for the comfort of self-identity, since any work of art, whether a novel, a poem, a sculpture, a painting, a symphony, or anything else, exceeds the signification that the artist herself can know. One communicates with others through art because as an artist the self must abandon its pretense of being an objective interpreter and open itself to interpretation by the world and by others. I wrote above that art is not exactly a way out of madness: this is because art compels the self to end its obsession with guaranteeing its own sanity—that is, its position as the impassive judge of the world. For that same reason, art is a way out of the madness that treats the Other as an object like an automaton or a piece of furniture. Dialogue with the Other is a wager against the madness of solipsism and for what Ricœur calls "linguistic hospitality [. . .] where the pleasure of dwelling in the other's language is balanced by the pleasure of receiving the foreign word [*parole*] at home, in one's own welcoming house" (OT 20/10). This hospitality does, however, entail a certain alienation, an encounter with the uncanny, for it means welcoming foreignness into "one's own" language—but this alienation is a creative, life-giving one, a holy madness, that frees the self from the empty wasteland of solipsism.

Here it bears repeating that not all interpretations are equally valid: linguistic hospitality decidedly does not oblige one to accept whatever interpretation of oneself the Other offers. It does not, for instance, oblige Albertine to accept Marcel's attempts to interpret her as an object. The self need not and must not cut out its tongue in favor of the Other's. For that matter, hostility turned against the self fails even to serve the Other, for it does the Other no good to become a tyrant; likewise, hostility against the Other harms the self precisely because creativity requires an openness to the Other. Whether primarily directed against the Other or the self, hostility is always an unholy madness that harms both.[12] To write is to embark on a mutual giving of narratives and interpretations, and for this mutual giving, the writer, the reader, and the text itself are all necessary. As Kearney puts it in *On Stories*, "the story is not confined to the mind of its author alone [. . .]. Nor is it confined to the mind of its reader. Nor indeed to the action of its narrated actors. The story exists in the interplay between all these. Every story is a play of at least three persons (author/actor/addressee) whose outcome is never final" (156). The reader of a text is also summoned to linguistic hospitality: she has the responsibility of welcoming the text by interpreting well, which requires listening to the Other and letting oneself be called into question. In addition, interpreting the *Search*, or any text, is itself a creative act that amounts to countersigning a text, precisely because the text's meaning exceeds what anyone can comprehend.[13] Thus reading as well as writing, if done well, is an act of friendship to language.

Involuntary Memory and the Dispossession of the Self

As we return to the text of the *Search* to further consider this dispossession of the self, this holy madness, that is necessary for writing, the key questions that remain are these: if writing is a dispossession of the self, what does it mean for the self to seek to write? And what does it mean for the self to seek friendship? Let us read a key scene from the beginning of the *Search*, whose import it is now possible to appreciate:

the celebrated episode of the madeleine, which introduces the notion of involuntary memory. The depiction of involuntary memory indicates that we must reject the possessiveness that demands presence—and thus it suggests that the only way to gain friendship is to risk not finding it. For it is precisely when the narrator is *not* in control of his memory that he has the decisive experience in which one may read in microcosm the beginning of the search for lost time.

Although the whole *Search* is told from the point of view of Marcel looking back on his past, he is unable to remember his childhood in Combray with any clarity until, at a moment when he is neither willing nor even expecting the return of these memories, he tastes a madeleine dipped in tea, like the ones his aunt gave him on Sunday mornings when he was a boy: "And soon, mechanically, afflicted by the dreary day and the prospect of a depressing morrow, I raised to my lips a spoonful of the tea in which I had let soften a morsel of the madeleine. But at the very instant that the mouthful of liquid mixed with the crumbs of cake touched my palate, I shivered, attentive to the extraordinary thing that was happening in me. A delicious pleasure had invaded me, isolated, with no suggestion of its cause" (S I.44/I.60, trans. mod.). It is crucial to realize that this event whose cause is hidden is not, as the novel's title might lead one to suppose, the restoration of lost time: on the contrary, it is a disruption of time. Attempting to recount this disruption, the narration moves from the past tense to the present, a switch that suspends the event of recollection between the past and the future:

> I drink a second mouthful, in which I find nothing more than in the first, a third, which gives me a bit less than the second. [. . .] It is clear that the truth I am seeking lies not in the beverage but in myself. [. . .] It is up to [my mind] to find the truth. But how? What grave uncertainty, whenever the mind feels overtaken by itself; when it, the seeker, is at the same time the obscure country through which it must seek and where all its equipment will avail it nothing. Seek? Not only that: create. It is face to face with something which does not yet exist, which it alone can make actual, then bring into its light. (S I.45/I.61, trans. mod.)

Once again, the event of involuntary memory is not what the title of the *Search* would have led us to expect: it is "not only" a matter of searching for the past but of creating it so that it may be read in the future. The point is not to make the past become present but to create, from its absence, a work that itself calls for creative interpretation. And this task is a difficult one: "Ten times I must begin again, lean down toward this memory. And each time the cowardice that deters us from every difficult task, every important work [*œuvre*], advised me to leave the thing alone" (S I.46/I.63, trans. mod.). By appearing in the present tense, the "not yet" of creation reveals itself as eternal. The work of creation is never finished but must always be begun again; no interpretation will close the dialogue. The temptation to abandon the work will surely remain with us as well, but, interestingly, it is only the creative work itself that is granted the eternity of the present. The memory itself arrives in the past tense—"And suddenly the memory appeared to me" (S I.46/I.63, trans. mod.)—and as Marcel remembers the madeleines his aunt gave him, and with them all of Combray, the narration remains in the past.[14] The use of the present tense for the work of seeking and creating the memory stands as a reminder that Marcel's narrative is an invitation, and not an end, to creation. Every text calls for interpretation, and interpretation itself is a creative work.

This complex interplay of the voluntary and the involuntary that we see in the episode of the madeleine is essential to artistic creation and to friendship. The initial pleasure is involuntary, but Marcel responds to it by seeking its reason—and "not only" by seeking but also by creating. Then the memory of his aunt's madeleines comes to him "suddenly," indicating that it is not simply the product of his will. In the episode of the madeleine, Marcel experiences a dispossession of the self that summons him to artistic creation, and the resulting creation—the memory—exceeds the work that he consciously put into it, thereby renewing the dispossession of the self. This point corroborates the preceding discussion of friendship to language: the author must put in the effort of writing, yet her own writing always escapes her control, and even the possibility of putting in the effort of writing depends on a prior revelation from the Other. Though Marcel says that "the truth" is "in [himself]," it bursts in on him as a revelation from outside—which is to say that he himself is constituted by the Other. The self is this dispossession of itself, and to put in the effort of writing is to embrace the impossibility of controlling that writing. Far from being incidental, the impossibility of controlling one's artistic creation is the uncanny strangeness that lies at the heart of any artistic creation and on which art depends.[15] The initial, involuntary moment of pleasure commands Marcel to commit himself to a creative process whose outcome he does not yet know and never will know fully, thus foreshadowing the *Search*'s end, in which Marcel glimpses darkly, as through a glass, the possibility of the novel he finds himself summoned to write. When seeking and creating the memory, he did not know what would come; so too, at the final volume's close, he, and we, do not know what will come. If we were sure that he had written his novel and that it was given to us as the *Search*, we could imagine that the creative task the final volume proposes had been satisfactorily completed once and for all; since we do not and cannot know this, that task of creation falls to us. Like Marcel, we find ourselves solicited:[16] reading calls us to the friendship with the text that is interpretation.

Friendship between humans likewise arises beyond our comprehension—beyond any reason—yet demands commitment. In the episode of the madeleine, we encounter in microcosm the drama of the self's constitution through friendship: one is involuntarily summoned to voluntarily commit oneself to a relation whose significance one cannot measure, now or ever. What is more, the will with which I respond to the call I involuntarily received and with which I choose to welcome the Other's gifts is itself constituted, without my willing it, through my relation to the Other.[17]

Note further that the self's creation through its relation to the Other is continual: the self I am called to commit to the Other is not simply always already dispossessed but is always already in the process of dispossession, a dispossession that is a creation. The dispossession is never over and done with. To speak of the self is therefore something of a paradox: even and especially at the moment when its will seems to be most definitively committed, as when Marcel was seeking the memory of Combray after the initial moment of pleasure, the self remains unfinished, held in suspense. The moment when Marcel receives his newly created past is, after all, also involuntary—and the creation of his childhood in Combray is, of course, not the end of the creation of Marcel, which continues as long as he exists in time. It is little wonder, then, that the self's singularity is unknowable, even to the self itself, and that we must call the *Search*'s narrator by a pseudonym: because the self is never a completed work, an individual's singularity is never caught and fixed in place that we might study it.

Even so, it is indeed as the unknowable singularity that he is that Marcel is summoned to the task of creation. In the episode of the madeleine it is, after all, a matter of one of his own memories. True, we know by now not to read the words "his own" too literally, since he does not control the creation of the memory and in any case the memory, being created, is a fiction. As Beistegui observes in *Proust as Philosopher*, "What characterizes involuntary memory is the fact that what resurfaces like this hasn't ever been experienced or perceived as such. It's a paradox: something resurfaces or returns that has never actually happened" (125–26/63). It would, however, be a different fiction if anyone else had been convoked to participate in its creation. Not only is each language singular, when it comes to my relation to language, no one else can stand in for me. Recall Marcel's conclusion in the final volume that "we have at our disposal as many worlds as there are original artists" (S IV.474/VI.299.). If anyone refuses the task of creation, an entire world is lost. The self's singularity is so deeply implicated in this task that the self's relation to language is indeed a matter of friendship, and not only of Levinasian ethics. Recall that the Levinasian Other does not mourn the self's death and that although self and Other are both singular, Levinas does not propose that the Other would have an essentially different relation to different selves by virtue of their distinct singularities. Language, however, does have an essentially different relation to different selves by virtue of their singularities because no two people will inhabit or create the same world. Thus language constitutes each person's death as worthy of mourning: each death is the death of an entire world that might have been given to others. In the final volume it is precisely the discovery of his artistic vocation that reveals to Marcel the significance of his own death: he realizes that he is "the only person capable" of writing his book, since "with [his] death would have disappeared not only the one and only miner capable of extracting these minerals but also the deposit itself" (S IV.614/VI.514, trans. mod.). He does not fear the cessation of his own existence precisely because the self is ever-changing: "since my childhood," he reflects, "I had already died many times" (S IV.615/VI.515). The self's multiplicity does not contradict its singularity: singularity means that no one can stand in for me and that I cannot be assimilated to a totality, not that I am wholly self-identical, a totality unto myself. The tragedy of death is the loss not of a fixed essence, of a self-contained, self-identical entity, but of the unforeseen creation to which one is summoned by the Other. It is only because the Other calls me out of myself that I am a singular individual in the first place. Hence my death, like my life, is not "my own" but is constituted in and through my relation to the Other—and, indeed, to the friend, for it is the friend who mourns my death.

The Fidelity of Translation

Another way to say that the self is constituted in and through its relation to the Other is that the self is translated in and through its relation to the Other. No original self preexists the relation to the Other; even the self's own interpretations of itself do not preexist that relation, for the self is not its own origin. Again, this is not to say that any interpretation the Other offers or seeks to impose is correct—one can and must judge interpretations against each other—but there is no way to avoid interpretation. One knows the Other and even oneself only across absence; neither Other nor self are ever fully present to the self. I observed earlier that writing is revealed in the *Search* as a dangerous supplement to the seemingly direct human relations that appear to give us knowledge of each other but that are in fact illusory. In fact, it is when writing of the "dangerous supplement" that is writing that Derrida famously remarks, in *Of Grammatology*, that "*there is no outside-the-text* [*il n'y a pas de hors-texte*]" (220/158, trans. mod.).[18] There is no way out of translation, no way to unmediated union with the Other, no way to self-identity. It is essential to resist the temptation to despair that may arise with this realization. It is all too easy to misread the statements that the end of translation would be the death of language, that union with the Other would destroy the Other and therefore the self, and that self-identity would be the self's destruction: one may suppose that these assertions are a command to resign oneself to the impossibility of absolute presence to self and others. They are not. They are a summons to rejoice in the mystery of the Other and to respond to the gift of a translated world with translations of one's own.

To say that "there is no outside-the-text" is also to say that the world itself is a text that pleads for translation, a point Marcel recognizes when he reflects, in a passage that must be quoted at length,

> If reality were indeed this sort of waste product of experience, more or less identical for each one of us, since when we speak of bad weather, a war, a taxi rank, a brightly lit restaurant, a garden full of flowers, everybody knows what we

mean, if reality were no more than this, no doubt a sort of cinematograph film of these things would be sufficient and the "style," the "literature" that departed from their simple data would be superfluous and artificial [un hors d'œuvre artificiel]. But was reality indeed thus? If I tried to realize what actually happens at the moment when a thing makes some particular impression upon us—on the day, for instance, when as I crossed the bridge over the Vivonne the shadow of a cloud upon the water had made me cry: "Damn!" and jump for joy; or the occasion when, hearing a phrase of Bergotte's, all that I saw of my impression was this, which did not particularly suit it: "It is admirable"; or the words I had once heard Bloch pronounce that did not suit such a vulgar affair at all: "I must say that that sort of conduct seems to me absolutely fffantastic!"; or that evening when, flattered at having been well received by the Guermantes and also a little intoxicated by the wines which I had drunk in their house, I could not help saying to myself half aloud as I left them: "They really are delightful people with whom it would be pleasant to spend one's life"—I perceived that to express these impressions, to write this essential book, the only true book, a great writer does not, in the ordinary sense of the word, have to "invent" this book—since it exists already in each one of us—but has to translate it. The duty and the task of a writer are those of a translator. (S IV.469/VI.290–91, trans. mod.)

The world is not made of bare facts that present themselves directly to the mind for comprehension. If it were, then literature would quite literally be an hors d'œuvre, an outside-the-work: the world would be the original, and in that case literature would be unnecessary to the task of seeking the truth. In reality, however, we discover the world through impressions that are different for each one of us and that, moreover, must be translated even for the self to realize its own experience: note in particular Marcel's remark, concerning his impression of a phrase by the writer Bergotte, "all that I saw of my impression was this, which did not particularly suit it: ' 'It is admirable.' " Without translation, even the self will not know what happened, for the self encounters only an impression of an impression that, by its very inadequacy, begs for interpretation. And if the "essential book [. . .] exists already in each one of us," it is as a work whose translation the self has already experienced and that the self must now translate for others. The Combray of Marcel's childhood becomes real only in becoming a fiction, for if one seeks the original, his actual childhood and not the remembered one, one will find that it was as a fiction—that is, a work of the creation that is interpretation—that he experienced Combray in the first place.[19] So too with our other impressions. The truth of the world is in the acknowledged translation of it: to be faithful to the fact that the world is constituted by interpretations, one must recognize that one does translate the world.

One passage of the *Search* that might initially seem to contradict this reading is Marcel's analysis of the painter Elstir's work, which he describes by writing of "Elstir's effort to exhibit things not as he knew them to be but according to the optical illusions of which our first sight is made" (S II.194/II.570, trans. mod.) and "the effort Elstir made to strip himself, in the presence of reality, of all the notions of his intelligence" (S II.195/II.572, trans. mod.). A closer reading, however, indicates that "the notions of his intelligence" are those seemingly commonsense notions that take the world to be composed of bare facts that do not result from any interpretation. For "our first sight" consists of "optical illusions," and, moreover, Marcel describes Elstir's work in terms of metaphor, writing that "the rare moments in which we see nature *as she is, poetically*, were those from which Elstir's work was made. One of his most frequent *metaphors* in the seascapes which he had close by him then was precisely that which, comparing land with sea, suppressed all demarcation between them" (S II.192/II.567, trans. mod., emphasis added). To paint the world truly, one cannot simply paint it as it is because it is always already translated; or, to put it another way, painting the world as it is means painting it in a way that makes clear that it is translated.

Writing to the Friend

To speak of translation as fidelity may surprise. It is more common to describe it as betrayal—as I myself have done in this book, for even the most faithful translation can never be perfectly faithful to the text it translates. Certainly the old problem of betraying the singular by speaking or writing of it, thereby bringing it into the universal, makes its appearance in the *Search*: consider, in particular, Marcel's pessimistic reflection, "Thus I had to resign myself, since nothing can last save by becoming general and if the mind dies to itself, to the idea that even the people who were most dear to the writer have in the end done no more than pose for him as for a painter" (S IV.484/VI.311, trans. mod.). How indeed can one depict in a work of art, without building deceptive images of them, people whom one does not know? Even if the writer does not directly depict those he loves, is he not subordinating the singular individual to the universalizing power of language by dedicating his life to writing and therefore to language? This pessimism is not, however, the last word on art. Shortly thereafter, describing the task of writing that faces him, Marcel reflects that "what it is a matter of causing to emerge, of bringing to light, are our feelings, our passions, that is, the feelings and passions of all" (S IV.485–86/VI.316, trans. mod.). That language always enters into the universal does not only mean that it betrays the singular; it also means that language can speak to more than one singular individual and in more than one language. Still later, he refers to "my book, thanks to which I would furnish [the readers] with the means to read in themselves" (S IV.610/VI.508, trans. mod.).[20] Addressed to everyone and no one—to everyone by virtue of language's generality and to no one because the readers are necessarily strangers to the writer—the work itself is singular and received by strangers, each of whom is singular, and who in countersigning it with their readings, their interpretations, will enter into a dialogue with the work through which they too will be interpreted. To write, to translate, is to be faithful to the stranger, including the strangers "who were [or who are] most dear to the writer," because to write is to give a gift without asking for anything in return, not the recipient's name, nor even—since a text calls out for translation—that the recipient know its language. Translation is even the greatest possible fidelity, as translating the world for another means recognizing both that he or she is Other and that it is good that this is so. It is the contrary of the attempt to absorb the Other into oneself: it is the affirmation that the Other will always be Other, that self and Other will never inhabit quite the same world. One cannot translate if one demands that the Other become the Same; one can translate only if one loves that the Other is Other.[21]

Where, then, does this leave friendship and eros? By revealing the folly of the shallow relation that one might easily mistake for friendship, the *Search* prepares us, as Katharina Münchberg argues, to realize that if genuine friendship is possible, it must be a love for the Other's alterity—or, as she puts it, that "the friendly relationship is a relationship of distance and separation."[22] Granted, Marcel never seems to realize that his narrative may lead us to this realization, but the preceding analysis of writing shows that no narrator will understand the full force of his own account. As for eros, Marcel credits it with being useful to the artist, but let us beware of drawing too direct a line between the lover and the artist: Swann, Charlus, and Robert de Saint-Loup all display intense jealousy, and none of them even has the ambition to create art. Marcel, reflecting on "that happiness suggested by the little phrase of the sonata to Swann," states that Swann "erred by assimilating it to the pleasures of love and had not known how to find it in artistic creation" (S IV.456/VI.272, trans. mod.). That Swann makes the mistake of seeking in love a happiness like that he found in the "little phrase" of Vinteuil's sonata shows how far eros can lead us astray if we take it as an end in itself and fail to realize that art demands a recognition of alterity that contrasts with the possessiveness of erotic desire. This point holds whether or not Marcel has misinterpreted Swann's conduct: even if Swann himself did not actually believe that the pleasures of art and eros were alike, the error remains a possible one. Recall that eros fuels art only if one moves beyond it: it is not the jealous quest to absorb the Other into the Same that is valuable for the artist, but rather the failure of eros to end in the absolute ipseity it seeks. When the writer who initially pursued eros discovers, through its failure, the unknowability of the Other and lets the revelation of this unknowability inspire his or her art, he or she leaves eros behind for the love across distance that is true friendship. Moreover, since writing is an act of friendship, the *Search*, by portraying eros in writing, operates a transmutation of eros into friendship. This is not to say that romantic or sexual love must be rejected or that lovers cannot also be friends but that lovers must leave behind eros understood, as it so often has been, as the desire for the absolute union of the Other with the Same.[23] Because friendship qua friendship does not seek even a physical union, however, it is friendship that stands as the most complete example of the love of the Other *as wholly Other*. The key point here is that distance is central to friendship in a way that it is not central to eros.

This book opened by asking how one could write of friendship. Now it turns out that, however difficult or impossible it may be to write *of* friendship, one is always writing *to* a friend: for writing is always striving for fidelity, always a friendship to a language that remains strange even and especially to those who know it best, always, too, a friendship to the unknown readers, each one singular, to whom the author offers his or her world as a gift. There is no adequate answer to the question "Who is the friend?" but the impossibility of giving a definitive answer to that question in no way prevents the act of friendship that is the translation of the world for the ultimately anonymous friend. Every such gift is, of course, imperfect. But if it will not do to forget that translation betrays, let us not forget either that translation is faithful. Friendship is translation between worlds, and translation is impossible because it can never be wholly faithful; so be it. Yet friendship is translation, and translation also takes place and is faithful.

5

Fidelity in the Dark
On Presence and Knowledge

Being-There-For

Friendship is impossible, and yet it takes place. Indeed, the distance between friends that renders perfect fidelity impossible is the very condition of friendship: friendship is love across distance, a struggle in the dark to testify to the unknowable Other. We might say with truth, therefore, that friendship takes place because it is impossible. To put it another way, friendship is possible for those who admit its impossibility, who renounce possession and who love precisely that the Other escapes them. Translation is the giving of one's world to another within finitude—translation between languages is only one manifestation of this giving—and although it can never be perfectly faithful, it remains a gesture of fidelity insofar as it affirms that the Other is Other. What, though, are we to make of the common idea that friendship involves being there to aid the friend when she is in difficulty? If pure presence is impossible, does anything remain of presence in the friend's hour of need?

Such presence is at the heart of Gabriel Marcel's distinction between fidelity and constancy, which he draws in the essay "Creative Fidelity." Defining fidelity, he writes that "when I assert of so-and-so: he is a faithful friend, I mean above all: he is someone who does not fail me, someone who stands up to the test of circumstances; he does not slip away, far from it, but one finds him there when one is in difficulty" (CF 230/153–54, trans. mod.). The presence that is essential to fidelity is not, however, a state in which the friend is wholly given phenomenally but rather is the act in which the friend actively turns toward me, or in which I actively turn toward her. Thus the crucial difference between constancy and fidelity is that constancy is directed toward the self, fidelity toward the other. In constancy and fidelity alike I consider myself as bound forever, despite any obstacles that may arise, to the other person, but whereas constancy is for my own sake, fidelity is for the sake of the other. In Marcel's words, "I am constant for myself, in relation to myself, to my project—whereas I am present for the other, and more precisely: for *thou*" (CF 230/154, trans. mod.). If I display mere constancy in my relation to another, I am motivated by my own desire to be the sort of person who fulfills obligations. To preserve this image of myself, I keep my promises to the other person, I help her when she needs it, and I may well have the external appearance of being faithful—yet my concern is for myself, and not for the other. Fidelity, in contrast, means that I am motivated by care for the other person. I act faithfully not to preserve an image of myself but because I love the one to whom I am faithful. Being present, in this sense, is listening to the call of the person to whom I am bound in fidelity. It is, as Marcel indicates, a matter not of being present as a chair or table is present but of being present *for* the other person.

The preposition is crucial. Being present *for* or being there *for* takes place precisely across the distance that conditions fidelity. In employing the term "being-there-for," I take a cue from Falque's discussion of being-there in his "Toward an Ethics of the Spread Body." Though the essay focuses on bodily suffering, and this particular passage concerns the relation between patient and caregiver in palliative care, his notion of being-there is more broadly applicable and may, I argue, be further developed as being-there-for. Falque writes that "the gaping of the sick body's chaos means that one is never truly 'with' ['*avec*'] but only 'next to' ['*à côté*'] or 'at its side' ['*à ses côtés*']. One does not share the 'mineness' of suffering and of death" (TE 75/107). The meaning Falque gives the word *with* here is deliberately narrow: to be with another, in his sense, would be to enter into her experience of suffering such that I suffer precisely as she does. Such a thing is, however, impossible: between her experience and my experience of her experience, there always remains a gap. I can come alongside her but cannot be with her in the sense of entering inside her own experience. Falque therefore concludes that "in this context, where the caregiver might have believed to be 'with' (*Mitsein*), it emerges that one can really only be 'there' (*Dasein*). To accompany does not mean to walk the same path but to operate from 'sideways' [*opérer le 'pas de côté'*]" (75/107, trans. mod.). Though Falque's point applies with particular force to suffering, insofar as the senselessness of suffering defies comprehension, it remains that one never knows another's experience, good or bad, from the inside. At first glance, the notion of being-there may seem to widen too much the gap between self and other; one may ask how mere being-there could bring aid or comfort. As Falque conceives of it, however (and note that the senses he gives being-with and being-there are not the same as Heidegger's),[1] being-there means being-beside or being-alongside (these two prepositions are other possible translations of *à côté*). Introducing the directionality of the *for* serves, moreover, to clarify the self's relation to the Other in this "thereness": being-there-for means directing oneself toward the Other such that one's care is first for the Other rather than for the self. Note that although it is possible to be there for a particular person on only a few occasions, or even only once, without undertaking a more lasting commitment, fidelity entails pledging oneself to being there for a particular other person for all time and unto eternity.

In being there for another, one is not absorbed into the Other because the self's experience of the situation is not interchangeable with the Other's: being-there-for means also that I come to the Other from the outside. Considering being-there-for in the context of suffering, we see that it is precisely because I come from the outside that I can help: one who was caught inside another's suffering could only suffer equally. One who is suffering does not need a second self to suffer in the same way, so that there would be twice the suffering. If I am trapped in a pit, what serves me is not someone jumping in with me but someone helping me get out. Granted, there are problems with no immediate way out, or no way that can readily be found, such as the situation of the person in palliative care who can be helped to live unto her coming death but who cannot be restored to health. One might also think of a chronic illness that can be managed but not cured or of grief over a loss, which will eventually lessen but that one cannot simply bring to an end. Even when there is no way for the other person to help me out of the pit, however, what truly serves me is not the duplication of my suffering but the gift of a world that is not reducible to my suffering.

When overwhelmed and submerged by pain, one risks losing everything else, to the point of becoming less a sufferer than a prolonged suffering.[2] In being there for the other person, however—going out from myself and my concern with myself toward her, coming alongside her to respond to her problems in ways that will be helpful to her—I remind her that the world is not structured only by suffering but also by love and fidelity. Or, better, I remind her that there is a world and that the world is a gift, for it is suffering that undoes the world and, as this chapter and the next explore in more detail, it is the promise of fidelity that constitutes the world. One who is there for a friend who is suffering does not demand a quicker recovery than is actually possible, but neither will she condone avoidable weakness, and she will not let her friend be given over to despair if she can help it (unfortunately, through no fault of one's own, one cannot always help it). Being there for someone in trouble is offering a strength that, rather than being overwhelmed by her burden along with her, will help her bear it. Being-there-for means, to borrow a Levinasian phrase, saying to the Other, "Here I am."

Being-there-for is not confined to times of trouble. In joy as well as in sorrow one can care for the other. It might initially seem absurd to complain that someone is there only when I am in difficulty, yet friendship involves sharing both pleasures and pains. Again, this sharing does not mean experiencing them in the same way but experiencing them alongside each other and in the light of the other's experience, and as it comforts one who suffers so too does it add new joys to one who is happy. Because the other's experience of my pleasures is not identical to my own, my happiness takes on, thanks to her, new dimensions that I could not have experienced on my own. Moreover, for the other's sake I particularly desire that she share in my pleasures so that she can also experience happiness she would not otherwise have had. Thus the friend is there for me by coming to share in my pleasure, and I am there for her by inviting her to share in it. Crucially, this sharing of joy, far from dividing a set amount of joy between friends, in fact multiplies joy. It is not "the transmutation of the other into the Same" that according to Levinas "is in the essence of enjoyment [*jouissance*]" (TI 113/111): it is a turn toward the Other that delights in her pleasure. My primary aim is to explore the conditions of possibility of friendship, rather than the day-to-day experience of it, but we must not forget that, while fidelity may at times be difficult, friendship is a source of pleasure and indeed of great joy.

Fidelity in Separation

Here we must consider the role of physical presence in being-there-for and in friendship. Certainly mere physical presence is not the same as being-there-for—one can be physically present while conducting oneself extraordinarily selfishly—but does the latter require the former? One might initially assume so. In his discussion of *philia*, Aristotle places a premium on physical presence, asserting that for friendship "there is also need of [. . .] the habits formed by living together [συνηθείας]; for as the adage has it it is not possible for people to know [εἰδῆσαι] each other until they have eaten together the proverbial salt, nor is it possible, before this occurs, for them to accept each other and to be friends [φίλους] until each appears to each as lovable [φιλητὸς] and is trusted" (NE 1156b26–30). The verb here translated as "to know," εἰδῆσαι, is a conjugation of οἶδα, "I know," which shares a root with εἶδον, "I see," and so also with εἴδωλον: *eidolon*, image, apparition, phantom. Thus in this insistence on physical presence we glimpse a hint of its dangers. Indeed, the more time one spends with another, the better one knows her, in a good sense of "knowing" that includes recognizing her ultimate unknowability. And it is true that knowing the friend is always, to a degree, a joint work of imagination: dialogue, the exchange of stories, is an imagining and reimagining of one's own possibilities and of the friend's possibilities, of the past, present, and future of our worlds. This imagining of self and Other creates new possibilities for the pursuit of justice by revealing the limits of my own understanding and by summoning me to respond to the Other. Imagination, when attuned to the Other, helps me to see the impact of my action and inaction on the Other and to create, together with the Other, new paths toward greater justice. At the same time, there is always a risk that knowing the friend will become the harmful sort of imagining that sees the friend only as I want her to be, that subordinates her to my selfish desires.[3] When the narrator of the *Search* supposed that he possessed Albertine as she lay sleeping, that too was a work of imagination. Physical distance between friends need not, therefore, be wholly regretted, for it can serve as a reminder of the limits to our capacity to know the Other: when separated, we see more clearly than ever that we do not possess each other.

Despite this potential risk of presence, physical distance does forestall certain manifestations of being-there-for—but, crucially, does not render being-there-for impossible. Although the above-noted root of εἰδῆσαι suggests a privileging of sight, Aristotle, as Kearney has reminded us, is also the ancient philosopher who first wrote of the importance of touch.[4] Touch frequently plays a role in both consolation and celebration—one thinks of the hug, handshake, or high-five—and physical distance deprives us of these gestures. And fewer shared activities are possible for friends separated by physical distance than for friends who are physically together. For that matter, the very language we use to speak of friendship across separation hints at the importance of physical presence, of being alongside each other in the flesh: when friends cannot literally be together, they speak of staying in touch or in contact. Yet when physical separation is for all practical purposes unavoidable, it does not prevent friends from continuing to place care for the other above care for the self. The gestures of care that are possible through mail, telephone, email, social media, and videoconference may be more limited than those that are possible in person—at any rate they are different, and it does seem that friends who are apart often wish to encounter each other in person—but they are not nonexistent.[5] Through these media, both old and new, friends can communicate their fidelity—can communicate, that is, that they are committed to each other, come what may; that they are still attentive to each other's joy and sorrow; and that they are and will remain ready to do whatever they can to aid each other, though their ability to act is restricted by the distance between them.

That being-there-for is not the same as literal physical presence accords with Marcel's take on the matter in "Creative Fidelity": he writes, "Of course, by presence I do not mean here the fact of externally manifesting oneself, but the much less objectively definable fact of giving me to feel that he is *with* me" (CF 230/154, trans. mod.). Here his choice of preposition differs from Falque's and my own, but my point in preferring the formulation "being-there-for" is not to insist that "with" can have only the meaning Falque employs in the particular context of his essay. Rather, I write "being-there-for" instead of "being-with" to emphasize at once the distance that in fact constitutes friendship and the turn toward each other and away from the self that friends must make. Marcel's phrase, as for that matter the word *com-passion* (suffering with), points not to an impossible identity of experience (as in Falque's sense of being-with) but to a manner of being that makes clear that I have set love for the other person higher than love for myself. As Marcel indicates, no words can wholly describe this manner of being. In speaking of being with (in Marcel's sense rather than Falque's), of coming alongside, of being beside, of being there, and of being there for, we are groping after a mystery that exceeds our powers of expression. Yet the very hesitations and failings of our words permit us to glimpse the greatness of the task of fidelity that they seek to express.

The friendship that is writing always arises across and through the text, such that the writer and reader are always at a distance from each other, even when the writer knows some of her readers or is friends with them prior to the writer/reader/text relation. The writer will not be there directly for the reader qua reader, but the text may, in a sense, be there for the reader. Certainly a text cannot be there in the same way that a person can, but the text, understood as the gift of the world and the beginning of a dialogue, may have a great influence on the reader's life. The act of writing a book to an unknown reader is an exemplary instance of giving the world to an unknowable one across distance: even if the writer knows that a certain person will read her book, she always writes without knowing everyone who will read it, and very often she does write not only without knowing who will read it but even before knowing whether anyone will read it. The gift of the world arises, not between the writer and the reader directly, but through the relation of the writer, the reader, and the text. Furthermore, since no two people will receive the text in the same way, the text has an essentially different relation to different people by virtue of their singularities. Hence the text, like language, constitutes the faithful writer and each faithful reader as worthy of mourning. In calling out for interpretation, it gives the world to all who come to interpret it faithfully. At the same time, because it is a translation, it does not duplicate the experiences of the writer or the reader, and it is precisely because the text is thus external to both the writer and the readers that the creative work of interpretation may bring them lasting insight, comfort, or joy. Once again, distance proves essential to the gift of the world—and writing, understood as a task of creation, again reveals itself as an act of friendship even though it differs from friendship between people who are also personally acquainted.

Knowing the Other through Empathy: Edith Stein's Account

Being-there-for requires that one be able to recognize in some way how the other person experiences the world, in order that one might respond appropriately. What makes this recognition possible is empathy, of which Edith Stein offers a compelling account—although I ultimately go beyond her analysis to argue that the recognition of similarities between self and Other depends on the Other's originary alterity. Empathy [*Einfühlung*] is, according to Stein, "the perceiving [*Erfahrung*] of foreign subjects and their experience [*Erleben*]" (PE v/1); used as a technical term in this sense, it does not mean "compassion," as it often does in colloquial use, nor does it imply any emotional reaction to other people's experiences. Empathy in Stein's sense is a crucial concept because if I had no sense of others' experience, neither would I know how to be there for another. How indeed could I possibly commit to valuing a wholly non-understandable being above myself? If I were utterly ignorant of another person's experiences, I would have no way of knowing what sorts of actions were appropriate or how she might respond to anything I did. For instance, if her experiences were wholly unfathomable, I would not even know whether she would object to being slapped. My promise to be faithful would be empty if I could not even understand whether the Other welcomed my gestures. Nor could I write if I had no idea at all how others would receive what I had written. Certainly the Other is not reducible to my awareness of his or her experiences, and this awareness will always be incomplete and may be erroneous. But while fidelity depends on the very gap between self and Other, it also depends on the dialogue that crosses that gap again and again without ever closing it. Although ultimately the friend is unknowable and exceeds any possible name, it does not follow that I cannot call her anything or say anything about her. Recall that we are given a name for the narrator of the *Search*: he himself invites us to call him Marcel, and although the name is pseudonymous, it is a name. When I bear witness to the Other, I always do so based on an incomplete and mediated understanding—my understanding is never a com-*prehension* that would directly grasp or seize (*prehendere* in Latin) the Other—but it does not follow that I have no basis whatsoever for my witness. It is impossible to adequately answer the question "Who is the friend?" not because there is nothing to say about the friend but because he or she surpasses everything I could say.[6]

Indeed, the particular force of Stein's account of empathy is her insistence that empathy takes place across distance. My perception of another's experience is never identical to her experience, yet I do have a perception of her experience that is distinct from my reaction to her experience. To clarify the point, consider Stein's example of my empathy for a friend who is happy because he has just passed an exam. I may myself react to his success with happiness, and I may also react to his happiness by being happy that he is happy, but neither reaction is empathy. As Stein puts it, "his joy is neither given to us as primordial [*originäre*] joy over the event nor as primordial joy over his joy" (PE 13/14). Both sorts of joy are my experiences, not his. Neither is empathy a matter of imagining how I would feel in his place and then attributing these imagined emotions to him (PE 14/14). Empathy does not overwrite another's experiences with the self's. Rather, in empathy the self goes outward to encounter one who is truly Other—though Stein would not capitalize *other*, and I argue that she ultimately does not go far enough in recognizing the Other's radical alterity. Stein explains that "empathy in our strictly defined sense as the experience of foreign consciousness can only be a non-primordial experience that announces a primordial one" (PE 14/14). Empathy is non-primordial because that of which I am aware is another person's experience and not my own. One's own joy is primordial, according to Stein, precisely because it is one's own, whereas the other's joy is always distinct from one's own even as one is aware of it. Thus empathy does not lead to an identification of self and other, but it does still take place. Both points are equally crucial. On the one hand, if empathy were impossible, then, as noted above, fidelity would become meaningless. On the other hand, if empathy resulted in the identification of self and other, then fidelity would become mere constancy, to use Gabriel Marcel's terminology: it would be loyalty to the self and not to the Other.

Empathy, Stein argues, arises through the self's recognition of the other person as a living body [*Leib*], which enables me to interpret his or her gestures and expressions and thereby be aware, through empathy, of his or her experiences. I realize that "my physical body and its members are not given as a fixed type but as a chance realization of a type that is variable within definite limits" (66/59, trans. mod.). The encounter with other people reveals the contingency of my own embodied existence in the world: my own experiences are not privileged but arise alongside others' experiences. The recognition of other people as such permits the interpretive acts that make empathy possible, acts Stein characterizes as "the comprehension [*Erfassen*] of a single instance of a known type [*Typ bekannten*]": "in order to understand a movement, for example, a gesture of pride, I must first 'link' it to other similar movements familiar to me" (PE 66–67/59, trans. mod.). This "linking" is to be distinguished from an "'inference by analogy [*Analogieschlüssen*]'" (PE 66/59) such as I might employ when, faced with a mathematical problem with which I am unfamiliar, I conclude through abstract reasoning that it is like another sort of problem that I do know and then infer that it may be solved in the same way. Thus my awareness that the other person is also a subject who experiences the world does not arise from my comparing her to myself and realizing that she is like me: such a process of comparison would be an inference by analogy. Rather, this awareness arises when I recognize "a known type" in the other person's gesture or expression, yet without needing to go through a process of inference.[7] My experience of myself tells me that there are subjects who experience the world, and I immediately recognize, without needing to reason my way to this conclusion, that the other person is also that sort of being. It is this recognition of known types that makes it possible for me to perceive others' experiences, and it is the perception of others' experiences that is empathy. Importantly, this recognition that is the condition of empathy is a matter of interpretation, a reading of others' bodies. Because empathy depends on interpretation, it is subject to error, as Stein recognizes (PE 96–99/84–87).

For Stein, recognition of similarity and recognition of difference are equiprimordial and always accompany each other. I cannot recognize that someone else is also an experiencing subject without also recognizing that she is other than myself. Indeed, Stein argues that empathy decenters the self, writing that "inasmuch as I now interpret [the foreign physical body] as 'like mine [*meinesgleichen*],' I come to consider myself as an object like it [*gleich ihm*]" (PE 100/88). The ego cannot possibly be the ground of all knowledge because it does not occupy a privileged position; it too is subject to interpretation, and "it is possible for another to 'judge me more accurately' than I judge myself and give me clarity about myself" (PE 101/89). Thus empathy confirms the folly of egoistic Cartesianism and compels me to recognize that the Other interprets me. Because empathy decenters the self in this way, it also confirms that my own empathic awareness of the Other never gives me a full understanding of the Other: since my perspective is never all-encompassing, my empathic awareness of the Other can never have the last word. Empathy itself reaffirms, therefore, my inability to ever adequately answer the question "Who is this Other?"

On Not-Knowing and Knowing the Other

Here, however, it is necessary to examine more closely the relation between sameness and difference. For Stein, one encounters the other person as both like oneself and different from oneself; the experiences of similarity and distinctness cannot be separated and are equiprimordial. I argue rather that the self first encounters the Other as incomparably Other. This encounter with radical alterity fundamentally conditions the self's relation to the Other, such that the realization of similarity is grounded in the encounter with alterity.[8] Indeed, the recognition of similarity cannot be fundamental, for similarities are always a mark of an underlying difference: it is precisely by virtue of that difference that they are similarities and not identities. To say that the Other is in some way like me is, therefore, first to say that the Other is not me. It is true that empathy depends in part on the recognition of similarity, and empathy does make it possible for me to have some practical understanding of how to be there for the Other. Yet empathy also depends on the Other's difference from me, precisely because the Other's experience is not my own. Thus empathy also testifies to the gap between myself and the Other that my understanding can never close.

To understand more adequately why difference and similarity cannot be equiprimordial, it is crucial to realize that the meaning of the Other's difference from myself cannot be wholly set forth, precisely because I do not know what will come of the encounter with the Other. Considering the Other solely as a being of the same sort that I am, yet distinct from myself, is insufficiently fundamental because it disregards this profound non-knowledge. As we have seen throughout the discussion of translation, the other person confronts me with an *other* world that my own categories can never subsume. Indeed, it is this very confrontation that grounds my world: as the previous chapter indicated, the self *is* only insofar as it is continually dispossessed of itself. Saying that I recognize the Other as a being like myself but distinct from myself takes for granted my recognition of myself as a particular sort of being, and it thus fails to reckon with this dispossession of the self. So too does it take for granted my recognition of the Other—but recall also that friendship resists interpretation. Only when the self and its powers of interpretation and recognition are radically disrupted by the Other can mutual recognition come. Recognition, in short, depends on disruption. In the encounter with one whom I do not and cannot fully recognize, I find that I am myself subject to recognition and interpretation, and I recognize that I am a stranger to myself. I recognize the Other first not as a being like myself but as one who recognizes and interprets me. And from this encounter, who knows what may come? For the encounter destabilizes the very notions of knowledge and of the *who* who does or does not know.

One might press the point, asking whether this destabilization does not depend on similarity. After all, I could not recognize the Other as one who interprets me if we did not share this capacity for interpretation. A table, for instance, is not open to this radical disruption by alterity: unlike me, it cannot become aware that it is subject to interpretation, and it cannot recognize the Other as a being who interprets it. Is it not the case, therefore, that I can be disrupted by the Other only because we are both interpreting beings? Such an argument, however, proceeds backward: it is, rather, because I am subject to disruption by the Other that I am an interpreting being. For it is precisely my capacity to interpret the world that the encounter calls into question yet also founds—or, better, that it founds by calling into question. The Other summons me to the witness stand, questioning me and thereby calling me to the task of interpretation, of the testimony that is translation. And in this way I am given the world, not as a set of bare facts or as a chaos that overtakes me but as the arena within which I am responsible to and for the Other.

Thus the encounter with the Other is first an encounter with one who is different from me to the point of being radically Other, and only on the basis of this encounter does it become possible to speak of similarities. True, it is impossible to avoid universalization—nor should we wish to, for without some sort of in-common, no communication would be possible. If, though, it is possible for the self and the Other to communicate, and if it is possible to be there for another, that is so only because I find myself always already summoned, always already promised to the Other. I am given myself as dispossessed of myself; or, to put it another way, in being dispossessed of myself I become a self. And the self that I am given is a self that is given to the Other and that is called to give to the Other. The very world comes into being that I might give it to the Other. Here one might point out that since absolute hospitality does not demand that the Other speak my language, we should not move too quickly from the gift to communication. Indeed. But saying "Here I am" is already seeking to speak the Other's language, seeking communication not for my sake but for the Other's. Recall, moreover, that friendship is a deeper self-giving than ethics and that friends do not demand reciprocity but give it freely. In friendship, I find myself promised beyond even what ethics asks, promised to give my world so wholly that my friend's world comes to be bounded not only by the horizon of his or her death but by the horizon of my own death as well. The gift of friendship is the gift of mutual translation, which is not a demand for monolingualism but is communication across distance. Therefore it is the promise of friendship that most profoundly calls forth the possibility of communication and of being-there-for.

Crucially, I do not know what will come from the possibility of communication and of being there for another. At the heart of what one might be inclined to call my knowledge of the friend—my recognition of him or her—is this great not-knowing. Being-there-for, let us recall, is not being-with, in Falque's strong sense of *with*. To meaningfully be there for another, I must have some sense of how he or she may interpret my actions—but this sense, this power of interpretation, arises only because I am summoned across distance. It is because his conception of friendship disregarded this distance that Proust's narrator believed friends could not communicate. Communication, however, is always a wager or venture: I do not know, when I seek to communicate, what will come of the attempt, since I can make the attempt in the first place only by virtue of the promise that calls me to the witness stand before I can even begin to know what it is to bear witness. Although fidelity involves empathy, fidelity also precedes empathy, for the initial encounter with the Other that is the call precedes and grounds my recognition of the Other. Because my relation to the Other—whether in ethics or friendship—thus depends on a call that precedes me and that promises me prior to my conscious awareness of the promise, I can never wholly know the origins of that relation.

The Beginning of Philosophy

This discussion of not-knowing—of a primordial dispossession of the self that founds one's power of interpretation by calling it into question—returns us to the question of what it might mean to think philosophy as friendship. For in Plato's *Theaetetus*, Socrates proclaims that philosophy begins in a radical disorientation. It is no coincidence, moreover, that the *Theaetetus* is a dialogue about knowledge, as any discussion of knowledge must reckon with the dispossession of the self that calls the very possibility of knowledge and interpretation into question. So too must any discussion of discernment, since discernment suggests knowledge—yet if we do not know in advance what will come of the promise, how then can discernment play any role in friendship? On the other hand, how can discernment not play a role in friendship, considering the distinction between creative and destructive madness, and also considering that friendship does involve some capacity to determine how, in practice, one ought to be there for another? Considering the radical disorientation that is the origin of philosophy will, therefore, permit us to better understand in what sense we might speak of discernment in friendship.

While a full analysis of the *Theaetetus* is well beyond the scope of this book, if we are to consider what it means to *not* know one's friends, we cannot disregard the statement that wonder is the origin of philosophy. Asking what knowledge is, Socrates and Theaetetus become embroiled in a discussion of being and becoming, and Socrates, summing up three points on which they agree but which seem to conflict, says, "I presume you're following, Theaetetus; at any rate it seems to me that you are not untried in such things" (T 155c, trans. mod.). Theaetetus replies, "Yes indeed, Socrates, by the gods, and it's beyond what's natural (ὑπερφυῶς), so that I'm in a state of wonder (θαυμάζω) at what in the world these things are. To tell you the truth, sometimes when I look at them I whirl around in the dark (σκοτοδινιῶ)" (T 155c). Thus he affirms that he is following the discussion yet adds that when he considers these matters he at times experiences astonishment to the point of dizziness ("become dizzy" being a common but less etymologically exact translation of σκοτοδινιῶ)—which may appear to suggest that he did not follow what Socrates just said. In answer, however, Socrates declares that this disorientation is philosophy's source: "So, dear fellow, Theodorus appears to have placed your nature (φύσεώς) not badly, for this experience (πάθος), wondering (θαυμάζειν), belongs very much to the philosopher (φιλοσόφου), since there is no other source (ἀρχὴ) of philosophy (φιλοσοφίας) than this" (T 155d). Note what Socrates does not say: he does not say that the experience of *thaumazein* (θαυμάζειν)—which means to wonder, to marvel, to be astonished, or even to venerate—makes one a philosopher, only that it is an experience that "belongs very much to the philosopher" or, more literally, that it is "very much of the philosopher." That Theaetetus has had this experience tells us something of his nature, according to Socrates, but it does not follow that he may say definitively that he simply is a philosopher, as though lover or friend of wisdom were a status that could be acquired once and for all and then proudly displayed. If philosophy's source is a disorientation that, as Theaetetus realizes, exceeds nature, one should hesitate to proclaim too quickly that one is a philosopher, lest one fall into an error like that of Robert de Saint-Loup, who proclaimed his friendship with Proust's narrator but did not let friendship dispossess him of himself.

What is more, if this disorienting wonder is philosophy's *arché* (ἀρχή)—its source, beginning, or origin—then we should also hesitate to speak too quickly of that origin, even to definitively name it an origin. One might dare to call this *arché* an-archic, for it is a beginning prior to every first principle (another meaning of *arché*) or originary condition deducible by our reason. The darkness (σκότος) beyond nature that Theaetetus encounters warns us that no transcendental deduction can lead us to the origins or conditions of philosophy. To be a philosopher—if one may speak of being a philosopher—is to have one's powers of comprehension and communication called into question. In *Proust and Signs*, Deleuze remarks that "Proust offers the same critique of philosophy as of friendship [. . .P]hilosophy, like friendship, is ignorant of the dark regions in which are elaborated the effective forces that act on thought, the determinations that *force* us to think; a friend is not enough for us to approach the truth" (116/95). Friendship with other persons does, however, confront us with the darkness in which signs vanish; so too, suggests the *Theaetetus*, does philosophy, rightly understood.

Discerning in the Dark

We cannot, however, disregard the danger posed by the counterfeit friendship or the counterfeit philosophy that insists on readily legible signs and affirms the self in its egoism and its pleasure. Hastily asserting that true friendship and true philosophy do disrupt the self risks implying that it is easy to avoid their counterfeits—but this very destabilization of the self calls into question any conception of discernment that presupposes an independent ego that freely interprets signs and judges them. Indeed, the fact that Socrates and Theaetetus spend a considerable portion of the dialogue grappling with the ideas of Protagoras suggests a certain haunting of philosophy by sophistry. Although they conclude that Protagoras is wrong, it remains that philosophy and sophistry do not exist in clearly separated spheres. What is more, the dialogue warns that friendship, or what appears to be friendship, may conflict with the pursuit of philosophy: because Protagoras was a friend of his, Theodorus refuses to participate in any conversation that seems likely to refute him, saying, "Socrates, the man was a friend (φίλος), as you said just now. So I wouldn't take kindly to Protagoras's being refuted by my agreeing, nor on the other hand to resisting you contrary to my opinion" (T 162a). Then he tells Socrates to continue the discussion of Protagoras's ideas with Theaetetus instead, so while he does not wish to shut down the conversation entirely, he does exclude himself from it in the name of friendship. The *Theaetetus* thus presents friendship, philosophy, and sophistry as far more entangled than one might hope.

Interestingly, both Socrates and Protagoras claim certain powers of discernment. Socrates professes to be a midwife like his mother, but a "midwife to men and not to women" who "look[s] to their souls when they are giving birth, and not to their bodies," for he has "the power to put to the test in every way whether the thinking of the young man is giving birth to something that is an image and false (εἴδωλον καὶ ψεῦδος), or to something that is generated and true (γόνιμόν τε καὶ ἀληθές)" (T 150b–c). And he has this power even though he is himself "barren of wisdom" (T 150c). If, then, he is or may be said to be a *philosophos*, a friend of wisdom, it is very much across absence. As for Protagoras, who does not appear in the dialogue, Socrates states that "he says somewhere that a human being is 'the measure of all things, of the things that are, that they are, and of the things that are not, that they are not'" (T 152a). From this claim, Socrates and Theaetetus agree, it follows that "perception is always of what is, and, being knowledge, is without falsity" (T 152c). Knowledge, according to the Protagorean position, does not arise across irreducible gaps but is immediate. There is, moreover, no suggestion of the chiasm in the notion that a human being is the measure of all: the human knows and perceives without him- or herself being known or perceived. We see again, in Protagoras's reported views, a refusal to be called into question. The sophists, let us remember, accepted money in exchange for their teachings, as if they knew the worth of their words from the start. It truly is crucial that friendship is not an exchange: not only does one demand nothing from one's friend, but one dares not claim to know in advance, or even at all, the true worth of either one's own actions or the friend's.

The darkness of philosophy's an-archic origin suggests that discernment, if it takes place at all, can do so only across a gap, only across a radical and primordial absence of knowledge. The one who seeks to discern cannot know what will come of the attempt. Indeed, discernment itself is chiastic: to discern, one must oneself be open to the discernment of others. To know the friend, insofar as such knowledge is possible, is to be known by the friend—again, insofar as such knowledge is possible. More profoundly, to be open to discernment is to confess that one is not the measure of all things, that one's very powers of discernment are limited, that one might be wrong. Discernment is necessary: recall from the first chapter the danger that hospitality to some might be hostility to others. Yet discernment is always a risk precisely because one might be wrong. Our powers of discernment are never adequate for determining what will happen. Consider Socrates's own claim that "the god (continually) forces [him] to be a midwife" (T 150c), and recall that friendship with the divine is hardly safe or easy, as the story of Abraham shows.

In addition, it bears noting that Socrates explicitly excludes women from the sphere of his art of midwifery: he works only with men. The female stranger seems to find herself unwelcome. To discern—from the Latin *dis* (apart) and *cernere* (to separate)—is in fact always to exclude. Exclusion may, in a given case, be right or wrong: one does, for instance, want to keep a would-be murderer apart from his or her proposed victim. Refusing to attempt to discern is refusing to accept one's responsibility for both the Other and the third. One finds oneself in the dark, already promised, unable to predict what will come of that promise—and one must venture forth in the darkness in the name of the promise. Again, therefore, philosophy reveals itself as a struggle in the dark, like Jacob's struggle with the angel. It is fitting that the name of *philosophy* means—if I might here take the risk of translating across languages, cultures, and centuries—*friendship of wisdom*, for the task of testifying to the Other in friendship is above all one that calls for wisdom. This wisdom does begin in wonder before the promise, and not in knowledge of what is to come: it is the wisdom of the one who seeks, as best he or she can, to be faithful to the friend instead of being paralyzed by the uncertainty of not knowing what will come. Such wisdom is not a possession but a gift, a grace. And if indeed philosophy is like Jacob's struggle with the angel, then it is also a prayer and even a demand for a blessing, for that wondrous grace by which one may meet the Other in peace as Jacob/Israel then met Esau. To discern how one ought to be there for the friend, one must first accept the limits of one's powers of discernment—which means accepting the risk that one may indeed be wrong—and one must rely on the grace by which alone one may seek to be there for another.

6

The Creation of Impossible Friendship

The Promise of Fidelity as the Ground of the Self

It remains, finally, to ask directly what it means to promise fidelity or to be promised in fidelity. What sense is there in proclaiming at one moment that one will always be there for the friend, or even that one will always strive to be there for the friend? It is one thing to be there for another in one particular moment, and quite another to find oneself committed to another person unto eternity when both self and other may change in wholly unforeseen ways. For that matter, it is not even clear that there is a self to commit: the previous chapter emphasized that friendship involves a dispossession of the self and that I find myself promised without knowing in advance what that promise entails. It seems, then, that I am in fact absent from the supposed commitment of myself that binds me to another in fidelity—but in that case, am I even the one bound by fidelity?

What this question fails to recognize is that fidelity constitutes the self—as the episode of the madeleine in Proust's *Search* has already indicated. In the *Search*, we see that the work of artistic creation in fact creates the narrator in all his multiplicity: insofar as he can give any truthful, though always partial, answer to the question "Who are you?" it is because this task of creation gives him a self. On one level, he is a creator and must be faithful to his work; on a deeper level, the task of creation that demands his fidelity is greater than he and creates him. Although saying that I am bound by the promise of fidelity risks giving the impression that fidelity has taken possibilities from me, in truth fidelity takes possibilities away only in the sense that any choice necessarily eliminates certain possible courses of action. Embarking upon an artistic project, I take a number of decisions that restrict the work, yet these very restrictions are essential for the work to exist as such. If I begin writing a traditional sonnet, I have committed myself to writing a particular number of lines, and I have a few variations on a basic rhyme scheme to choose from. If I begin writing a novel, I am initially freer, but I must soon make decisions about style, plot, and characters that will affect the book's future shape in ways that are not yet apparent to me. These restrictions are creative, however, because it is through them that the work of art becomes what it is. So too, while I can hardly predict all the ways that fidelity to the friend will shape my life—and while I am bound prior to any conscious choice—the boundaries it sets in place are not burdens but rather provide structure for the creation of my self. Thus I am the one bound by fidelity because I am the one fidelity creates. Recall Montaigne's famous phrase, "If I were pressed to say why I loved him, I feel that it could be expressed only by replying: 'Because it was he, because it was I'" (E 186–87/97, trans. mod.). But *he* and *I* are *he* and *I* only by and through the promise—which is precisely why Montaigne cannot explain their friendship. In his inability to account for their friendship, then, we see a hint of the wonder with which one must respond to the promise.

That the limits fidelity imposes on my actions are not burdens is an essential point. Listing certain concrete responsibilities that being there for the friend may include, one might say, for example, that if someone she cares about dies, I must provide what consolation I can; that if she publishes a book, I must congratulate her; or that if I move, I must provide her with my new contact information. As Marcel argues in "Creative Fidelity," however, my friend has every right to be displeased if I am acting only out of duty. Just as a work of art must appear organic and not seem to be the result of the artist grimly following undesired rules, Marcel explains that "fidelity can be appreciated as such by the person to whom it is vowed only if it presents an element of essential spontaneity, which in itself is radically independent of the will" (CF 232/155, trans. mod.). If I make myself perform my duties for the other person out of sheer force of will, and nothing more, then something is lacking—which is not to say that fidelity will always be easy or pleasant. Suppose, for instance, that I have promised to visit a grieving friend, but I have had a long and frustrating day and want only to relax; then someone invites me to the theater that evening to watch a comedy, which seems an altogether more pleasant way of spending my time; and on top of all that certain of my friend's more irritating qualities are currently uppermost in my mind. But if I, by an effort of the will, refuse the invitation, fix my mind on the qualities I admire in my friend, and make the promised visit, have I really acted contrary to fidelity? For it is not in fact my changeable emotions that determine whether I am faithful. I have acted faithfully if my effort of the will derives from the bond that commits me for the sake of the other. As Marcel observes, when I have committed myself to being faithful to another, "the possibility which has been barred or refused will thereby be demoted to the rank of a temptation" (243/162, trans. mod.). It may take an effort of the will for one to reject a temptation, but first one must recognize it as a temptation. The commitment to recognizing any possible deviation from fidelity as a temptation is made for the other's sake and is more fundamental than any emotion or act of the will. Recall that friendship is more a secret to which one is summoned than a choice one makes. Marcel's phrase "element of essential spontaneity" is another way to indicate that fidelity exceeds one's own ability to account for it.[1]

This spontaneity of fidelity proves to be essential to life itself. One might claim that fidelity is impossible because I can never be sure that I will not change such that the fidelity that at one instant seemed right becomes a betrayal of myself. Against this view that upholds the changeable self as the ultimate value, Marcel writes that this "radical instantaneism [. . .] can be grasped only as an absolute rejection of the *I believe*" (251/168, trans. mod.). It is belief in God that he especially has in mind here, since he maintains that God is the ultimate ground of all fidelity—a position that echoes Aelred's and Thomas Aquinas's view that friendship is grounded in Christ and will be most fully expressed only in heaven—but the point may be understood more broadly. In the fear of committing oneself lest one later change such that one wishes to reject the commitment, we recognize once again the Cartesian ego that will not believe anything of which it cannot be certain. Precisely because it rejects commitment, however, this solitary self does not manage to truly exist as a self: it refuses to be dispossessed of itself, not realizing that this dispossession alone can save it.[2] This dispossession is precisely the creation of the self as faithful: in committing myself to another, I promise that fidelity to the other person will shape me throughout the rest of my life. The self that refuses fidelity is dissolved into a mere series of ever-changing whims, each one subject to annihilation by the next—and, ultimately, to annihilation in a death that renders the entire series derisory.

For if the self is not dispossessed through fidelity, it will indeed be utterly lost in death. As Marcel explains, "despair and betrayal lie in wait for us at every moment, and death, too, at the end of our visible career, like a permanent invitation to absolute defection, like an incitement to proclaiming that nothing is, that nothing has any value" (257/172, trans. mod.). But belief—and for Marcel, "*believing* in the strong sense of the term [. . .] is always believing in a *thou*" (253/169, trans. mod.)—gives the lie to the nihilism that lets death have the last word: Marcel writes that "it is not entirely true that I am my life, since it is sometimes given to me to judge it, and to not recognize myself in it; this judgment is possible only on the basis of what I am, that is to say, of what I believe. Therefore it seems that the movement is freed by which I can free myself from the objective pessimism of death" (258/173, trans. mod.). "Life" here refers to the life that is extinguished in death. As for this judgment that my belief—my fidelity—makes possible, it is not to be confused with the judgment of a detached ego: this judgment steps back from the life that will be annulled in death only so it can affirm the value of the human person. It affirms that I and the other person[3] are not reducible to the life whose meaning death denies and hence that there is more to human life than a steady progress toward death. Crucially, this affirmation is grounded in fidelity because in fidelity I defy death by committing myself to the Other beyond her death. Through this commitment to the Other, I myself am saved from the abyss of despair: refusing commitment is abandoning oneself to despair, whereas commitment is a rejection of nihilism and an expression of hope—specifically, for Marcel, of hope in God.[4] To embrace the promise of fidelity is to wager that death, with its apparent nullification of life's value, does not have the last word. One who is faithful to another may or may not believe that this wager will in fact be fulfilled in an actual resurrection of the dead. Regardless, fidelity insists, against death and against the progress of entropy that will degrade and destroy all our attempts to record meaning, that the Other's life is meaningful. For human beings, fidelity is inseparable from betrayal, at least in this life—but all the same, fidelity is a promise that life is not reducible to betrayal, to meaninglessness, to decay. Thus when I am summoned to fidelity I am also summoned to life—or, better, fidelity is the very sense of human life.

The Self's Creation through Friendship

What, though, of ethics? Since Levinasian ethics is an affirmation of life's meaning against death, does it not suffice for the constitution of the self? Recall, however, that friendship implicates the self in its singularity more profoundly than does ethics. Ethics does call me to life, since by establishing me as responsible for the Other it keeps me from existing as a mere series of fleeting whims, and it is an utter rejection of nihilism. While the ethical relation does not in practice entail a lifelong commitment to one particular Other, ethics is undeniably a commitment. Indeed, it is a promise, and one that shapes me rather than one that I make: from the start I am promised to serve faithfully in response to the Other's call, and that there are many Others who call to me makes my obligation considerably more complicated but does not lessen it. Ethics may therefore justly be understood as a call to fidelity even though it does not necessarily establish a lifelong bond between the self and a specific Other. Insofar as I am intrinsically irreplaceable, however—that is, irreplaceable by virtue of my own singularity and not only because I am bound to act as if there is no one else who can respond to the call of the Other—it is because the fidelity of friendship creates me as such.

Friendship, unlike marriage, does not necessarily involve an explicit pledge on the part of those involved. Even when people do explicitly make a decision that is meant to indicate that they will always be friends, they do not and cannot know in advance that all parties will remain faithful to that commitment. Fidelity can be recognized as such only in retrospect, if at all. Retrospectively, it may still be difficult to determine what constitutes fidelity or a breach of it: for instance, even a seemingly short-lived relation of hospitality may be a transformative gift of the world that shapes those involved for their whole lives, such that they are faithful to each other, even if they lose contact, if they remember each other in gratitude for the gift. What matters, though, is less identifying fidelity than striving to be faithful. Granted, the two are not wholly separable: I must have some notion of what fidelity demands in order to strive to be faithful. At the same time, however, I can never identify in advance to what, exactly, fidelity may commit me, for I am faithful not in the abstract but as a specific person related to another specific person within concrete situations. Moreover, if I wonder whether I am being faithful in the manner of ethics or of friendship, I may not be able to answer. This certainly does not mean that I may decide at any moment that a relationship is not a true friendship and therefore abandon my responsibilities. Rather, it means that I am bound to care for the Other and that I will not know in advance whether this care will be the care of ethics or of friendship. It may be unclear for some time whether a given relation is a friendship or simply an acquaintanceship, but I remain responsible to and for the Other regardless; I must act and wait to see whether my actions will prove to be part of the profound, mutual giving of the world that is friendship.

At this point, it is necessary to recognize that Marcel, rightly, discusses both friendship and marriage in terms of fidelity.[5] Although the two are not mutually exclusive—consider that Aelred regards Adam and Eve as friends (see SF 1.57)—they do not form the self in the same way. In the erotic relation the creation of the self is inseparable from a certain unity of the flesh that friendship does not seek. Even when the lovers leave behind the false notion of eros as absolute union, eros, thought with or without reference to marriage, remains characterized by a turn inward that does not mark friendship. For Marcel, this inward turn is apparent in marriage's relation to family and to the home. He writes, for instance, that "we must make ourselves aware of the primitive *us*, this archetypal and privileged *us* which is only normally realized in family life. This *us* is in general inseparable from a home of our own [*un chez nous*]" (TMF 107/77). The inward turn is not an egoistic one insofar as it is marked by fidelity; notwithstanding, the marital erotic relation is less directly related to justice than is friendship because it represents a move away from the world and the Other into the shelter of the home. Recall that friends spur each other on toward justice and that friendship points me outward to my responsibility toward others: friendship does not seek shelter and security as eros does in the home. The self is not as fully created in eros insofar as eros is less directed toward justice, although the lovers may subsequently make an outward turn if they do raise a child, who must be brought up to go out into the world to pursue justice. I certainly do not propose that lovers do not seek justice or that they cannot spur each other on in the pursuit of justice, but it is not, or not primarily, by virtue of being lovers that they do so.

In addition, if one thinks eros as procreative, as Levinas does, its temporality differs from friendship's: consider Levinas's reflection that "love and friendship are not only felt differently; their correlative differs: friendship goes unto the Other; love seeks what does not have the structure of a being, the infinitely future, what is to be engendered" (TI 298/266, trans. mod.). Lovers, on this view, are directed toward the always-future messianic time more than to the Other who will die and whose death I will mourn. Even leaving aside the point about messianic time and turning to a more concrete temporality, the engendering of the child directs the lovers to a future that will exist in this world beyond their death. We observe that faithful lovers do mourn each other, but given the different temporalities of eros and friendship, it is reasonable to consider that in this way eros partakes of friendship. As the temporality of eros is directed beyond the lovers through the child, they themselves cannot escape the extinguishing of their own individual timelines in death or, therefore, the obligation of memory. Because the friend qua friend is memorialized only in the other friend's memory and not in the new timeline of a child, the obligation of memory is most characteristic of friendship; and insofar as the obligation of memory is common to eros as well, it marks a likeness of eros to friendship or a partaking of eros in the nature of friendship.

If one thinks eros without reference to the marital or to procreation, as Kearney does, its temporality remains different from that of friendship. Kearney maintains that "the matrimonial is not the first or last paradigm of eros. The primary paradigm is the nuptial, meaning a binding of two beings (of whatever sex or gender) in an interplay of togetherness."[6] He points to the Song of Songs, arguing that "chapter 8 of the Song of Songs speaks of a free play of love (eros) that is stronger than death (thanatos)—a sacred erotic liaison that is prior to duties and responsibilities of marriage contracts, laws and norms relating to childbearing, property and the economy of a home."[7] On this account, however, eros still stands apart from the temporality of being toward the death of the other; indeed, it is located in or constructs for itself a temporality of immediacy, free of the obligation of mourning because it is free from the oncoming of the future. These lovers are directed toward each other, and not toward the future of the child, but neither are they directed toward the future of memory and mourning. Time is summed up in the instant of their union. The obligation of memory is once again, therefore, most characteristic of friendship, and so insofar as the lovers' temporality is not fulfilled in the immediacy of their union—insofar, that is, as each one is toward the other's death—their relation partakes of the nature of friendship. It is true that much more could be said on these matters, and

I do not pretend that it is possible to wholly distinguish what belongs to eros from what belongs to friendship. Still, these remarks serve to indicate why I refer specifically to the self's creation through friendship.

As it is the friend, and not the Levinasian Other, who mourns my death, it is fidelity to the friend, and not ethics, that creates me as a being whose death will be the end of the world. Hence the self's constitution through its relation to others occurs through both ethics and friendship: ethics does create the self, summoning it to a meaningful life, but friendship creates the self more profoundly still. Through fidelity to the friend, I become a self in the fullest sense of the word—which is not to say that this becoming is ever complete. Because friendship is an enduring bond, never a finished project, I am always in the process of creation—which means that I am ever multiple and always changing, but changing through and in accord with my fidelity to the friend. Friendship is at once constant and dynamic: constant because it lasts unto eternity, and dynamic because it is always creating me through time. And time, for friendship, is assuredly real, not an illusion: it is the time of a coming mourning, the time of being toward the friend's death. Likewise eternity, for friendship, is no illusion, though friendship necessarily unfolds within time, since it is only because friends' commitment to each other endures that time has for them the meaning that it does: it is because they are friends unto eternity that they are promised to mourning. Temporal and eternal, constant and ever in motion—friendship gives us to see, even if darkly, as through a glass, the meeting of Heraclitus and Parmenides.

On the Friend's Absolute Alterity

The above discussion of ethics and fidelity should not be taken to elide the differences between Levinas and Marcel. Most notably, Marcel admits of reciprocity in fidelity and does not regard the other person as absolutely Other. I have already argued that reciprocity in friendship is not incompatible with ethics, and both Marcel and Levinas do emphasize wholly giving oneself to another.[8] Still, bringing Levinas and Marcel into dialogue provides me an occasion to explain why I consider it important to maintain the Levinasian and Derridean language that speaks of the Other as absolutely or wholly Other even as I also draw on philosophers, including Marcel, Ricœur, and Kearney, who are less inclined to this language or who do not use it at all. Brian Treanor, in

Aspects of Alterity, raises a critique of the language of absolute Otherness that merits a response: proposing to preserve the term "absolute alterity" while denying the absolute Otherness of which Levinas and Derrida write, he suggests that "*similitude* is that aspect of things, and others, that is in some way familiar or understandable. [. . .] Alterity is that aspect of things, and others, that is (absolutely) unfamiliar, alien, or obscure. [. . .] *Otherness*, then, is the chiastic relationship of alterity and similitude. Thus, qua alterity, the other is that which can reveal or bring about something new and unforeseen; however, qua similitude, the other is also susceptible to some measure, imperfect though it may be, of understanding" (229). Indeed, given the role empathy plays in fidelity, one's experience of the Other must involve a certain degree of similarity. It bears noting, also, that for Levinas and Derrida one never does directly experience the Other as absolutely Other: for Levinas the Saying never was and has always already become the Said, and for Derrida absolute hospitality never actually takes place. Treanor contends that "the advocates of absolute otherness seem to imply that alterity is different than, independent of, and more important than similitude" (233). Without it being necessary to suppose that similitude is independent of alterity, however, one reason to maintain the language of absolute Otherness is precisely that, as the discussion of empathy also indicated, alterity underlies both my experience of similitude and indeed similitude itself, since I would not even exist as a self to consider myself and the Other as similar if I had not received the Other's call. That this call comes from wholly and utterly outside myself is essential, since otherwise there would be no way to explain why the call itself was not lost in totality.

A second reason to maintain the language of absolute Otherness is that the phrases "wholly Other" and "absolutely Other" emphasize that the Other can in no way be absorbed into the self: it is not only that the Other cannot be completely absorbed but that the Other, even in his or her similarities, utterly resists being absorbed into the self. I write, therefore, of translation between self and Other rather than employing Treanor's terminology, which raises the question of what is being translated: if there is no translation from the aspect of otherness that is alterity, but only from the aspect of otherness that is similitude, then the concerns he raises about absolute Otherness recur, this time with regard to absolute alterity. And if there is translation from absolute alterity, then it is not clear why there could not be translation from absolute Otherness. One could perhaps reply that translation from absolute alterity proceeds via similitude, and Treanor does argue that "any other with whom we have, or could have, a relationship cannot be absolutely other. [. . .] Absolute otherness, being absolutely incommensurable with the world in which we perceive and think, would not register on our radar screens, so to speak, *not even as a 'trace'*" (230). If one accepts this argument, however, one must also ask how absolute alterity could both be absolute and cross over into similitude: again, the concerns about absolute Otherness recur with regard to absolute alterity. If one does not accept the argument and continues to speak of absolute Otherness, then one is, I grant, left with a mystery as to how translation is possible. But as translation grounds the self, it is not surprising that the self cannot fully explain the possibility of translation. Translation is an unaccountable gift that precedes, calls into question, and grounds the self's very powers of explanation. One might even risk theological language by calling miraculous the creation of my world through the encounter with the wholly Other.

Indeed, since the encounter with the absolutely Other does call into question the self's capacity to understand and explain, it is little wonder that the self cannot explain how that encounter is possible. The encounter is the condition of possibility for all else, and the self can but receive it in wonder. Here it is worth quoting at length Derrida's remark, in his reading of Levinas in "Violence and Metaphysics," that

> the other, then, would not be what he is (my neighbor as foreigner [*étranger*]) if he were not alter ego. [. . .] A necessity due to the finitude of meaning: the other is absolutely other only by being an ego, that is, in a certain way, the same as I. [. . .] And this contradiction (in terms of a formal logic which Levinas follows for once at least, since he refuses to call the other alter ego), this impossibility of translating my relation to the other into the rational coherence of language—this contradiction and this impossibility are not the signs of "irrationality": they are the sign, rather, that one may no longer draw inspiration from within the coherence of the *Logos*, but that thought's breath is cut off in the region of the origin of language as dialogue and difference. (187/127–28, trans. mod.)

Thus Derrida admits that the encounter with the absolutely Other cannot be explained within the *Logos*—yet this does not mean that the Other is not absolutely Other. Rather, it means that the *Logos* cannot explain its own ground. The reference to formal logic is instructive in light of Gödel's incompleteness theorems, which show that no system of mathematical axioms can be both consistent and complete. The mathematician and physicist Roger Penrose explains in *The Road to Reality* that "Gödel shows us how to transcend any [formal system] we are prepared to trust"—that is, Gödel's theorems show that any formal system of axioms points beyond itself to a statement that we must accept if we accept the system but that we cannot prove within the system (377). So-called "natural language," named "natural" in opposition to the formal systems of mathematical logic, cannot suffice unto itself either, though its incompleteness cannot be demonstrated with a formal theorem like Gödel's. The *Logos* points beyond itself to what it cannot prove or even account for. It does not follow, however, that we should abandon the notion of absolute Otherness; far from it, we should embrace the impossibility of accounting for either the absolutely Other or our encounter with the absolutely Other, for on this impossibility does the *Logos* depend.

The Promise as Origin

Let us revisit, in light of the understanding of fidelity as that which creates the self, the problem of the inevitability of betrayal. The question of betrayal is a question of origins, as the case of translation between languages highlights with especial clarity. It is normal to think of the translated work as secondary and of the work it translates as the original, and then to conceive of the inevitable infidelity of translation as a fall from the supposedly pure original. As we have seen, however, the original itself is already a translation: it, too, is unfaithful and appears as a fall from a pure union of sign and sense—yet once again, this pure union, far from being originary, never was. In translation understood more broadly as a fundamental way of encountering the Other, of which translation between languages is one manifestation, we find this same pattern. Friends translate the world for each other, and yet the world the friend receives from me is never my world, nor is the world I receive from her ever her world. No originary union binds us; far from it, we are separated by an originary difference. Thus when I must bear witness to her, I cannot but fail. Yet we have also seen that, much as I am other than myself, in the Other I encounter multitudes: in truth we should speak not of my world and her world but of my worlds and her worlds—myriad changing, shifting, dissolving worlds. Language, necessarily universal, betrays the singular—in Levinasian terms, the Saying never was, only the Said—but where then can the singular be found? Who is the singular? Where is the *who* that is betrayed? And where is the *who*, the *I*, that betrays by failing to adequately bear witness? The problem of fidelity, in its most fundamental form, comes down to this: there is no stable, predetermined original to which to be faithful, nor is there anyone to practice fidelity, and thus fidelity can never be. Or if the first clause of that statement speaks too confidently about the Other, then the problem comes down to this: I will never encounter an original to which to be faithful, nor yet an *I* that might have such an encounter, and thus fidelity can never be.

This way of stating the problem conceals a key assumption, however, that we have yet to fully consider. We have already seen that it is false to imagine that fidelity demands union or at least perfect imitation: union and perfect imitation would be only another kind of betrayal. What is more, the notion that fidelity is union or perfect imitation itself depends on the assumption that what is originary must already contain within itself everything that arises from it—that, in other words, any creation, any novelty, marks a fall from a purer origin. Again, the case of translation between languages furnishes a particularly clear illustration of the point. Claiming that the gap between the so-called original and the translation means that the translation has betrayed the original amounts to saying that the ideal translation would reproduce the original, bringing forth nothing new. Put another way, it amounts to saying that the content of the translation must be wholly predetermined by the content of the original. And describing the original itself as unfaithful implies that ideally it would contain neither more nor less than what is meant, that the text ought to be wholly predetermined by the mythical union of sign and sense. For the text is supposedly unfaithful precisely insofar as it exceeds what it was meant to say—insofar, that is, as it brings something new into the world that could not be calculated in advance. Likewise, saying that the gap between self and Other renders fidelity impossible amounts to saying that every contour of the self's relation to the Other must be fixed in advance by their prior union—which, again, is mythical. The assumption is that the self in bearing witness to the Other must not bring forth anything new and unforeseen—as if the Other were not essentially unforeseeable, as if the self ought simply to download and transmit an exact report on the Other's immobile essence.

Proceeding from this assumption and finding no stable ground on which the promise of fidelity might stand, one despairs of fidelity, declares the promise broken from the start, and characterizes translation only as betrayal. In truth, however, it is misguided to look for the origin of the promise because the promise is the origin. I refer not to the promise that the self consciously makes but to the promise that creates the self: any promise the self makes comes second, in response to the primordial promise that summons it forth to life, already promised to the Other. The promise, in a lightning-flash of eternity, calls me into existence and summons me, not to the task of the copyist, but to a never-ending creation of the new in and through my relation to the Other. It is, moreover, through the promise that the Other appears to me as a *who*, as a singular individual: the Other appears to me as *the one to whom I am promised*, by ethics alone or by friendship as well. Who is the Other? The one to whom I am promised. Who am I? The one who is promised. Whatever further account I might seek to offer is made possible only by the promise that relates us to each other and that creates us through that relation. The impossibility of directly perceiving the Other in his or her singularity, without the mediation of the universal, is most problematic if I want to possess him or her, as Proust's narrator sought to possess Albertine. From the standpoint of friendship, or indeed of ethics (for ethics is a self-giving, albeit a more limited one than friendship), this impossibility is a call to the work of translation. The universal does betray the singular, but this betrayal is not simply opposed to fidelity because it is the condition of fidelity: only through the generality of language can I testify to and speak with the Other. Already I have argued that translation is fidelity because it recognizes and affirms the alterity of the Other. Here I go further, arguing that the creativity of translation, the way it deviates from its supposed model, is itself a faithful witness to the creation and the creativity of the Other: if the Other is never wholly foreseeable, my witness to the Other must not be either. And in testifying to the Other I cannot simply imitate her, not only because one cannot imitate what cannot be wholly foreseen or comprehended, but also because a mere imitation would lack the Other's spontaneity and would thus fail even to be an imitation. A testimony that attempts to merely imitate falls into the trap of the literal translation that fails altogether to convey the liveliness of the work it translates. The translation also lacks *the Other's* spontaneity, of course, but the translation's spontaneity, arising through dialogue with the Other, is a better testimony to the Other's than a rigid literalism could ever be.

Destruction and Creation in Translation

At stake here is something like the relation between fidelity and freedom that Walter Benjamin and Paul de Man discuss, though my question concerning fidelity and infidelity is not exactly the same: I am considering as infidelity deviations from either the sense or the idiom, or both, of the original. De Man, reading Benjamin, asks, "Does translation have to be faithful, or does it have to be free? For the sake of the idiomatic relevance of the target language, it has to be free; on the other hand, it has to be faithful, to some extent, to the original. It can only be free if it reveals the instability of the original, and if it reveals that instability as the linguistic tension between trope and meaning" (C 91–92). Freedom reveals "the instability of the original" because the act of translating shows that there is no way to leave language behind to access meaning in itself, which means that in the original also there is a gap between meaning and what it wants to say. My argument is that an unfree translation, too bound to the original, is also unfaithful precisely because it tries not to reveal "the instability of the original": it pretends that the language from which one translates is originarily united with itself and that this unity can then be copied. Such a translation is thereby unfaithful to the original, for the original is unstable, always at a distance from itself.

It is necessary, however, to pursue Benjamin's and de Man's arguments a bit longer, as the relation between fidelity and freedom is not as straightforward as it might seem. Having initially defined freedom (*Freiheit*) and fidelity (*Treue*) as "freedom of the sense-measuring reproduction [*sinngemäßin Wiedergabe*] and, in its service, fidelity to the word" (TT 17/259, trans. mod.), Benjamin goes on to write that

> in this pure language [*reinen Sprache*]—which no longer means [*meint*] and no longer expresses [*ausdrückt*] but rather is, as expressionless and creative [*schöpferisches*] Word, that which is meant [*Gemeinte*] in all languages—all information, all sense, and all intention finally encounter a stratum in which they are destined to be extinguished. And in this very stratum the freedom of translation finds confirmed [*sich bestätigt*] a new and higher justification. This justification does not derive from the sense of the message, for the emancipation from this sense is precisely the task of fidelity. Rather, freedom proves its worth for the sake of the pure language in its effect on

its own language. It is the task of the translator to release in his own language that pure language which is exiled among alien tongues, to liberate the language imprisoned in a work in his re-creation of that work. (TT 19/261, trans. mod.)

Freedom, at first understood as departing from the word to express the sense, now becomes departing from the word to liberate the pure language. Note, however, that the pure language is here not an originary union of sign and sense but rather a freedom from sense, a pure creativity. One must not take the phrase "pure language" too literally. As de Man points out, "Least of all is there something like a *reine Sprache*, a pure language, which does not exist except as a permanent disjunction which inhabits all languages as such, including and especially the language one calls one's own" (C 92): the pure language *is not* because it is the distance between a language and itself. Benjamin proceeds to state that "a translation touches the original lightly and only at the infinitely small point of the sense, thereupon pursuing its own course according to the laws of fidelity in the freedom of linguistic flux [*Sprachbewegung*]" (TT 20/261). Thus freedom becomes an expression of "linguistic flux": this creative movement is language itself—and because the word of the original is in flux, so too must be the word of the translation if the latter is to be faithful to the former. The dichotomy between fidelity and freedom does not account for the flux.

It remains that this creative movement is also a destructive one. As de Man emphasizes, "translation, to the extent that it disarticulates the original, to the extent that it is pure language and is only concerned with language, gets drawn into what [Benjamin] calls the bottomless depth, something essentially destructive, which is in language itself" (C 84). De Man remarks also that "the process of translation, if one can call it a process, is one of change and of motion that has the appearance of life, but of life as an afterlife, because translation also reveals the death of the original" (C 85). For, as he observes later, "meaning is always displaced with regard to the meaning it ideally intended" (C 91). And it is here that I insist on the creativity as well as the destructiveness, thereby making—very carefully—a different move from that found in Benjamin and in de Man's reading of him, or at any rate placing the accent differently. This move must be made carefully indeed, for one cannot escape the danger of destructiveness: recall that there is no way out of madness and that one's efforts at discernment always come too late insofar as one is promised without being able to know what will come of the promise. But from danger and even death may come the life or afterlife of a translation that by its own freedom testifies to the freedom of the original—or to the freedom of the Other who saves me from destruction by constituting me. In this death of language we encounter the finitude of language, a horizon that limits it—and yet within and thanks to this horizon there is the possibility of an encounter with the genuinely new, with that which is not inscribed in advance in the order of things, not predetermined by an originary union of sign and sense. De Man suggests that "at the moment when translation really takes place, for example Hölderlin's translation of Sophocles, which undid Sophocles, undid Hölderlin, and revealed a great deal—that's an occurrence. That's an event, a historical event" (C 104). The event, which does take place in history and not in the futurity of messianic time, both undoes and reveals, even creates.

The Fidelity of Unfaithful Translations

Thus the dichotomy between fidelity and infidelity proves to be too simplistic a way to conceive of translation because it cannot account for the creation of the new. That it cannot do so is unsurprising, since the desire for a pure origin is closely related to the notion of time as degeneration: if all of history appears as a fall from a mythic, atemporal past, then all that remains good is predetermined by the mythic point of origin and so is good despite temporality. Time, on such an account, can bring forth nothing new that has a positive existence of its own; anything that emerges within and through time, rather than having been present already at the origin, has only the negativity of error and confusion. Friendship, however, is made possible by finitude, which is essentially temporal: hence, if indeed friendship is good, time cannot be only degenerative. Here I have in mind Henri Bergson's remark in *The Creative Mind*, "Would not [time] then be a vehicle of creation and of choice? Would not the existence of time prove that there is indetermination in things? Would not time be that indetermination itself?" (102/75). He answers the question in the affirmative, maintaining that the possible does not exist before it is realized: only after an event occurs does it become possible, for it is radically new and not inscribed beforehand in the order of things. Time is therefore the undetermined creation of the new. What is new is not necessarily good, to be sure, or even better than what came before, but it cannot be defined as degenerative simply by virtue of being temporal. Bergson too turns to the example of art to clarify his thesis, though it applies to all events: "Let a man of talent or a genius arise, let him create a work: it will then be real, and by that very fact it becomes retrospectively possible. It would not be possible, it would not have been possible, if this man had not arisen" (110–11/82, trans. mod.). Proust made À la recherche du temps perdu possible only by writing it; that he would write it was in no way predetermined.[9] One could not have beaten Proust to writing it by studying the prior state of the world and finding data that, rightly interpreted, told what the novel would say, for there were no such data. What is more, Proust only exists as such because he wrote the *Recherche*. The "genius" arises from his or her work, created by it as much as he or she creates it. Bergson does not address translation directly, but I add that any translation of Proust's *Recherche* became possible only in the writing of the translation, and because the *Recherche* itself is an unforeseeable creation, it is absurd to think that one could translate it faithfully by producing a translation that itself had nothing of the unforeseeable, even if such a thing were possible. On the one hand, this newness makes the translation unfaithful, since it departs from the work it supposedly renders. On the other hand, however, the translation must be a new creation—which also creates the translator, just as friends are constituted by the promise—to testify faithfully to the fact that the text it translates is a new creation.

Moreover, to suppose that Proust's *Recherche* contains within itself its ideal translations into other languages is to radically disconnect it from the French language in which it was written, as if the language were merely incidental to the work, as if the work had some nonlinguistic essence. Thus the inadequacies of a translation may turn out to be not infidelities but fidelities, since they testify to the irreplaceable singularity of each language. The English translation is faithful to the French by not attempting to be the French text; and when an English text is translated into French, the French translation is faithful to the English by not attempting to be the English text—while at the same time each is transformed by the other. The process of translation between languages reveals each language's singularity even more than a work written in a single language. Hence the notion of singularity must not be confused with the idea that any one particular language has a genius that makes it uniquely suited to thought, over and above other languages. As Marc Crépon observes in *Le Malin*

Génie des langues [The Evil Genius of Languages], "Languages alone, taken individually, have no genius. Their genius is revealed only in the crossing [*passage*] from one to another and belongs to none" (220). Translation is the glory of language: each language calls for translation, and it is through translation, through "the crossing between them," that we discover each one as singular and irreplaceable. Thus it is not only that languages call for translation; also, translation calls languages to the creativity by which alone they can live.

As in the case of translation between languages, imagining that the Other contains within herself the ideal witness that I ought to bear to her amounts to detaching her from herself, as though any singular individual could represent her equally. The apparent perfect fidelity of imitation would be infidelity; and conversely, the very infidelity of my testimony is fidelity, for it reveals that I cannot replace her. This infidelity keeps the promise by bearing witness to the unforeseeable singularity of the Other. A strict dichotomy between fidelity and infidelity cannot account for this dynamic in which my failure to bear witness to the Other is in fact the very fidelity to which I am promised.[10] Earlier, when I described translation as the greatest possible fidelity, I defended this claim by arguing that translation loves that the Other is Other. This is true, but it is not the whole story: the very infidelity of translation may in fact be the greatest possible fidelity, for only an unfaithful witness makes clear that the Other is inimitable and irreplaceable.

Friendship is impossible, and yet it takes place. Friendship is impossible because it is never realized—never brought to completion. Neither self nor Other ever ends the dialogue. And yet friendship takes place: it takes place precisely for those who recognize its impossibility, who recognize that it is never a completed project. Friendship takes place as the never-completed creation of the impossible. Consider the phrase Derrida borrows from Montaigne, who in turn borrowed it from Diogenes Laertius's attribution of it to Aristotle: "O my friends, there is no friend." In response to the preceding analysis, and in conversation with the many other possible interpretations of this inexhaustible enigma, I propose the following gloss: O my friends, there is no friend because friendship is always future, because friendship is an unending process of creation, because the title of friend can never be awarded to one who still lives, and yet I call you friends as a hope and as a sign of the promise: I call you friends to mark my commitment to the promise of friendship and in the hope that when I die I will have lived in fidelity to the promise, as far as fidelity is possible.[11]

As far as fidelity is possible: in arguing that the dichotomy between fidelity and infidelity or betrayal is too simplistic, I do not mean to suggest that there is no betrayal. It is not inherently contrary to fidelity that in a translation, in an act of bearing witness to the Other, there is always a novelty that does not derive from the Other, for only such novelty can point to the Other as an unforeseeable creation and respect the Other's irreplaceability. But that novelty or spontaneity is necessary for fidelity does not entail that it is always faithful; for this reason I stated only that the infidelity of translation *may be* the greatest possible fidelity. It may also be only an infidelity. To take an extreme example, if I translate *Pourquoi le chien mange-t-il si vite?* (Why does the dog eat so quickly?) as *Trees were climbed by green lightbulbs*, I have produced a sentence that is not inscribed in the original, and I have also been decidedly unfaithful to the French sentence. It is certainly possible to bear false witness about the Other, and the impossibility of fully knowing the Other means that there is no way to be sure that one has been as faithful as one can be, that any particular infidelity is a mark of fidelity and not merely a betrayal. After the friend's death, it will become even harder to know if I am and have been faithful, as the friend will be altogether absent and I will have only the vagaries of memory—my own and perhaps others'—to rely on.

To say that friendship is never realized does not mean that it is betrayed, that the promise is broken from the start, for the promise binds me precisely to a continuous work of creation. It remains, however, that I am free to violate the promise, though not to release myself from it, and that I will at times, even often, be unable to know whether I honestly have striven as best I can to keep it. If, though, I truly love the friend I will not wish to reject the friendship in a misguided attempt to preserve my innocence. Faced with such uncertainty, I can only keep striving and rejoice that the task of fidelity has been given to me. On the one hand, this striving is to be undertaken in fear and trembling because of the importance of the promise; and yet it is also to be undertaken in joy and thankfulness because of the goodness of the promise.

The Fidelity and Infidelity of Memory

A brief digression on the question of fidelity and infidelity as regards one's memory of the friend is worthwhile here, as memory is far less reliable than we generally think. Though we know that memory fades with time, we tend to assume that what memories we retain are accurate, or at least that they accurately represent our past perceptions, however erroneous those perceptions may have been. In fact, as Proust's *Search* indicated even before most scientific studies of memory took place, memory is a matter not of simple recall but of re-creation and interpretation. As the psychologist Daniel L. Schacter, who specializes in the study of memory, observes in *The Seven Sins of Memory*, to remember the past "we extract key elements from our experiences and store them. We then recreate or reconstruct our experiences rather than retrieve copies of them. Sometimes, in the process of reconstructing we add on feelings, beliefs or even knowledge we obtained after the experience" (9). Simply remembering an event can suffice to alter one's memories: as Schacter explains, "the act of retrieving information from memory can inhibit subsequent recall of related information" (81). Thus remembering certain details about the friend may make one more likely to forget other details that one once knew but did not try to call to mind as often. Furthermore, it is normal not only to forget things that did happen but also to remember things that did not, thanks to the errors of misattribution, suggestibility, and bias. "Misattributions in remembering are surprisingly common," reports Schacter: "Sometimes we remember events that never happened [. . .]. Sometimes we recall correctly what happened but misattribute it to the wrong time or place" (90). In the latter sort of misattribution, one's memory contains some correct elements, but in the former sort one mistakes a product of one's imagination for a memory of past reality. Suggestibility is a specific sort of misattribution in which the formation of the false memory is prompted, often inadvertently, by "external sources—other people, written materials, even the media" (100). Merely being asked questions about the friend might lead me to develop false memories, incorporating into my memories information from the questions that is not actually true. As for bias, people tend to "reconstruct the past as overly similar to, or different from, the present" ("consistency and change biases"), unwittingly alter their memories based on "current knowledge" ("hindsight biases"), misremember the past in ways that make their current self look better ("egocentric biases"), and misremember the past based on stereotypes ("stereotypical biases") (139; see 149–53 on egocentric biases and 153–57 on stereotypical biases).

Yet these infidelities of memory are inseparable, Schacter argues, from the proper functioning of memory, for if we remembered everything, our memories might become jumbles of trivial, disconnected data points

(193). The very act of constructing a narrative requires privileging some information and leaving out other information that seems less important, which means that falsity may creep in. Yet we must construct narratives to make sense of our lives—and to bear witness to the Other. Memory's capacity to be faithful and its capacity to be unfaithful are both rooted in our nature as storytelling beings. It is certainly possible to deliberately lie about the friend, to be too careless about one's biases, or to be too quick to accept an implausible memory as truthful, but even when one is careful one cannot be certain that one's narrative is wholly true; odds are good that it is not, and it certainly cannot be complete. Even so, fidelity demands that I remember the friend—demands, therefore, that I accept the risk and responsibility of a partial infidelity in order to avoid the still greater betrayal that is complete forgetfulness. And the very fallibility of my memory does testify to the impossibility of producing an accurate copy of the Other.

To the Unknowable Friend

The moment has come to highlight certain tensions that are central to my analysis of friendship and that reveal still more starkly the unknowability of the friend. On the one hand, it is as the singular individual that I am, and indeed because I am the singular individual that I am, that I am summoned—promised—to friendship, yet on the other hand, it is that very promise that creates me as a singular individual. This creation, moreover, is genuinely unforeseeable. How, though, can I be called because of a singularity that is continually created by the call, the promise? That I am called because of who I am means that I am called to give the Other my world, the world that will be created through the call. With the Proustian madeleine, moreover, we have already seen that the promise operates both backward and forward in time, creating the self's past anew and binding the self to the task of a continuing future creation. Indeed, the backward and forward movements are inseparable precisely because the summons, no matter when it occurs, creates the self's world in order that the self translate its world as a gift to the Other. This creation and translation are never complete and are likewise inseparable: the world that I translate for the Other is a world creatively transformed by the Other's translation of her world for me, and the translation of my world is a creative transformation of the Other's world.

No one could own the copyright on these creations/translations: there is no way to disentangle the claims to authorship. This point clarifies the appeal of the idea that the friend is another self: so it may seem when two are so closely bound. Rather than suggesting an absorption of the Other by the self, or vice versa, however, the fact that one cannot disentangle the claims to authorship highlights that self and Other are both other than themselves.

Fidelity, because it binds the self to this continuing task of mutual creation/translation, must be fidelity through change. But this point raises another concern. Since both self and Other are caught up in this continuous transformation, one might fear that fidelity devolves into fidelity not to the Other but to some reified notion of fidelity: if I am bound to the Other through all the changes the Other may undergo, in what sense is it the Other to whom I am bound? This question can, however, be turned on its head: if I am *not* bound to the Other through all the changes the Other may undergo, in what sense is it the Other to whom I am bound? For if I am not thus bound—if I may legitimately end the friendship when the Other changes—then I am bound not to the unknowable singularity of the Other but only to certain visible phenomena, such as the Other's opinions, habits, beliefs, or overall behavioral tendencies. It is the Other to whom I am bound because the Other is not reducible to phenomena; the Other exceeds my knowledge. That the self must be faithful to an Other who can never be fully known is an objection to this account of fidelity only if one takes epistemology as first philosophy. If, however, the self is constituted in and through its relation to the Other, then so too is the self's capacity to know, and so one must, following Levinas, begin with ethics rather than epistemology. Furthermore, if, as I have argued, the self is constituted in and through friendship, then so too is the self's capacity to know—and so friendship precedes epistemology. That I am bound in advance of knowledge and beyond the possibility of knowledge is essential to friendship. Precisely because friendship is a dispossession of the self and hence cannot depend on the self's perceptions or claims to knowledge, it cannot be contingent on that which the self is capable of perceiving and knowing.

That the ultimate unknowability of the Other does not stand as an objection to this account of fidelity does not mean that it is not the source of a tension. At stake here is, again, the question of recognition and discernment. The question of change in the friend is a particularly serious one when it comes to changes in virtue, and I have already argued that if the friend proposes some vicious design, one is bound by fidelity itself to oppose the friend. Thus the friendship continues, in the form of opposition, through the friend's loss of virtue. We are then faced, however, with the problem of discerning virtuous designs from vicious ones in order that friendship be a spur toward true justice and not away from it—and if friendship is, as I have maintained, a relation that directs us toward the justice that is higher than political justice, this problem in turn raises the problem of recognizing whether a relation does direct us toward justice. We face, therefore, the problem of recognizing, if not true friendships (a phrase that risks assuming that friendship can be established once and for all), then friendships that are directed toward justice more truly than not. On the one hand, it is a betrayal to seek to determine exactly what the word "friend" names; on the other, it is also a betrayal to refuse to let the name of "friend" signify at all, lest it thereby lose its relation to justice.[12] It bears repeating, however, that in such a dilemma we should see not simply a double possibility of failure but a responsibility to be undertaken in fear and trembling yet also in gratitude and joy. For we can escape the dilemma only by escaping finitude, and escaping finitude would entail abandoning friendship and its goodness.

It is because the friend is ultimately unknowable that friendship is not a lesser or easier love than love of one's enemy. If I do not know what may come of the promise or who the friend may be or become, I do not even know whether I may not at some point find myself bound in friendship to one who has also become, in a sense, an enemy. For a grave breach of fidelity on the part of another whom I called a friend does not release me from the task of mourning and of memory. Jean-Luc Marion argues in *Being Given* that the gift is not possible within friendship, writing that "if the gift does not die, it is not given absolutely, therefore is not manifest as such. The gift owes its loss to the enemy. Only the enemy makes the gift possible; he makes the gift evident by denying it reciprocity—in contrast to the friend who involuntarily lowers the gift to the level of a loan with interest. The enemy thus becomes the ally of the gift, and the friend its adversary" (151/89). When, however, I give my world to the one whom I dare to call a friend, I never wholly know to whom I am giving it; or what I am giving, since I also receive my world from the friend; or what will come of the gift, not even that it will be reciprocated. Thus the gift to the friend is lost—although if I refuse to give it, then I lose my world by refusing the friendship that constitutes it. It is only by losing my world through giving it to the friend that I receive my world, though not according to the temporality of exchange, but rather according to the temporality of mutual gratitude. For that matter, I do not know that the gift to the enemy will never be returned in gratitude, that enmity will not be transformed into friendship. In light of the Other's unknowability, the distinction between friend and enemy cannot be drawn so sharply as to diminish friendship in comparison to love of enemies. It remains, of course, that one always does risk falling into the temporality of exchange when giving a gift—but, as ever, the risk is no reason not to make the attempt.

Faced with the risk and responsibility of friendship, let us return, at last, to the quotation from Baudelaire's prose poem "The Stranger" with which this book began:

> Whom do you love best, enigmatic man, your father, your mother, your sister, or your brother?
> I have neither father, nor mother, nor sister, nor brother.
> Your friends?
> Now you are using a word whose sense has remained unknown to me unto this day.[13]

It should be clear by now that friendship is anything but a matter of mastering a definition, and to the degree that friendship is impossible, a friend must say, with the "enigmatic man," that "friend" is "a word whose sense has remained unknown to me unto this day." But what the "enigmatic man" does not say is as interesting as what he says: he does not deny that the word signifies, even if it also exceeds signification. Still more importantly, he does not deny that the question asking after his friends and, implicitly, his love for them is one worth asking.[14] Neither he nor his interlocutor pursues the question,[15] but that does not mean we cannot or must not. The question and the reply give us to hear, if we will, the possibility of a secret that may begin a dialogue in the course of which we may dare to speak the name of friend.

Or, then again, we may not. We cannot be sure whether, in a given instant, we should or should not thus dare: we cannot know what will come of such speech or such silence. Yet though for the friend's sake one should fear infidelity, one should not fear it because for one's own sake one fears to err. We must speak in faith, in fear and gratitude both; and we must be silent in the same way, for even in the silence the unspoken name may resonate. Indeed, silence and speech are inseparable, for what one does not say echoes in the interstices of what one says. Silence and speech must intertwine to testify to the friend, and I dare to let the name of friend resonate through speech and silence because I care for the friend still more than I care about the danger of doing so. The fidelity (from the Latin *fides*, faith) of this intertwining is indeed a faith: I testify to the friend's unknowable singularity, without perceiving it. And, crucially, this witness is not *to an unknown friend*, as if I were testifying to *a* member of some genus that is unknown because I never encountered it; rather, it is *to the unknowable friend*, for the friend is beyond the possibility of comparison and remains unknowable in the reiterated encounter that continually transforms my world.

Conclusion

Risking Friendship in the Twenty-First Century

Friendship and the Facebook Friend

Never wholly realized, friendship is a promise that I will always strive to be faithful in giving the Other my world (which I have already received from the Other). In this it is a double risk: I risk failing in this striving, and I risk the refusal of the gift. Yet because friendship summons me to life in all the depth of my singularity, it is by this risk that I live. Returning, by way of conclusion, to the question of social media and the Facebook "friend," I propose that a great danger of social media is that it seems to offer the possibility of friendship without risk. Social media such as Facebook and Twitter present exposure as an ideal; though one can set one's page to private so that only selected people can see it, the basic principle behind many social media platforms remains the public presentation of one's life. True friendship, being a secret that even those it binds can never fully know, utterly refutes the notion that all can and must be public. By announcing one's doings to everyone, one gives oneself to no one; the refusal to acknowledge the essentially secret is a way of holding oneself back, of refusing to risk oneself for fear of being led astray by that which one does not comprehend.

Certainly we have realized that social media does not reveal everything—that, for instance, people tend to present themselves as happier than they really are. But this very realization often tempts us to want to know the truth about other people's lives, to wish that they would confess everything. Faced with the realization that some things have remained secret, we wish they would become public.[1] It is true that the choice to portray only the best aspects of one's life on social media may be motivated by the perverse desire to elevate oneself above others, but the wish to know about others' sorrows and failures may be motivated by the equally perverse desire of the voyeur or, worse yet, by the sincere belief that everything ought to be public. I say that this belief is worse than the voyeur's desire because the voyeur does not question the basic notion that some things should be secret: her pleasure lies in the fact that she knows, or thinks she knows, a secret to which she has no right, and it would be altogether spoiled if even she, let alone everyone, actually had a right to the secret. Insofar as friends share their troubles with each other, moreover, the motivating force is not the view that all must be public; rather, one desires to be there for the friend, and because one is motivated by care for her, one does not demand that she share her troubles but rather holds oneself ready to receive whatever disclosures she makes. A mark of one's trustworthiness is precisely that one does not demand such disclosures; to demand indicates possessiveness. The most fundamental danger of social media is not, however, the idea—already dangerous enough in its possessive greed—that everything that can be public should be made public; rather, it is the idea that all that is worthwhile is of such a nature that it could be made public. Social media offers the illusion of an all-encompassing being-with, in Falque's sense of the phrase, that would comprehend the totality of the Other's experiences. Thus social media does worse than tempt us to demand the secret of friendship, the promise that binds the friends and that they can never explain: it tempts us to deny the secret. It tempts us to reduce to a nullity all that cannot be exposed.

    The above is not a demand that everyone delete their social media pages, a declaration that social media is never good for anything, or the assertion that being Facebook friends and being real friends are mutually exclusive. It is a warning about a certain dynamic that underlies social media regardless of how wisely one uses it and of which one should therefore be aware in deciding whether and how much it is worth using. In truth, though, the notion that all that is worthwhile can be made public was not born with social media. A notable testimony to this fact comes from Kierkegaard, who in his 1848 work *The Two Ages* remarks that "in contrast to the age of revolution, which took action, the present age is an age of publicity [*Avertissements*], the age of miscellaneous announcements [*Bekjendtgjørelsers*]; nothing happens but still there is instant publicity [*Bekjendtgjørelse*]" (68/70). The words translated as "publicity" are not related to the Danish words that may be translated as "public," but the point remains that Kierkegaard saw in his own era a valorization of that which can be presented to everyone in announcements and a corresponding devaluation of the singular individual. His warning against abundant disclosures that actually disclose nothing, precisely because they deny the secret that cannot be wholly disclosed and that is the basis for all worthwhile disclosures, still holds. Indeed, his warning is not rooted in empirical observations of an era; whenever and in whatever form it occurs, publicity is always a risk insofar as it tempts us to imagine that all has been or can be disclosed. It is worth noting that today even anonymous social media platforms may also contribute to this devaluation of the individual, rather than resisting it, insofar as they permit the individual to disappear more readily into a mass group—which is not to say that anonymity or pseudonymity, on or off social media, is inherently bad. The key is to remember that any person's name, whether real or pseudonymous, stands for a singularity that is never wholly given and to remember that friendship, if it is to have the hope of taking place, can never be wholly brought to light and so made safe.

Beyond Calculation

One may have up to 5,000 "friends" on Facebook. That one does not have the time or the mental capacity to commit oneself to that many people is clear enough, but whether one can have more than one true friend is less so. A book may reach more than 5,000, but what of those friendships that do not essentially involve a written work? Indeed, as mysterious as friendship is, it is not altogether surprising that there should be some disagreement about how many people can be friends. Friendship has often been thought as a relation that holds between two and only two people; Montaigne, for instance, argues that one cannot have more than one friend, for "if two called on you for help at the same time, to which of them would you run? If they required contradictory services of you, how would you reconcile them? If one of them told you a secret which it would be useful for the other to know, how would you get out of the quandary?" (E 188/101, trans. mod.). Aristotle, however, does not limit friendship to two people only, suggesting rather that "intense [σφόδρα] friendship [. . .] is only with a few [ὀλίγους] people" (NE 1171a12–13), though he does note that "celebrated" friendships "are spoken of in terms of pairs" (NE 1171a15). What, indeed, are we to make of the question of number when friendship is a relation to the absolutely singular? Noting that Aristotle does not give us an actual number to mark the maximum possible quantity of friends, Derrida asks, "What knowledge could ever measure up to the injunction to choose those whom one loves, whom one must love, whom one can love? Between them? Between them and the others? All of them?" (PF 40/22, trans. mod.). These questions resemble Montaigne's but are not the same: Montaigne notes the impossibility of choosing between friends to conclude that it is impossible to have more than one friend, whereas Derrida, by asking also how one could choose the one and only friend, implicitly questions whether it is possible to put a numerical limit on friendship. I have already argued that friendship is not primordially a matter of choice or preference, but when even the friends cannot explain how their friendship begins, it becomes still harder to argue that this mystery cannot occur multiple times in a person's life; and if one replies that strictly speaking it never does occur and that true friendship, insofar as it can be said to occur, is exceedingly rare, such an answer still does not tell us whether in principle even the hope for friendship might not bind one to more than one person.

The question of number is in fact a question of political justice, for it is political justice that numbers the singular, as if multiple singularities could be brought under a single genus. Montaigne's objection to the idea that one could have more than a single friend indicates, rightly, that there is no place for political justice in friendship: there must be no calculation of the friend's interests against those of others, for the friend cannot be compared to others. Yet is not limiting the number of friends one may have to one and only one already a calculation? Moreover, it is a calculation that attempts to neatly separate friendship, which concerns only the two involved, from political justice, which concerns everyone else.[2] Here it is worth noting that writing is an act of friendship that is directed to more than one but that is prior to calculation, as the writer must write without knowing how many will read the book or even if there will be any readers at all. As for friendship between people who, unlike writer and reader, are personally acquainted, it is easiest to conceive of fidelity to a single Other, for the reasons Montaigne states. Nevertheless, one is never truly alone with the friend: recall once more Levinas's observation that "the third party looks at me in the eyes of the Other" (TI 234/213). It is therefore impossible to altogether avoid the calculations and comparisons of politics, even in friendship with only one Other—yet friendship, as I have argued, resists the political and points one to ethics by affirming that calculation is impossible where singular individuals are concerned. This affirmation still holds when one is bound in friendship to more than one Other. The multiplicity of friendships marks a promise not to calculate among the friends, and that such a promise can never be kept perfectly does not mean it is not worth making—particularly given that the promise makes us more than we make it. It is certainly dangerous to employ the word "friend" too casually, yet there is also a danger in fearing its use too greatly: friendship is the mutual giving of a world, and while there are certainly practical limits on the number of people with whom one can practice this mutual giving, one should not be too hesitant to give or to receive. The notion that the ideal friendship is between only two people, each of whom counts only the other as a true friend, may in fact contribute to a harmful reification of friendship in which one regards friendship as a sort of thing to be attained, as does Robert de Saint-Loup, who is clearly influenced by this ideal, in Proust's *Search*.

In an era of both nation-states and globalization, friendship's resistance to the political takes on a double importance. Friendship summons us to a hospitality that takes no account of the borders of the nation-state, without either the disregard for the foreign that tends to accompany globalization or the emphasis on exclusive national identity with which states may respond to the pressures of globalization. For friendship depends neither on everyone speaking the same language nor on a valorization of national identity but rather on translation. It is crucial to note, moreover, that in destabilizing the political, friendship does not operate in the manner of a revolution, which remains within the political: friendship points us to a higher justice than any revolution, however justified, can accomplish. Whereas the revolution essentially aims at some goal and so finds itself obliged to calculate in order to reach that goal, friendship arises beyond any reasons one can assign it and so directs us to a love of the Other that arises beyond calculation, a love that is not apolitical (for to be apolitical is to not care how political justice measures up to ethics) but that calls us to transcend the political by recognizing the absolute singularity of each Other. Any discussion of the relation between the friendship and the political carries with it a certain danger, however, lest one give the impression that the goodness of friendship reduces to a call to transcend the political. A call to transcend the political can arise only within the political, and so reducing friendship to this call would amount to reducing it to a dialectic by which the political would hope to transcend itself. But friendship—or let us rather say the promise of friendship, for it can never be wholly realized—is superior to any importance we could give it, however justly, and to any reasons we could cite, however rightly, to justify it: therefore striving to keep that promise is one of the greatest joys that our existence within finitude offers us.

The stakes of friendship in the twenty-first century are not as novel as we might think when we consider how the world has changed since the ancient Greeks first spoke of *philotes*. Certainly we can no longer attempt to locate the relation we call *friendship* within the *polis*, the *polis* having long since given way to the nation-state, and it is undeniable that *philotes*, *philia*, *amicitia*, and *friendship* are not simply synonymous. But none of these words are entirely synonymous with themselves either. It is not only that different authors understood them differently—that *philia*, for instance, is not quite the same in Plato's *Lysis* and in Aristotle's *Nicomachean Ethics* or that *amicitia* undergoes a shift in meaning when Christian authors such as Aelred and Thomas Aquinas think it in relation to God's kingdom. Nor is it only that there are multiple possible referents of *friendship*: eternal fidelity between human persons; the relation to God; the writer/translator's relation to language; the relation between writer, text, and reader; even philosophy, *philosophia*, itself. It is also that there is always a remainder toward which these words gesture but that they cannot quite express: they are all attempts to speak of a secret that, even when one tries hard to tame it, dispossesses the self. Even referring to *a* secret is too narrow: a bond that binds singular individuals precisely by virtue of their singularity must itself be singular, and thus there are many secrets. "O my friends, there is no friend": for *friend* is a generic noun, and you and I are bound not as members of a genus but as absolute singularities, yet I call you *friends* because, being obliged to speak, I dare to hope that this word, which signifies more than it or I can say, is least inadequate or most suitable. I dare to hope that the very infidelity of my words testifies faithfully to the impossibility of saying what I want to say, of bearing witness to each of you in your singular alterity. And in truth (for this enigmatic phrase has the air of a passionate outburst, which may be of joy or despair; let us wager on the former) if I speak it is not from mere obligation but because I rejoice in risking the impossible alongside you.

Notes

Introduction

1. Charles Baudelaire, *Paris Spleen*, trans. Louise Varèse (New York: New Directions, 1970), 1, translation modified.

"— *Qui aimes-tu le mieux, homme énigmatique, dis? ton père, ta mère, ta sœur ou ton frère?*

— *Je n'ai ni père, ni mère, ni sœur, ni frère.*

— *Tes amis?*

— *Vous vous servez là d'une parole dont le sens m'est resté jusqu'à ce jour inconnu*" ("L'Étranger," in *Le Spleen de Paris* [*Petits Poèmes en prose*], Œuvres complètes, vol. 1, ed. Claude Pichois [Paris: Pléiade, 1975], 277).

2. I write *different* rather than *distinct*: when people are bound by both friendship and eros, or even when one person feels both friendship and eros for another, not only may there be no way to determine whether a particular aspect of their bond derives from friendship or from eros, but friendship and eros themselves may be so bound together that it would be impossible, even senseless, to strictly distinguish between them. It nonetheless remains that, blended though they may be in certain cases, friendship and eros are not the same. It is also possible for someone to be uncertain whether he or she feels eros or friendship for another, but the very uncertainty as to which is felt suggests their difference, however difficult it may be to distinguish between them. Moreover, eros is not the *telos* of friendship. I return to the difference between friendship and eros in chapters 4 and 6.

Chapter 1

1. Note that *hôte* can mean either "host" or "guest" and that *étranger* means both "stranger" and "foreigner." See also Pierre Chantraine's remark that the word *philos* "properly expresses not a relation of sentiment but belonging to a social group" (*Dictionnaire étymologique de la langue grecque: Histoire des mots* [Klinksieck: Paris, 1991], 1204, my translation).

2. Specifically, the two parties who wished to establish a bond of *philotes* between themselves would break the ring, and each would take one half. On subsequent meetings they would prove their identities by showing that their two halves fit together. Proof of identity thus derived from a prior break. The word *sumbolon* referred to any token broken in half to prove identity in this manner and was not necessarily a ring; indeed, it was originally a vertebra (*astragalos*). See Henry George Liddell and Robert Scott, *A Greek-English Lexicon*, rev. Sir Henry Stuart Jones and Roderick McKenzie, 9th ed. with a revised supplement (Oxford: Clarendon Press: 1996), 1676.

3. Benveniste notes a striking example of this danger that a relation of *philotes* with one person may lead to hostility to others: he points out that according to Homer, Achilles refuses a bond of *philotes* with Hector when the latter requests "an agreement that the corpse of the loser should not be thrown to the beasts" (D 343/280). Achilles, of course, is fighting to avenge Patroclus, his *philos* (see D 349/285). For Achilles, then, hospitality to Patroclus is linked to hostility to Hector.

4. Although the two authors discussed here as representatives of the Christian tradition wrote in Latin, the term *amicitia* is certainly not associated only with Christianity. There were, of course, Christian authors who wrote in Greek and non-Christian authors who wrote in Latin. Indeed, Aelred recognizes his debt to Cicero's *De Amicitia* (see SF, Prologue).

5. James McEvoy, "The Other as Oneself: Friendship and Love in the Thought of St Thomas Aquinas," in *Thomas Aquinas: Approaches to Truth*, ed. James McEvoy and Michael Dunne (Cornwall: Four Courts Press, 2002), 20.

6. McEvoy, "The Other as Oneself," 20.

7. McEvoy in fact goes so far as to say that "St. Thomas was obliged by the nature of the Latin language to place the discussion of *amicitia* within the context of *amor*, thus making friendship a form of love" (McEvoy, "The Other as Oneself," 27).

8. McEvoy renders *amor concupiscentiae* as "love of desire" and takes care to note that this form of love is not necessarily wrong, although it lacks the perfection of *amor amicitia* (McEvoy, "The Other as Oneself," 24–25).

9. Note that the term *amor*, in Thomas Aquinas, is not restricted to human love: he in fact states that "in God there is love [*amorem*]" (Thomas

Aquinas, ST I q. 20 a. 1 resp.). It is by virtue of *amicitia* that human *amor* can be directed toward God.

10. Jean-Pierre Torrell, *Saint Thomas d'Aquin, maître spirituel: Initiation 2* (Freiburg: Éditions Universitaires Fribourg Suisse, 1996), 408.

11. That said, Aelred does suggest that friendship arises because God designed the world such "that peace should guide all his creatures and society unite them" (SF 1.53). *Amicitia*, though personal and intimate, still occurs within the context of a broader society. For his part, when Aristotle suggests that the maximum possible number of friends "is perhaps the greatest number someone would be able to live together with" (NE 1171a1–2), and when he explains that friends are eager to assist each other, he does portray a certain form of *philia* as an intimate personal bond.

12. This analysis is partly inspired by Emmanuel Falque's discussion of Richard of St. Victor's account of the Trinity, in which Falque oberves that "only the sharing of love with a *third loved one* definitively removes all pretensions of egoity" (*Le Livre de l'expérience: D'Anselme de Cantorbéry à Bernard de Clairvaux* [Paris: Cerf, 2017], 258–59). This theme appears in Aelred as well, though not with explicit reference to God's triune nature.

Chapter 2

1. As Levinas explains, "there is always a third party in the world: he or she is also my other, my neighbor. Hence, it is important that I know which of the two takes precedence. Is the one not the persecutor of the other? Must not human beings, who are incomparable, be compared? Thus justice, here, is prior to the taking upon oneself of the fate of the other" (EN 113/104, trans. mod.).

2. As Levinas explains, "the *moral* relation with the Master who judges me underlies the freedom of my adherence to the true. Thus language commences" (TI 104/101, trans. mod.).

3. "This infinity, stronger than murder, already resists us in his face, is his face, is the primordial *expression*, is the first word: 'thou shalt not commit murder'" (TI 217/199, trans. mod.).

4. See also Levinas's statement that "absolving himself from all essence, all genus, all resemblance, the neighbor, *the first one who comes along*, concerns me for the first time (even if he is an old acquaintance, an old friend, an old lover, long caught up in the fabric of my social relations) in a contingency that excludes the a priori" (OB 137–38/86, trans. mod.). One Other bears no resemblance to any other Other; the Other is absolutely individual.

5. Jean-Luc Marion denies that the Levinasian Other is an individual, maintaining instead that for Levinas the Other remains within the universal such

that any Other can substitute for any Other. According to Marion, it is love, not ethics, that individualizes, and we must therefore go beyond Levinas. For this criticism, see Marion, *Prolégomènes à la charité*, 3rd ed. rev. (Paris: Éditions de la Différence, 2007), chapter 4, "L'intentionnalité de l'amour," 93–125; in English as *Prolegomena to Charity*, trans. Stephen E. Lewis (New York: Fordham University Press, 2002), chapter 4, "The Intentionality of Love," 71–101, as well as Marion, "D'autrui à l'individu: Au-delà de l'éthique," *Studia Phaenomenologica* 2 (2002): 11–30; in English as "From the Other to the Individual," trans. Arianne Conty, *Levinas Studies* 1 (2005): 99–117. The preceding paragraph makes clear my reasons for contesting such an interpretation of Levinas. Christina Gschwandtner ably defends Levinas against Marion's critique in her "Ethics, Eros, or Caritas? Levinas and Marion on the Individuation of the Other," *Philosophy Today* 49, no. 1 (2006): 70–87. She points out that Levinas rejects the Kantian emphasis on the universal that Marion attributes to him (see in particular Gschwandtner, "Ethics, Eros or Caritas?" 76–78) and convincingly shows that for Levinas, "the universal itself becomes individuated in the eyes of the specific, particular other who appeals to me and also gives me to myself" (ibid., 77).

6. Scotus explains that "we will know singulars in their own reasons in the fatherland (*in patria*) [. . .] but in the present state (*sed pro statu ipso*) our intellect knows nothing but what can be produced by an image" (*Ordinatio* III d. 4 n. 5, cited and translated in Emmanuel Falque, *Dieu, la chair et l'autre: D'Irénée à Duns Scot* [Paris: PUF, 2008], 464; *God, the Flesh, and the Other: From Irenaeus to Duns Scotus*, trans. William Christian Hackett [Evanston: Northwestern University Press, 2015], 274).

7. In this passage Scotus is using the example of a stone, but his claim applies to all that exists. He writes "that it is necessary through something positive intrinsic [*per aliquid positivum intrinsecum*] to this stone, as through a proper reason [*per rationem propriam*], that it be incompatible with the stone for it to be divided into subjective parts. That positive feature [*illud positivum*] will be what will be said to be by itself the cause of individuation. For by 'individuation' I understand that indivisibility—that is, incompatibility with divisibility" (*Ordinatio* II d. 3 p. 1 q. 2 n. 57, in *Five Texts on the Medieval Problem of Universals: Porphyry, Boethius, Abelard, Duns Scotus, Ockham*, trans. and ed. Paul Vincent Spade [Indianapolis: Hackett, 1994], 71).

8. It does not follow that the friend is simply self-identical. This second claim, drawing as it does on the Scotian idea that a thing is *this* thing by virtue of itself and not of its differences from other things, may appear suspect to readers of Saussure or, especially, Derrida. But as the play of *différance* precedes identity, it necessarily precedes any attempt to compare supposedly self-identical persons or things. I am not denying difference or differance in favor of identity but am arguing that all comparisons of the friend to others, far from being a

condition of friendship, do not belong essentially to friendship. Originarily if not historically, friendship arises without comparison.

9. As Sartre writes, "However, there can be no doubt that in one sense I *am* a café waiter—otherwise would it not be equally possible to call myself a diplomat or a journalist? [. . .] I am the waiter in the mode of *being what I am not*" (Jean-Paul Sartre, *L'Être et le Néant* [Paris: Gallimard, 1976], 95; *Being and Nothingness*, trans. Sarah Richmond [New York: Washington Square Press, 2018], 104).

10. See C. S. Lewis, *The Four Loves* (New York: Harcourt Brace, 1960): "Friendship arises out of mere Companionship when two or more of the companions discover that they have in common some insight or interest or even taste which the others do not share and which, till that moment, each believed to be his own unique treasure (or burden). The typical expression of opening Friendship would be something like, 'What? You too? I thought I was the only one'" (65).

11. Angelus Silesius, *Der Cherubinischer Wandersmann* (Jena: Diederichs, 1905), 39, my translation. Friendship, like the rose that blooms, is greater or better than any reason could ever say, but there may also be a "without why" that is inferior to reason. Consider Primo Levi's account of an incident during his imprisonment in a concentration camp: "Driven by thirst, I eyed a fine icicle outside the window, within hand's reach. I opened the window and broke off the icicle but at once a large, heavy guard prowling outside brutally snatched it away from me. '*Warum?*' I asked him in my poor German. '*Hier ist kein warum*' (there is no why here), he replied, pushing me inside with a shove" (Primo Levi, *Survival in Auschwitz: The Nazi Assault on Humanity*, trans. Stuart Woolf [New York: Touchstone, 1996], 29). Evil has no why because it is unjustifiable in the most common sense of the word: it is below any possibility of justification. A great good is without why because it is better than any justification can explain.

12. Blanchot, *Pour l'amitié*, 19.

13. The French title of Derrida's *The Work of Mourning* is *Chaque fois unique, la fin du monde*, meaning "Each time unique, the end of the world."

14. It is not wrong for the Other to not be interested in friendship with me, and I stand by my prior argument that the Levinasian Desire of the Other is a gift, is an occasion for joy, and is good for the self: see Sarah Horton, "The Joy of Desire: Understanding Levinas's Desire of the Other as Gift," *Continental Philosophy Review* 51, no. 2 (2018): 193–210. On my view, it is good for me to be called as the one who must aid the Other, and the gift that is Desire is no less good for me because it would be offered to anyone in the position of the self, but friendship still implicates me in my singularity to a greater degree than ethics. The Other summons me to goodness and makes my freedom meaningful by calling on me to use it responsibly, but the friend goes farther than the Other

in his or her gladness that I, specifically, exist—and in friendship I go farther by being faithful as one who is called because I am myself, not just as one who is called because I alone am there to receive the call.

15. Tatranský, "A Reciprocal Asymmetry? Levinas's Ethics Reconsidered," *Ethical Perspectives* 15, no. 3 (2008), 304.

16. Melissa Fitzpatrick, "Disruption, Conversation, and Ethics: A Study on the Limits of Self-Legislation" (PhD diss., Boston College, 2019), 215.

17. Also drawing on Ricœur to argue for the legitimacy of friendship despite the asymmetry of the ethical relation, Tatranský uses the phrase "reciprocal asymmetry." See Tatranský, "A Reciprocal Asymmetry? Levinas's Ethics Reconsidered," 301–7 in particular.

18. Mutuality can also characterize relations that we would not ordinarily call friendships, such as familial or erotic relations. I suggest that when these relations involve mutuality and lasting fidelity, they partake in the character of friendship. Although it is possible to identify differences between friendship and these other relations (for instance, friends do not raise each other as parents raise children, and friends qua friends do not, like lovers, become one flesh), it is a mistake to rigidly demarcate them as if it were always clear what belongs to friendship and what to another sort of relation.

19. See Levinas's essay "A Man-God?" whose final paragraph begins, "The idea of the hostage, of expiation of me for the Other, [. . .] cannot be extended outside me" (*ENE*, 71; *ENT*, 60).

20. Elsewhere I have argued, via a reading of Kierkegaard's *The Concept of Anxiety*, that although the self may lose its individuality through language, language is also the only way for the self to be opened to alterity and thereby be saved from the abstractions of the universal. See Sarah Horton, "Illegible Salvation: The Authority of Language in *The Concept of Anxiety*," in *Authorship and Authority in Kierkegaard's Writings*, ed. Joseph Westfall, 121–37 (London: Bloomsbury, 2018).

21. *Epieikeia* is often translated as "equity"; I have preferred "decency" here to avoid the connotation of comparisons among persons.

22. In this connection it is worthwhile to note Claire Elise Katz's remark, in an article on Levinas and Kierkegaard's *Fear and Trembling*, that "this moment in the story [when Abraham obeys God's command to not kill Isaac] could be read as the need for our attention to be focused on the victims, those who suffer the violence, not the administrators of that violence, even if, or maybe especially if, that violence is administered in the name of God. [. . .] Abraham needs to be able to see Isaac's face, and he needs to be able to see his responsibility to God precisely as a responsibility to Isaac" ("The Voice of God and the Face of the Other," *Journal of Textual Reasoning* 2, no. 1 (2003), http://jtr.shanti.virginia.edu/volume-2-number-1/the-voice-of-god-and-the-face-of-the-other/). In Thomistic terms (which Katz does not employ), Abraham must let his friendship for

God lead him to *caritas* for Isaac. This *caritas* must also be understood in terms of ethical responsibility.

23. Willow Verkerk thoughtfully examines Nietzsche's understanding of friendship in *Nietzsche and Friendship* (London: Bloomsbury, 2019). See in particular chapter 2, "Nietzsche's Re-evaluation of Friendship," 29–65, in which she points out that "Nietzsche believes that conflict promotes shared enhancement and that to grow, we require companions who are capable of questioning and potentially defeating us" (45).

24. For an insightful reading of Nietzsche and Levinas that argues that they are not as different as they seem when it comes to caring for others, see Melissa Fitzpatrick, "A Nietzschean Ethics of Care?" in *(mis)Reading Nietzsche*, ed. M. Saverio Clemente and Brian J. Cocchiara, 88–111 (Eugene, OR: Pickwick Publications, 2018).

Chapter 3

1. Aristotle's remark that "happiness is in need of nothing but is self-sufficient [αὐτάρκης]" (NE 1176b6–7) must be read in context to avoid confusion. The preceding sentence asserts that "one must posit happiness as being among the activities that are choiceworthy in themselves and not for the sake of something else" (NE 1176b4–6). The claim that "happiness is self-sufficient" thus means that happiness is a good in and of itself: it is "in need of nothing," or "self-sufficient," because it is an end in itself, not a means to an end, and so nothing need be added to it to make it good. It does not follow that human beings have no need of other people in order to be happy.

2. See Merleau-Ponty, VI 192/138, and Richard Kearney, "The Wager of Carnal Hermeneutics," in *Carnal Hermeneutics*, ed. Richard Kearney and Brian Treanor (New York: Fordham University Press, 2015), 38–39.

3. See Levinas's observation that "this presentation [of the face of the Other] is nonviolence par excellence, for instead of hurting my freedom it calls it to responsibility and founds it" (TI 222/203). It is only because I am responsible to and for the Other that my actions matter at all. In the absence of the Other, therefore, I would be lost in a solipsistic, nihilistic world where nothing I do would have any significance because there would be no one to whom it could matter.

4. Thus Derrida writes that "the other's death, especially but not only if one loves him, does not signal an absence, a disappearance, the end of *this or that* life, that is, the possibility of a(n always unique) world appearing to *this* living one. Death proclaims each time *the end of the world in totality*, the end of all possible worlds, and *each time the end of the world as a unique, irreplaceable, and therefore infinite totality*" (Jacques Derrida, *Chaque fois unique, la fin du monde*

(Paris: Galilée, 2003), 9; this line is from Derrida's introduction to the French edition, which does not appear in the previously published English edition, *The Work of Mourning*).

5. One might ask here how this point, and the situating of friendship within finitude more broadly, relates to friendship to God, as God is infinite and not subject to change. From a Christian theological perspective, one might also ask how this view of friendship can account for the relation among the persons of the Trinity. I reply that neither the relation among the persons of the Trinity nor God's relation to humans who are friends of God are univocal with human friendship. The human experience of friendship is essentially constituted by finitude. God's relationships with human beings cannot add to his happiness, as he is perfectly happy in himself, nor can they transform him. The account of friendship that I propose here can describe only the human experience of friendship with God, and that only partially, because God created the world and will not die. As for the Trinity, one might hazard the remark that God would not be perfectly happy if he were not triune, but according to the traditional Christian conception, he is essentially triune; the proposed condition—God not being triune—cannot be true any more than it could be true that a hexagon had fewer than six angles. In other words, the relation that holds among the persons of the Trinity is a necessary one, whereas the relation that holds between human friends is contingent: one or more of them might never have been born, they might never have met, one of them might have died the moment they met, or any number of other events could have prevented the friendship from forming. In addition to being necessary and infinite, God knows himself perfectly, and the importance of the fact that human friends can never know each other perfectly will soon become clear. Christians have often maintained that we are communal because God himself is communal; still, the relation among the persons of the Trinity is sufficiently different from any relation we experience as friendship that a further study of it is outside the scope of this book.

6. See in particular Emmanuel Falque, *Parcours d'embûches: S'expliquer* (Paris: Éditions Franciscaines, 2016), §11, "Désir de Dieu et finitude de l'homme," 90–93; *By Way of Obstacles: A Pathway through a Work*, trans. Sarah Horton (Eugene, OR: Cascade Books, 2022), §9, "The Desire for God and Human Finitude," 38–40.

7. Stanislas Jullien in fact argues that the difference between Levinas and Derrida comes down to the fact that Levinas privileges infinity, whereas Derrida insists on an originary finitude that is the site of an originary mourning. See Stanislas Jullien, "Entretien discordant de Derrida et Levinas autour de la finitude originaire," in *Levinas-Derrida: Lire ensemble*, ed. Danielle Cohen-Levinas and Marc Crépon, 147–74 (Paris: Hermann, 2015). See also Marc Crépon's observation that Derrida adds to ethics the dimension of mourning, in Marc Crépon, *Vivre avec: La pensée de la mort et la mémoire des guerres* (Paris: Hermann, 2008), ch. VII, "Hospitalité et mortalité," 145–71.

8. Falque of course agrees wholeheartedly that finitude and temporality are not to be thought on the basis of eternity. Though he certainly differs from Derrida in that he admits the possibility of a transformation of our finitude by God, he maintains that "we experience ourselves first of all as beings of the 'very low'—that is to say, not as coming from God, even were He the 'Very Low,' but as belonging to the 'world,' to 'time,' and as 'simply man [*l'homme tout court*]'" (MF 226/40). And it is not here a matter of "an essence of man" understood from the start with reference to God and eternity but of an originary experience of the world and of man as temporal, without reference to God or eternity.

9. Derrida's translation of the phrase he quotes in Greek, "there is no friend without time," is fairly literal; Inwood and Woolf's less literal translation is "It takes time to become a friend" (EE 1237b17). The context does suggest that Aristotle is referring to the time required for friends to establish confidence in each other, but Derrida's reading reminds us that this temporal element, far from being an accident, is essential to friendship.

10. One might ask here about God's knowledge of us. A full answer to this question is beyond the scope of this book, but in short, God is, according to traditional Christian theology, the source of our being; he does not need a copy of us to know us because "in him we live and move and have our being" (Acts 17:28). That at Pentecost (Acts 3) each person heard the disciples speaking in his native language—instead of everyone being granted the ability to understand Aramaic—also suggests that God approves of translation and of the multiplicity of tongues.

11. Quoted in Joseph M. Perrin and Gustave Thibon, *Simone Weil telle que nous l'avons connue* (Paris: Éditions du Vieux Colombier, 1952), 146; *Simone Weil as We Knew Her*, trans. Emma Crauford (London: Routledge, 2003), 118.

12. Perrin and Thibon, *Simone Weil telle que nous l'avons connue*, 146; *Simone Weil as We Knew Her*, 118.

13. Jean-Louis Chrétien, *La Voix nue: Phénoménologie de la promesse* (Paris: Éditions de Minuit, 1990), 224.

Chapter 4

1. It bears noting that the name "Marcel" appears on one other occasion, when the narrator quotes a note Albertine sent him: "'My darling dear Marcel, I return less quickly than this cyclist, whose bike I should like to borrow in order to be with you sooner. How could you believe that I might be angry or that I could enjoy anything better than to be with you? It will be nice to go out, just the two of us together; it would be nicer still if we never went out except together. The ideas you get into your head! What a Marcel! What a Marcel! Always and ever your Albertine'" (S III.663/V.202–203, trans. mod.). Given

the deliberate indirectness of the previous reference to his name, however, we cannot take this note as proof of his name: Marcel may be his real name, in which case the previous indirectness was a ruse, or he may here have replaced his name with "Marcel" without informing readers that he was doing so.

2. Miguel de Beistegui, "From the Writing of Desire to the Desire of Writing: Reflections on Proust," in *Somatic Desire: Recovering Corporeality in Contemporary Thought*, ed. Sarah Horton, Stephen Mendelsohn, Christine Rojcewicz, and Richard Kearney (Lanham, MD: Lexington Books, 2019), 185.

3. As Sabine Fos-Falque observes, "Deceptive paradox: Albertine's sleep covers, in the end, her internal world even as it innocently exhibits a body without modesty and without reserve, a volume of body lasciviously spread out between the sheets. [. . .] The one who watches guesses nothing of it, wears himself out with trying to represent it to himself but can let himself also be taken up by the hallucinatory, thus entering into a dreaming thought." (Fos-Falque, *Une chair épandue sur le divan*, in Emmanuel Falque and Sabine Fos-Falque, *Éthique du corps épandu suivi de Une chair épandue sur le divan* [Paris: Cerf, 2018], 145–46).

4. Elizabeth Ladenson argues that lesbianism in the *Search* is not the female version of male homosexuality and that it is in fact "the sole context in the *Recherche* in which the otherwise unbridgeable chasm between subject and object closes," for only lesbians are "creatures who truly desire their like" (*Proust's Lesbianism* [Ithaca: Cornell University Press, 1999], 46). She further contends that "Gomorrhean [lesbian] sexuality thus presents the peculiar paradox of being at once exhibitionistic and yet impossible actually to see. Proust invests in Gomorrah not just an erotics of sameness [. . .] but also the novel's sole model of a sexuality in control of itself, or at least of its own representation" (*Proust's Lesbianism*, 68). I accept Ladenson's arguments that the *Search* portrays lesbianism as the one form of erotic relationship that truly unites the lovers, since they are alike, and that Marcel sees of lesbians only what they are willing for others to see. But from the fact that the lesbians in the novel are skilled at controlling their "own representation," as Ladenson puts it, does it follow that lesbianism truly unites the Same to the Same? And that Marcel only sees what he is allowed to see does not mean that he rightly interprets what he sees: if he interprets lesbian relationships as a union of the Same to the Same, must his interpretation be correct? I reply to both these questions in the negative. Unlike Ladenson, I argue that lesbian relationships appear as the union of the Same to the Same because Marcel imagines them thus. He knows, however little he wants to admit it, that no relationship that is possible for him permits the union for which he so ardently wishes, as anyone—man or woman—with whom he could enter into a relationship would always remain Other. (That he never considers entering into an erotic relationship with a man is beside the point; he has no need to consider it because he has seen that such relationships are as unsatisfying as heterosexual ones. Still, if

indeed he idealizes lesbian relationships because they are impossible for him, his awareness that male homosexual relationships are unsatisfying suggests that he is aware that he could theoretically pursue one even though he never consciously envisions such a possibility.) The only relationship in which he cannot possibly participate is that of a woman to a woman, and it would be even more unbearable for absolute ipseity to be utterly illusory than for it to exist out of his reach. Unable to accept that "every other is wholly other" (to borrow one translation of Derrida's famous phrase *"tout autre est tout autre"*) regardless of who the self is, he therefore imagines that lesbians have attained absolute ipseity and wishes all the more desperately to possess Albertine in order to master his own Otherness. The fear that lesbians, and only lesbians, have satisfied the desire that torments him ends up fueling his own longing to satisfy that desire by possessing Albertine. Marcel is not a wholly reliable narrator, and we should be all the more hesitant to trust his account when it concerns that which he desires. What is more, precisely because lesbianism lies wholly outside Marcel's experience—as Ladenson herself notes, when he tries "to understand what women do together, his comprehension is always blocked" (*Proust's Lesbianism*, 67)—we cannot trust his portrayal of it.

5. A passage in which Marcel observes two paintings by the artist Elstir is instructive in this regard: noting that a particular man appears in both paintings and that in one he appears "at some popular seaside festival where he evidently had no business to be," Marcel deduces that this man must be "a friend, perhaps a patron, whom [Elstir] liked to introduce into his paintings, as in the past Carpaccio introduced—and in perfect likenesses—prominent Venetian noblemen into his; in the same way as Beethoven, too, found pleasure in inscribing at the top of a favorite work the cherished name of the archduke Rudolph" (S II.713/III.576, trans. mod.). The economic exchange between artist and patron may perhaps occur within a friendship, and in any case it is not unreasonable to suppose that the man is a patron. Given Marcel's claim that friendship is useless to the artist, however, the fact that he so quickly introduces the notion of patronage and exchange suggests that he must find some way in which the man might be economically useful to Elstir to make sense of the thought that this painter he admires has a friend.

6. One need only consider Stéphane Mallarmé's poem *Un coup de dés jamais n'abolira le hasard* (*A Throw of the Dice Will Never Abolish Chance*), with its many blank spaces that are inseparable from the printed words, to see that the absence of text may be as meaningful as text itself.

7. The application of the phrase "dangerous supplement" to writing comes from Jacques Derrida, *De la grammatologie* (Paris: Éditions de Minuit, 1967), part 2, chapter 2, "'Ce dangereux supplément,'" 197–226; *Of Grammatology*, trans. Gayatri Chakravorty Spivak (Baltimore: Johns Hopkins University Press, 1997), part II, chapter 2, "'. . . That Dangerous Supplement . . . ,'" 141–64.

8. Elizabeth Ladenson, in "Proust's Case Against Friendship," *Romanic Review* 110, no. 1–4, 2019, 265–85, argues both that we must take the *Search*'s critique of friendship seriously and that Proust himself, despite his friendships, was genuinely inclined to regard friendship as an illusion. I contend, however, that the *Search* ultimately indicates that writing is an act of friendship, even if Proust himself would reject this conclusion.

9. Specifically, the first two lines feature an enjambment that was unacceptable according to French classical rules, and the alexandrins (lines of twelve syllables) of which the play is composed do not always have a caesura after the sixth syllable, as those rules required. The play also violates the three unities (unity of time, unity of place, and unity of action) essential to classical theater, but this point is less directly related to the linguistic style in which it is written.

10. Ricœur borrows this phrase from the title of a book by Antoine Berman, rendered in English as "the test of the foreign." Note that *étranger* can mean both "foreigner" and "stranger."

11. This point recalls Sartre's analysis of the look in *Being and Nothingness*: the experience of being looked at by another person reveals to me that there are other people in the world who are able to interpret and judge my actions differently than I do. For Sartre, to discover that other subjects exist is to discover myself as vulnerable to their judgments. See Sartre, *L'Être et le Néant*, part 2, chapter 1, § 4, "Le regard," 292–341; *Being and Nothingness*, part 2, chapter 1, § 4, "The Look," 347–408.

12. Kearney describes Ricœur's notion of linguistic hospitality as a "middle road" between "the impulse to assimilate and absorb the Other into the Same" and "the contrary temptation to evacuate one's own linguistic dwelling altogether, surrendering one's speech to the in-coming Other, even to the point where there is no longer a host at home to receive a guest at all": on this "middle road," he explains, "one honors both host and guest languages equally while resisting the take-over of one by the other" (Richard Kearney, "Linguistic Hospitality: The Risk of Translation," *Research in Phenomenology* 49 [2019], 1).

13. Kearney observes that "it is perhaps no accident that the novel becomes fragmented in a number of different directions in *Time Regained*, just when it appeared to reach closure and become whole (in the manner of some Hegelian Idea). Proust resists the Hegelian temptation. His book remains undecided as to whether Marcel's projected novel is actually the author's *In Search of Lost Time* or not. That is for the reader to decide. Indeed, it is curious how each philosophical reading of Proust—by Ricœur, Deleuze, Levinas, Benjamin, Ginette, Beckett, De Man, Blanchot, Kristeva, Nussbaum, Murdoch, Girard—manages, in every case, to *translate* the novel into its own hermeneutic. The ultimate definition, perhaps, of an open text" (Kearney, *Anatheism*, 116–17). That Marcel's novel never appears is precisely a reminder that a text never does simply appear in the mode of presence, that it is always an invitation to translation. If there is

a mark of great literature, it is perhaps that it invites and sustains translation, again and again and again. Readings of it can never wholly express its meaning, but they can hope to invite translation themselves.

14. "Advised [*a conseillé*]" and "appeared [*est apparu*]" are in the *passé composé*, a more informal tense, rarely used in literature; after the memory's appearance, the narration returns to the literary *passé simple*. The use of the *passé composé* for these verbs makes the temptation to stop and the appearance of the memory seem more immediate, though still past. Interestingly, the first line of the *Search*—"For a long time, I went to bed early [*Longtemps je me suis couché de bonne heure*]" (S I.3/I.1, trans. mod.)—also employs the *passé composé*. The *passé simple* tends to distance events from the reader; beginning with the *passé composé*, although nearly the entire book uses the *passé simple*, draws us into the story with the impression that the past in question is not simply over and done with but has effects that carry forward into our, the readers', present.

15. It is worth noting that the cake featured in this scene, the madeleine, bears the name of Mary Magdalene, called Marie-Madeleine in French: this name should call to mind the *noli me tangere*, "Touch me not," the resurrected Christ's command to Mary Magdalene when she encounters him in the garden on Easter morning. It is Marcel himself who here appears as a Magdalene who must not hold back "his own" created memory, which can emerge as a work of art only if he accepts that he does not control it. Moreover, Mary was looking for Jesus's body when she finds Jesus himself, and he also commands her to tell the disciples of his resurrection. For the writer as for Mary Magdalene, what one receives is far more and far better than what one had thought to look for. (Serge Doubrovsky and Kevin Newmark have both noted the religious significance of the name *madeleine*, though neither connects it with the *noli me tangere*. See Serge Doubrovsky, *La Place de la madeleine: Écriture et fantasme chez Proust* [Paris: Mercure, 1974], 110; *Writing and Fantasy in Proust: La Place de la madeleine*, trans. Carol Mastrangelo Bové with Paul A. Bové [Lincoln: University of Nebraska Press, 1986], 80, and Kevin Newmark, *Beyond Symbolism: Textual History and the Future of Reading* [Ithaca: Cornell University Press, 1991], 128.)

16. The word "solicit [*solliciter*]" in fact appears in the madeleine scene, between the initial pleasure and the coming of the memory, when Marcel is seeking and creating the memory of Combray: "Will it reach the surface of my clear conscience, this memory, this ancient instant which the attraction of an identical instant has come from so far away to solicit, to disturb, to raise up out of the very depths of myself?" (S I.46/I.62, trans. mod.).

17. For this reason I maintain that Doubrovksy is wrong to argue, as he does in *Writing and Fantasy in Proust*, that "the work of art" is "an autogenesis" (56/31). He does recognize that it is impossible to wholly free oneself from the other: as he puts it, "whatever I do, my words are always those of others; language is the Other as a code" (157/123, trans. mod.), and he later adds that

"if I dream of being myself, it is precisely because I never manage to be myself" (183/147, trans. mod.). Notwithstanding, he contends that writing is the attempt to create oneself, a declaration of independence from the Other even if this independence can never be fully realized: thus he states that "to write is to refuse to 'make' on command. In this way the rupture with the language-mother, the transgression of the code of the Other, takes place" (159/125, trans. mod.). For Doubrovsky, to write is to seek to be original, that is, an origin unto oneself (159–60/125–26). Certainly writing is not taking dictation from the Other, but since the very possibility of writing depends on the Other, the desire to be self-contained and independent of the Other is utterly inimical to writing well. Writing is not a matter of originality, if by that one means being an origin unto oneself, but of singularity: no one else can write in my place not because I am my own origin but because no one else can inhabit the world in my stead. To say that I receive the world from the Other is also to say that the Other, as giver, does not receive the world in my place. Far from being "a translation or transference of a masturbatory experience," as Doubrovsky would have it (30/8), the madeleine episode shows that the self's very powers of creation come from outside. Doubrovsky notes the similarity between the madeleine episode in the *Search* and the masturbation scene in Proust's *Contre Sainte-Beuve* (26–29/5–8), but the resemblance need not imply that the madeleine episode is autoerotic; on the contrary, the madeleine episode calls into question the masturbation scene by suggesting that the very notion of "self-pleasure" that would be wholly independent of the Other is a false trail that one must not attempt to follow if one wishes to create art.

18. It bears noting that Rousseau, from whom Derrida takes the phrase "dangerous supplement," actually employs it in his *Confessions* and in *Émile* to describe not writing but masturbation (*Of Grammatology*, 200–18/144–57). The autoerotic fantasy, in contrast to writing, seeks to supplement the absent Other with the present self. But though it is true that the Other is absent, so too is the self. As Derrida explains, "in what one calls the real life of these existences 'of flesh and bone' [the existences of Rousseau himself, of his mother, of his mistress Thérèse], beyond what one believes one can circumscribe as Rousseau's work, and behind it, there has never been anything but writing [*il n'y a jamais eu que de l'écriture*], there have never been anything but supplements" (*Of Grammatology*, 220/159, trans. mod.). That there are and ever have been only supplements means that the desired object has never been present. Because the self is absent from itself, the autoerotic fantasy, which depends on the self being present and so able to substitute for the Other, must fail. Artistic creation, in contrast to the autoerotic fantasy, is not a search for presence: to create well, the artist must embrace the necessity of translation across distance.

19. As Newmark observes, "according to Proust, true 'life' can never be consciously present at its own conception and maturation. Rather, it can only

be *re*cognized or *re*discovered by the subject, who must always stumble across it belatedly and as if by accident" (Newmark, *Beyond Symbolism*, 139). Because the experience of the initial impression exists only in translation, Bersani is wrong to state that "it is, furthermore, obvious that language itself and therefore the literary work are necessarily a fall from the paradise of involuntary memory" (Leo Bersani, *Marcel Proust: The Fictions of Life and Art*, 2nd ed. [New York: Oxford University Press, 2013], 210–11), or at least he is wrong insofar as he implies that the "paradise of involuntary memory" ever existed as such. Language and the literary work are a fall that was always already falling, for the instant of involuntary memory, over as soon as it is begun, could not be said to belong to one's conscious experience without itself being remembered and hence interpreted.

20. Ricœur also notes the significance of this line, writing that "time regained, I will now say, is *the impression regained*. [. . .] In order to be regained, the impression must first have been lost as an immediate enjoyment [*jouissance*], prisoner to its external object; the first stage of the rediscovery marks the complete internalization of the impression. A second stage is the transposition of the impression into a law, into an idea. A third stage is the inscription of this spiritual equivalent into a work of art. There would supposedly be [*il y aurait*] a fourth stage, which is alluded to only once in the *Search*, when the narrator evokes his future readers" (Ricœur, *Temps et récit*, vol. 2 [Paris: Seuil, 1984], 221; *Time and Narrative*, trans. Kathleen McLaughlin and David Pellauer [Chicago: University of Chicago Press, 1985], 149–50, translation modified). The work is not complete until it reads its readers. And it should not surprise us that this final stage in the finding again of lost impressions, of lost time, is mentioned only once, in the conditional, and as if in passing, for by the time this stage occurs the writer is effaced behind the text, and it is we, the readers, who are invited to let it be accomplished in ourselves. Here neither narrator nor author can tell us what to do; what takes place will take place through our reading of the text, which is also, and crucially, the text's reading of us.

21. Commenting on the *Search*, Levinas rightly observes that "Proust's most profound teaching—if, that is, poetry contains teachings—consists in situating the real in a relation with what forever remains absent—the other as absence and mystery. It consists in rediscovering this relation within the very intimacy of the *I*, in inaugurating a dialectic that breaks definitively with Parmenides" (Levinas, *Noms propres* [Montpellier: Fata Morgana, 1976], 155–56; *Proper Names*, trans. Michael B. Smith [Stanford: Stanford University Press, 1996], 104–5, trans. mod.). This lesson that Levinas draws from the *Search* is precisely the fidelity of translation: that it recognizes and loves the "absence and mystery" of the Other.

22. Katharina Münchberg, "Freundschaft ohne Freunde. Marcel Prousts *Recherche*," in *Freundschaft: Theorien und Poetiken*, ed. Katharina Münchberg and Christian Reidenbach (München: Wilhelm Fink Verlag, 2012), 210.

23. Merleau-Ponty in fact argues, in his reading of the *Search*, that "alienation (the failure) is one with love, but is its reality: love entails a beyond oneself, the very beyond of the false desire of possession" (*L'institution, la passivité: Notes de cours au Collège de France (1954–1955)* [Paris: Belin, 2015], 98; *Institution and Passivity: Notes from the Collège de France*, trans. Leonard Lawlor [Evanston: Northwestern University Press, 2010], 37).

Chapter 5

1. Falque in this essay uses "being-there" considerably more narrowly than Heidegger: he refers specifically to caring for the Other. One is not truly "there," in Falque's sense, if one is physically present but neglects the person for whom one ought to be caring. As for "being-with," Heidegger uses *Mitsein* to mean that I share a world with others, and although my world is the same world that others also inhabit, Heidegger does not imply that our experiences are the same. For Heidegger's use of *Mitsein*, see in particular *Sein und Zeit*, GA 2 (Frankfurt am Main: Vittorio Klostermann, 1977), part 1, division 1, chapter 4, §26, "Das Mitdasein der Anderen und das alltägliche Mitsein," 117–25; *Being and Time*, trans. John Macquarrie and Edward Robinson (New York: Harper and Row, 1962), part 1, division 1, chapter 4, §26, "The Dasein-with of Others and Everday Being-with," 153–63. Finally, Being-alongside (*Sein-bei*) for Heidegger has to do with Dasein's relation to "beings [*Seienden*] encountered within-the-world" (*Sein und Zeit*, 327; *Being and Time*, 375, trans. mod.), and not with caring for others.

2. As Falque puts it, "*I* become the *object* of my pain and by becoming it I accordingly *objectify* myself. The lived experience of suffering is practically no longer mine because the self [*le moi*] destroys itself [*se détruit*] through suffering. I who believed that here or there I had a hurt (pain), now I become *only this* hurt (suffering)" (TE 61/97, trans. mod.).

3. For an examination of both the dangers of imagination and its great value for the pursuit of justice, see Richard Kearney, *Poetics of Imagining: From Husserl to Lyotard* (London: HarperCollins Academic, 1991), especially "Afterwords: Vive l'imagination," 210–32.

4. See in particular pages 19–26 of Richard Kearney, "The Wager of Carnal Hermeneutics," in *Carnal Hermeneutics*, ed. Richard Kearney and Brian Treanor, 15–56 (New York: Fordham University Press, 2015). Later in this essay, discussing Merleau-Ponty, Kearney takes care to note that touch does not close the gap between self and other: "the gap makes all the difference, preventing fusion and keeping open the task of transit and translation between self and other" (ibid., 39). For a more in-depth account of Aristotle's analysis of touch, see Richard Kearney, *Touch* (New York: Columbia University Press, 2021), chapter 2, "Philosophies of Touch: From Aristotle to Phenomenology," 33–59.

5. Indeed, there is a long tradition of friendships by letter. Consider, for instance, Carolinne White's discussion of friendships by letter in the patristic era, "Friendship in Absence: Some Patristic Views," in *Friendship in Medieval Europe*, ed. Julian Haseldine (Gloucestershire: Sutton Publishing, 1999), 68–84. White observes that "there were deemed to be ways of counteracting the threat of friendship's dissolution through separation. It is clear that there was a belief, among Christians as among many pagans, that they could overcome separation if they continued to hold one another in their thoughts and affections. [. . .] A more practical way was to maintain communication by letter" (72–73). She notes further that "most fundamentally [fourth-century Christian friends] regard letters as offering the addressee tangible proof of his friend's affection and as providing a means of fostering that affection" (74), a view that remains as applicable today as in the fourth century. Even so, White points out that the patristics' letters to absent friends reveal that "besides the positive feeling that it is possible to maintain friendships by means of letters, there exists also a feeling that letters are in fact only a disappointing second best, unable to reproduce the satisfaction of meeting in person" (80).

6. Consider that the Name of God is unsayable not because it is meaningless but because it is too great for humans to say. At the risk of entering into theology, I propose that in the anonymity of the Other who exceeds any possible name, we may hear an echo of the divine Name and thus a reminder that each person bears the likeness of God.

7. To avoid confusion, it is also worth distinguishing Stein's account of empathy from "the theory of association [*Assoziationstheorie*]," which she describes and differentiates from her own position: "I see someone stamp his feet. I remember how I myself once stamped my feet at the same time as my previous fury is presented to me. Then I say to myself, 'this is how furious he is now.' Here the other's fury itself is not given but its existence is inferred. By an intuitive representation, my own fury, I seek to draw it near. By contrast, empathy posits being immediately [*unmittelbar*] as a perceived act, and it reaches its object directly without representation" (PE 26/24). According to the theory of association, I do not perceive the other's emotion but only her actions, and I then associate her actions with my own emotion. For Stein, however, it is because the self and the other person are beings of a similar type that the self is able to perceive what the other person is experiencing without relying on either analogies or associations—although those perceptions may well be erroneous. Perceiving others' experiences involves interpretation, but it is not a matter of establishing inferences or associations that relate others to the self, as if the self took precedence over others.

8. It is worth noting another, related point of disagreement with Stein's account of the self in *The Problem of Empathy*. She writes that it is "by the help of empathy" that I "obtain the same world's second and third appearance which are independent of my perception": my primordial perception of the world is

mine, and then by perceiving that others also perceive it I understand that it exists independently of myself (PE 72/64). I have argued, in contrast, that the self's perception of the world is always already conditioned by the self's relation to the Other. To be sure, Stein does nuance the point considerably, arguing that "the constitution [*Konstitution*] of the foreign individual [is] a condition for the full constitution of our own individual" (PE 99/88). I maintain, however, that there is no constitution of the individual, even a partial one, without the Other. Previous chapters have already discussed the constitution of the self and its world through the self's relation to the Other, and the following chapter further pursues these points by arguing that fidelity creates the self.

Chapter 6

1. One may ask whether the notion of spontaneity entails that fidelity precedes interpretation. In reply, I note first that to encounter spontaneity or the secret as such is already an interpretive act. Fidelity to the Other does constitute the self, however, and so without fidelity the self would not exist as interpretive. In that sense, fidelity precedes interpretation, but the self is constituted as interpretive from the start.

2. It is worth noting that Levinas does find in Descartes an encounter with the absolutely Other: Levinas writes that "the *cogito* in Descartes rests on the other who is God and who has put the idea of infinity in the soul, who had taught it, and has not, like the Platonic master, simply aroused the reminiscence of former visions" (TI 85/86). It remains, though, that Cartesianism, if not always Descartes himself, emphasizes the ego over the Other.

3. Marcel affirms elsewhere that the other person's death is of still greater importance than my own: "each one participates in being-against-death, not only in virtue of a *Drang*, an instinct of preservation, but much more profoundly and intimately against the death of the being whom he loves and who for him counts infinitely more than himself, to the point of his being, not by his nature but by his vocation, decentered or polycentered" (Gabriel Marcel, *Pour une sagesse tragique et son au-delà* [Paris: Plon, 1968], 309. *Tragic Wisdom, Including Conversations between Paul Ricœur and Gabriel Marcel*, trans. Stephen Jolin and Peter McCormick [Evanston: Northwestern University Press, 1973], 212, trans. mod.).

4. Thus for Marcel, a Christian, it is fidelity to God that anchors all other fidelities—much as for Thomas Aquinas, it is friendship for God that makes possible charitable love for all people. While I share this religious conviction and agree with Marcel that it is a legitimate subject of philosophical investigation, it is also my view that this analysis of how fidelity creates the self holds whether or not the wager against death is actually fulfilled in a final resurrection. A fuller analysis of the notion of resurrection and its implications

is outside the scope of this book, but it is worth addressing one possible concern that is immediately relevant to the topic of friendship. One might argue that the Christian is not genuinely toward-the-friend's-death, at least if the friend is also a Christian, because death no longer represents a genuine loss. Françoise Dastur concludes that because Christianity teaches that the dead will be raised, "one has to look elsewhere for an illustration of a real assumption of mortality" (*La Mort: Essai sur la finitude*, rev. ed. [Paris: PUF, 2007], 42; *Death: An Essay on Finitude*, trans. John Llewelyn [London: Athlone, 1996], 14). Her criticism is of the Christian view of death in general and so does not concern only the death of the Other, but her criticism does encompass the notion that the death of the friend is not a real loss. Regarding the death of the Other, my response is twofold. First, it is still true for the Christian that she did not choose to exist within finitude and that in this world one's own death and the friend's death stand as horizons of one's finitude. Religious faith in resurrection—one's own or the friend's—comes only after the primordial confrontation with death as the horizon of finitude. In this regard, my conclusion draws on Emmanuel Falque's remarks concerning one's own death in GG chapter 2, 31–49/10–21. Second, I argue that the friend's death is, for the Christian, a surrender of the friend even from the standpoint of faith in the resurrection; indeed, for the Christian it is a sign of the absolute renunciation of the friend to God that is demanded of us. The Christian must, therefore, assume the other's death as the sign of a radical separation even as she hopes for the friend's resurrection. The Christian's experience of mourning will differ from that of the atheist, but it does involve a genuine experience of separation and renunciation. Space does not permit a more detailed analysis of this point here, but I intend to take it up elsewhere.

5. Marcel also considers the parent-child relation as one that must involve fidelity (see TMF 124–26/90–92). The parents' rearing of the child and the child's obedience to the parents clearly differ from the responsibilities that friends have toward each other; mutual translation of the world does occur in parent-child relationships, and in this way these relationships resemble friendship, but this translation occurs within the context of these unique duties that the parents and child have toward each other. The parent-child relationship is also distinct in that parents are not inherently toward-the-child's-death: as the child is supposed to outlive the parents, when this expectation is defied, the parents mourn a violation of the natural order of events in mourning the death of their child.

6. Emmanuel Falque and Richard Kearney, "Embrace and Differentiation: A Phenomenology of Eros," in *Somatic Desire: Recovering Corporeality in Contemporary Thought*, ed. Sarah Horton, Stephen Mendelsohn, Christine Rojcewicz, and Richard Kearney (Lanham, MD: Lexington Books, 2019), 87. The text is a conversation between Falque and Kearney.

7. Falque and Kearney, "Embrace and Differentiation," 87.

8. For an insightful analysis of Marcel's understanding of love as "the total gift of self, in which the self forever surrenders itself to the other, for the sake of the other in service to the other," see Zachary Willcutt, "Marcel and Augustine on Immortality: The Nothingness of the Self and the Exteriorization of Love as the Way to Eternity," *Marcel Studies* 5, no. 1 (2020): 1–18 (quotation from page 9).

9. One might ask how this statement fits with the description of a text as the "so-called original." The point of the phrase "so-called original" is to indicate that any text is always already a translation, not to claim that it was unoriginal in the sense of being predetermined. The phrase in no way denies that the text is an unforeseen and unforeseeable creation; indeed, a translation from one language to another is also an unforeseen and unforeseeable creation and is in this sense original.

10. The question of fidelity and infidelity in translating becomes still more pressing when it is a matter of sacred scripture. The Christian tradition admits the translation of its scripture, and the Protestant branches of Christianity have been marked since their beginnings by an emphasis on translation into the vernacular. What, then, are we to make of the notion that infidelity in translating may be fidelity? A full examination of this question as it applies to translation of the Christian scripture is beyond the scope of this book, but I propose, in brief, that translation may be understood apophatically: the limits of translation force us to confront the impossibility of adequately speaking or writing of God. Note also that when I maintain that infidelity in translating may be fidelity, I am in no way recommending carelessness or the introduction of deliberate errors; the infidelity that is fidelity is the infidelity that is inevitable in translation. Because of the difficulty, even impossibility, of discerning what infidelities, specifically, are and are not inevitable, translation must, as I write below, be undertaken in fear and trembling; yet we should also be thankful that the task has been conferred upon us, for only by the risk of translation can one come to exist as a self.

11. Of Derrida's commentaries on this phrase, all of which wrestle with its paradoxical call to the friends it denies, the one most like the gloss I offer here is the following remark: "Let us note in passing that the logic of this call—'You-my-friends-be-my-friends-and-although-you-are-not-yet-my-friends-you-are-already-since-I-am-calling-you-thus'—comes under the structure and the temporality of what we have been calling on several occasions a messianic teleiopoiesis" (PF 262/235, trans. mod.). Friendship is a matter of creation—*teleiopoiesis*—and a creation that will never be accomplished: in calling out the name of "friend" one hopes in the always-future time of messianicity.

12. The name of justice is, of course, not one that can be taken for granted either. I have considered elsewhere, through a reading of Plato's *Cratylus*, the inadequacy of our accounts of justice, and have argued that "if seeking justice

means attempting to find a thing that could be circumscribed within language and made present, then such a search is misguided, but the *Cratylus* permits us to glimpse an alternative: praying to and for truth and justice, however poorly we may understand them" (Sarah Horton, "The Just as an Absent Ground in Plato's *Cratylus*," *Epoché: A Journal for the History of Philosophy* 25, no. 2 [2021]: 287). The name of "friend," though not mentioned in this dialogue, is another name that can be, as Socrates puts it, "assigned even as a prayer" (Plato, *Cratylus*, 397b4, my translation): one offers up the name of "friend" in hope, without knowing whether it is legitimate.

13. Charles Baudelaire, "The Stranger," in *Paris Spleen*, 1, translation modified.

"— *Qui aimes-tu le mieux, homme énigmatique, dis? ton père, ta mère, ta sœur ou ton frère?*

— *Je n'ai ni père, ni mère, ni sœur, ni frère.*

— *Tes amis?*

— *Vous vous servez là d'une parole dont le sens m'est resté jusqu'à ce jour inconnu*" ("L'Étranger," in *Le Spleen de Paris*, 277).

14. The canonical reading of the poem has interpreted the questions as clichéd demands imposed on the stranger, but as E. S. Burt points out, "Baudelaire [. . .] leaves open the question of which of the two interlocutors might best be called the stranger. The title of the poem, L'Etranger, doesn't say which of the two is the stranger" (E. S. Burt, "Question. Response? 'The Stranger,'" unpublished paper, Nineteenth-Century French Studies conference, Yale University, October, 2010). Her reading of the poem reminds us that we dare not take the questions for granted, that questioning need not be a demand for the sort of answers that would put an end to dialogue and to the play of language.

15. His interlocutor responds only by asking, "Your country? [*Ta patrie?*]" ("L'Étranger," 277; "The Stranger," 1).

Conclusion

1. Anne Dufourmantelle has insightfully commented on the way social media functions as a demand that everything be revealed. She writes that "confession [*l'aveu*] becomes the norm, and therefore whoever 'separates' herself from the communicational flux will potentially be reproached with the unconfessable [*l'inavouable*]. The new totems are Facebook, Instagram, Twitter" (*Défense du secret*

[Paris: Payot, 2015], 40). *Inavouable*, literally "unadmittable" or "unconfessable," generally signifies that which is too shameful to confess: Dufourmantelle's point is that when people are expected to reveal everything, those who do not may be suspected of hiding shameful secrets. That Facebook, Instagram, and Twitter are totems means that they serve to protect those who use them from the threat of shame, for the totem is that which denies the unconfessable: "the interdiction that [the totem] represents cannot even be formulated: it is absolute" (*Défense du secret*, 40). Here the literal meaning of *inavouable* becomes relevant again: it will be not only shameful secrets that are denied but all secrets, including those that quite literally cannot be revealed. For social media, on this analysis, protects against shame by proclaiming that only what is confessed is true; what cannot be confessed then appears as shameful or illusory, so one feels compelled to deny that it exists at all. In this specific passage Dufourmantelle does not refer to that which inherently cannot be fully revealed, but she questions the demand that all be revealed: "Must we always descend into crypts to shine light on them? At what cost will we know everything about ourselves?" (*Défense du secret*, 42). In a later chapter she pursues this consideration of the potential dangers of social media, noting that "the individual that social networks profile has no 'hidden side'; she is supposed to be, in real time, adjustable to changes in the rules of the game and anticipatable" (*Défense du secret*, 93). The obligation to have no secrets amounts to an obligation to be comprehensible for and pliable to the demands of the watching public.

    2. Derrida points out that if one adds an iota subscript and reverses the breath mark on the first letter of the Greek phrase that has been read as meaning "O my friends, there is no friend," it means instead "too many friends, no friend" (PF 235–36/208–09, trans. mod.). He explains, however, that "both [versions of the phrase] say that *one* friend is not (*oudeis philos*). And both declare it against a backdrop of multiplicity ('O friends,' or for him who has 'friends'). [. . .] This multiplicity renders inevitable the taking into account of the political, from the very depth of the most secret secret" (PF 243–44/215–16, trans. mod.). In either case, therefore, we find ourselves confronted with the political, unable to avoid the multiplicity that requires us to count beyond "one" and to calculate. Incidentally, since Derrida does consider both possible meanings of the phrase, Agamben is wrong to claim "not to find any trace of the problem" (the problem, that is, of the copyist's error that may have changed the phrase's meaning from "too many friends, no friend" to "O my friends, there is no friend") in Derrida's *Politics of Friendship* (Giorgio Agamben, *L'amico* [Milan: Nottetempo, 2007], 8; "The Friend," in *What Is an Apparatus? And Other Essays*, trans. David Kishik and Stefan Perdatella [Stanford: Stanford University Press, 2009], 28, trans. mod.). In any case, what each of these readings can teach us is more important than the historical question of what Aristotle actually said; as Derrida observes, "fortunately for us, no orthographic restoration or archived orthodoxy will ever

damage this other, henceforth sedimented archive, this treasure of enticed and enticing texts which will always give us more to think than the guardrails [*garde-fous*] to whose policing one would want to submit them" (PF 234/207, trans. mod.). And even the second, supposedly more straightforward, reading is not as simple as it looks, since it returns us to the question of the political.

Bibliography

Agamben, Giorgio. *L'amico*. Milan: Nottetempo, 2007. "The Friend." In *What Is an Apparatus? and Other Essays*, 25–37. Translated by David Kishik and Stefan Perdatella. Stanford: Stanford University Press, 2009.

Baudelaire, Charles. *Le Spleen de Paris (Petits Poèmes en prose)*. In *Œuvres complètes*, vol. 1, edited by Claude Pichois. Paris: Pléiade, 1975. *Paris Spleen*. Translated by Louise Varèse. New York: New Directions, 1970.

Beistegui, Miguel de. "From the Writing of Desire to the Desire of Writing: Reflections on Proust." In *Somatic Desire: Recovering Corporeality in Contemporary Thought*, edited by Sarah Horton, Stephen Mendelsohn, Christine Rojcewicz, and Richard Kearney, 183–200. Lanham, MD: Lexington Books, 2019.

———. *Jouissance de Proust: Pour une esthétique de la métaphore*. Paris: Éditions Michalon, 2007. *Proust as Philosopher: The Art of Metaphor*. Translated by Dorothée Bonnigal Katz, Simon Sparks, and Miguel de Beistegui. New York: Routledge, 2012.

Bergson, Henri. *La Pensée et le Mouvant*. 1934. Reprint, Paris: PUF, 1960. *The Creative Mind: An Introduction to Metaphysics*. Translated by Mabelle L. Andison. 1946. Reprint, Mineola, NY: Dover, 2007.

Bersani, Leo. "Death and Literary Authority: Proust and Klein." In *Reading Melanie Klein*, edited by John Phillips and Lyndsey Stonebridge, 223–44. London: Routledge, 1998.

———. *Marcel Proust: The Fictions of Life and Art*. 2nd ed. New York: Oxford University Press, 2013.

Blanchot, Maurice. *L'Amitié*. Paris: Gallimard, 1971. *Friendship*. Translated by Elizabeth Rottenberg. Stanford: Stanford University Press, 1997.

———. *L'Écriture du désastre*. Paris: Gallimard, 1980. *The Writing of the Disaster*. 2nd ed., translated by Ann Smock. Lincoln: University of Nebraska Press, 1995.

———. *Pour l'amitié*. Paris: Fourbis, 1996.

Burt, E. S. "Question. Response? 'The Stranger.'" Unpublished paper. Nineteenth-Century French Studies conference. Yale University, October, 2010.
Chantraine, Pierre. *Dictionnaire étymologique de la langue grecque: Histoire des mots*. Klinksieck: Paris, 1991.
Chrétien, Jean-Louis. *La Voix nue: Phénoménologie de la promesse*. Paris: Éditions de Minuit, 1990.
Crépon, Marc. *Le Malin Génie des langues: Nietzsche, Heidegger, Rosenzweig*. Paris: Vrin, 2000.
———. *Vivre avec: La pensée de la mort et la mémoire des guerres*. Paris: Hermann, 2008.
Dastur, Françoise. *La Mort: Essai sur la finitude*. Rev. ed. Paris: PUF, 2007. *Death: An Essay on Finitude*. Translated by John Llewelyn. London: Athlone Press, 1996.
Deleuze, Gilles. *Proust et les signes*. 3rd ed. Paris: PUF, 2014. *Proust and Signs*. Translated by Richard Howard. 1972. Reprint, Minneapolis: Minnesota University Press, 2000.
Derrida, Jacques. *Chaque fois unique, la fin du monde*. Paris: Galilée, 2003.
———. *De la grammatologie*. Paris: Éditions de Minuit, 1967. *Of Grammatology*. Translated by Gayatri Chakravorty Spivak. 1974. Reprint, Baltimore: Johns Hopkins University Press, 1997.
———. "Des tours de Babel." In *Psyché: Inventions de l'autre*, vol. 1, 203–36. Rev. ed. Paris: Galilée, 1987. "Des tours de Babel." Translated by Joseph F. Graham. In *Psyche: Inventions of the Other*, vol. 1, edited by Peggy Kamuf and Elizabeth Rottenberg, 191–225. Stanford: Stanford University Press, 2007.
———. "La Différance." In *Marges de la philosophie*, 1–29. Paris: Les Éditions de Minuit, 1972. "Difference." In *Margins of Philosophy*, 1–28. Translated by Alan Bass. Chicago: University of Chicago Press, 1982.
———. "Violence et métaphysique." In *L'Écriture et la Différence*, 117–228. Paris: Seuil, 1968. "Violence and Metaphysics." In *Writing and Difference*, 79–153. Translated by Alan Bass. Chicago: University of Chicago Press, 1978.
———. "Lettre à un ami japonais." In *Psyché: Inventions de l'autre*, vol. 2, 387–93. Paris: Galilée, 1987. "Letter to a Japanese Friend." Translated by David Wood and Andrew Benjamin. In *Psyche: Inventions of the Other*, vol. 2, edited by Peggy Kamuf and Elizabeth Rottenberg, 1–6. Stanford: Stanford University Press, 2008.
———. *Le Problème de la genèse dans la philosophie de Husserl*. Paris: PUF, 1990. *The Problem of Genesis in Husserl's Philosophy*. Translated by Martin Hobson. Chicago: University of Chicago Press, 2003.
Doubrovsky, Serge. *La Place de la madeleine: Écriture et fantasme chez Proust*. Paris: Mercure, 1974. *Writing and Fantasy in Proust: La Place de la madeleine*. Translated by Carol Mastrangelo Bové with Paul A. Bové. Lincoln: University of Nebraska Press, 1986.

Dufourmantelle, Anne. *Défense du secret*. Paris: Payot, 2015.
Falque, Emmanuel. *Dieu, la chair et l'autre: D'Irénée à Duns Scot*. Paris: PUF, 2008. *God, the Flesh, and the Other: From Irenaeus to Duns Scotus*. Translated by William Christian Hackett. Evanston: Northwestern University Press, 2015.
———. *Le Livre de l'expérience: D'Anselme de Cantorbéry à Bernard de Clairvaux*. Paris: Cerf, 2017.
———. *Parcours d'embûches: S'expliquer*, Paris: Éditions Franciscaines, 2016. *By Way of Obstacles: A Pathway through a Work*. Translated by Sarah Horton. Eugene, OR: Cascade Books, 2022.
Falque, Emmanuel, and Richard Kearney, "Embrace and Differentiation: A Phenomenology of Eros." In *Somatic Desire: Recovering Corporeality in Contemporary Thought*, edited by Sarah Horton, Stephen Mendelsohn, Christine Rojcewicz, and Richard Kearney, 71–89. Lanham, MD: Lexington Books, 2019.
Fitzpatrick, Melissa. "A Nietzschean Ethics of Care?" In *(mis)Reading Nietzsche*, edited by M. Saverio Clemente and Brian J. Cocchiara, 88–111. Eugene, OR: Pickwick Publications, 2018.
———. "Disruption, Conversation, and Ethics: A Study on the Limits of Self-Legislation." PhD diss., Boston College, 2019.
Fos-Falque, Sabine. *Une chair épandue sur le divan*. In Emmanuel Falque and Sabine Fos-Falque, *Éthique du corps épandu suivi de Une chair épandue sur le divan*, 87–165. Paris: Cerf, 2018.
Gschwandtner, Christina M. "Ethics, Eros, or Caritas? Levinas and Marion on the Individuation of the Other." *Philosophy Today* 49, no. 1 (2005): 70–87.
Heidegger, Martin. *Sein und Zeit*. 1927. GA 2. Reprint, Frankfurt am Main: Vittorio Klostermann, 1977. *Being and Time*. Translated by John Macquarrie and Edward Robinson. New York: Harper and Row, 1962.
Horton, Sarah. "Illegible Salvation: The Authority of Language in *The Concept of Anxiety*." In *Authorship and Authority in Kierkegaard's Writings*, edited by Joseph Westfall, 121–37. London: Bloomsbury, 2018.
———. "The Joy of Desire: Understanding Levinas's Desire of the Other as Gift." *Continental Philosophy Review* 51, no. 2 (2018): 193–210.
———. "The Just as an Absent Ground in Plato's *Cratylus*." *Epoché: A Journal for the History of Philosophy* 25, no. 2 (2021): 281–92.
Jullien, Stanislas. "Entretien discordant de Derrida et Levinas autour de la finitude originaire." In *Levinas-Derrida: Lire ensemble*, edited by Danielle Cohen-Levinas and Marc Crépon, 147–74. Paris: Hermann, 2015.
Katz, Claire Elise. "The Voice of God and the Face of the Other." *Journal of Textual Reasoning* 2, no. 1 (2003). http://jtr.shanti.virginia.edu/volume-2-number-1/the-voice-of-god-and-the-face-of-the-other/.
Kearney, Richard. *Anatheism*. New York: Columbia, 2010.
———. "Linguistic Hospitality: The Risk of Translation." *Research in Phenomenology* 49 (2019): 1–8.

———. *On Stories.* New York: Routledge, 2002.
———. *Poetics of Imagining: From Husserl to Lyotard.* London: HarperCollins Academic, 1991.
———. *Strangers, Gods and Monsters: Interpreting Otherness.* New York: Routledge, 2002.
———. *Touch.* New York: Columbia, 2021.
———. "The Wager of Carnal Hermeneutics." In *Carnal Hermeneutics*, edited by Richard Kearney and Brian Treanor, 15–56. New York: Fordham University Press, 2015.
Kierkegaard, Søren. *En literair Anmeldelse.* 1845. Reprinted in *Søren Kierkegaards Skrifter*, vol. 8, 5–106. Copenhagen: Gads Forlag, 2004. *Two Ages: The Age of Revolution and the Present Age: A Literary Review.* Translated by Howard V. Hong and Edna H. Hong. Princeton: Princeton University Press, 1978.
———. *Frygt og Bæven.* 1843. Reprinted in *Søren Kierkegaards Skrifter*, vol. 4, 73–168. Copenhagen: Gads Forlag, 1997. *Fear and Trembling.* Translated by Howard V. Hong and Edna H. Hong, 1–124. In *Fear and Trembling/Repetition.* Princeton: Princeton University Press, 1980.
———. *Kjerlighedens Gjerninger.* 1847. Reprinted in *Søren Kierkegaards Skrifter*, vol. 9. Copenhagen: Gads Forlag, 2004. *Works of Love.* Translated by Howard V. Hong and Edna H. Hong. Princeton: Princeton University Press, 1995.
Kristeva, Julia. *Étrangers à nous-mêmes.* Paris: Gallimard, 1988. *Strangers to Ourselves.* Translated by Leon S. Roudiez. New York: Columbia University Press, 1991.
Ladenson, Elizabeth. "Proust's Case Against Friendship." *Romanic Review* 110, no. 1–4 (2019): 265–85.
———. *Proust's Lesbianism.* Ithaca: Cornell University Press, 1999.
Levi, Primo. *Survival in Auschwitz: The Nazi Assault on Humanity.* Translated by Stuart Woolf. 1958. Reprint, New York: Touchstone, 1996.
Levinas, Emmanuel. *Noms propres.* Montpellier: Fata Morgana, 1976. *Proper Names.* Translated by Michael B. Smith. Stanford: Stanford University Press, 1996.
Lewis, C. S. *The Four Loves.* New York: Harcourt Brace, 1960.
Liddell, Henry George, and Robert Scott. *A Greek-English Lexicon.* Revised by Sir Henry Stuart Jones and Roderick McKenzie. 9th ed. with a revised supplement. Oxford: Clarendon Press: 1996.
Marcel, Gabriel. *Pour une sagesse tragique et son au-delà.* Paris: Plon, 1968. *Tragic Wisdom, Including Conversations between Paul Ricœur and Gabriel Marcel.* Translated by Stephen Jolin and Peter McCormick. Evanston: Northwestern University Press, 1973.
Marion, Jean-Luc. "D'autrui à l'individu: Au-delà de l'éthique." *Studia Phaenomenologica* 2 (2002): 11–30. "From the Other to the Individual." Translated by Arianne Conty. *Levinas Studies* 1 (2005): 99–117.

———. *Étant donné: Essai d'une phénoménologie de la donation*. 2nd ed. Paris: Presses Universitaires de France, 2013. *Being Given: Toward a Phenomenology of Givenness*. 2nd ed. Translated by Jeffrey L. Kosky. Stanford: Stanford University Press, 2002.

———. *Prolégomènes à la charité*. 3rd ed. rev. Paris: Éditions de la Différence, 2007. *Prolegomena to Charity*. Translated by Stephen E. Lewis. New York: Fordham University Press, 2002.

McEvoy, James. "The Other as Oneself: Friendship and Love in the Thought of St. Thomas Aquinas." In *Thomas Aquinas: Approaches to Truth*, edited by James McEvoy and Michael Dunne, 16–37. Cornwall: Four Courts Press, 2002.

Merleau-Ponty, Maurice. *L'institution, la passivité: Notes de cours au Collège de France (1954–1955)*. Paris: Belin, 2015. *Institution and Passivity: Notes from the Collège de France*. Translated by Leonard Lawlor. Evanston: Northwestern University Press, 2010.

Münchberg, Katharina. "Freundschaft ohne Freunde. Marcel Prousts *Recherche*." In *Freundschaft: Theorien und Poetiken*, edited by Katharina Münchberg and Christian Reidenbach, 205–16. München: Wilhelm Fink Verlag, 2012.

Newmark, Kevin. *Beyond Symbolism: Textual History and the Future of Reading*. Ithaca: Cornell University Press, 1991.

Nietzsche, Friedrich. *Also Sprach Zarathustra: Ein Buch für Alle und Keinen*. 1883–1885. Reprinted in Kritische Studienausgabe Band 4, edited by Giorgio Colli and Mazzino Montinari. Berlin: De Gruyter, 1999. *Thus Spoke Zarathustra: A Book for All and None*. Edited by Adrian del Caro and Robert B. Pippin. Translated by Adrian del Caro. Cambridge: Cambridge University Press, 2006.

———. *Die fröhliche Wissenschaft*. 1882. Reprinted in Kritische Studienausgabe Band 3, edited by Giorgio Colli and Mazzino Montinari. Berlin: De Gruyter, 1999. *The Gay Science*. Edited by Bernard Williams. Translated by Josefine Nauckhoff. Cambridge: Cambridge University Press, 2001.

Nygren, Anders. *Agape and Eros*. Translated by Philip S. Watson. Philadelphia: The Westminster Press, 1953.

Penrose, Roger. *The Road to Reality: A Complete Guide to the Laws of the Universe*. London: Jonathan Cape, 2004.

Perrin, Joseph M., and Gustave Thibon. *Simone Weil telle que nous l'avons connue*. Paris: Éditions du Vieux Colombier, 1952. *Simone Weil as We Knew Her*. Translated by Emma Crauford. London: Routledge, 2003.

Plato. Κρατύλος *[Cratylus]*. In *Platonis Opera*, edited by John Burnet. Oxford: Oxford University Press, 1903. Perseus Digital Library. http://data.perseus.org/citations/urn:cts:greekLit:tlg0059.tlg005.perseus-grc1:383a.

Ricœur, Paul. *Soi-même comme un autre*. Paris: Seuil, 1990. *Oneself as Another*. Translated by Kathleen Blamey. Chicago: University of Chicago Press, 1992.

Sartre, Jean-Paul. *L'Être et le Néant*. 1943. Reprint, Paris: Gallimard, 1976. *Being and Nothingness*. Translated by Sarah Richmond. New York: Washington Square Press, 2018.
Schacter, Daniel L. *The Seven Sins of Memory: How the Mind Forgets and Remembers*. New York: Houghton Mifflin, 2001.
Scotus, John Duns. "Six Questions on Individuation from His Ordinatio II. d. 3, part 1, qq. 1–6." In *Five Texts on the Medieval Problem of Universals: Porphyry, Boethius, Abelard, Duns Scotus, Ockham*, 57–113. Translated and edited by Paul Vincent Spade. Indianapolis: Hackett, 1994.
Silesius, Angelus. *Der Cherubinischer Wandersmann*. Jena: Diederichs, 1905.
Tatranský, Tomáš. "A Reciprocal Asymmetry? Levinas's Ethics Reconsidered." *Ethical Perspectives* 15, no. 3 (2008): 293–307.
Torrell, Jean-Pierre. *Saint Thomas d'Aquin, maître spirituel: Initiation 2*. Freiburg: Éditions Universitaires Fribourg Suisse, 1996.
Treanor, Brian. *Aspects of Alterity: Levinas, Marcel, and the Contemporary Debate*. New York: Fordham University Press, 2006.
Udoff, Alan. "Levinas and the Question of Friendship." *Levinas Studies* 1 (2005): 139–56.
Verkerk, Willow. *Nietzsche and Friendship*. London: Bloomsbury, 2019.
White, Carolinne. "Friendship in Absence: Some Patristic Views." In *Friendship in Medieval Europe*, edited by Julian Haseldine, 68–84. Gloucestershire: Sutton Publishing, 1999.
Willcutt, Zachary. "Marcel and Augustine on Immortality: The Nothingness of the Self and the Exteriorization of Love as the Way to Eternity." *Marcel Studies* 5, no. 1 (2020): 1–18.

Index

Aelred of Rievaulx, 8, 18, 21–23, 28, 33, 143, 146, 172, 174n4, 175n11–12
Agamben, Giorgio, 194n2
agape, 18–19, 50
alterity, 8–11, 14, 16, 18–19, 22, 33, 36–38, 64, 80, 94–95, 97–101, 107, 121, 130–31, 133–34, 148–50, 153, 172, 178n20
amicitia, 8, 18–23, 29, 172, 174n4, 7–8, 175n9, 11
amor, 18–21, 174n7–9, 174–75n9
Aristotle, 2–3, 8–9, 12–19, 21–22, 33, 36, 45, 56, 58, 63–66, 74, 76, 82, 84–85, 93, 127–28, 158, 169–70, 175n11, 179n1, 188n4, 194n2
art, 90, 91–94, 100, 104–108, 111, 114, 120–21, 139, 142, 157, 185n15, 185–86n17, 187n20; artist, 89, 91–94, 99, 103, 106, 108, 111, 116, 121, 142, 183n5, 186n18

Baudelaire, Charles, 2–3, 164
being-there-for, 123–29, 135
Beistegui, Miguel de, 94, 116, 182n2
Benjamin, Walter, 154
Benveniste, Émile, 9–10, 24, 174n3
Bergson, Henri, 156–157

Bersani, Leo, 98, 187n19
Blanchot, Maurice, 6, 36–37, 43–44, 86, 109, 184n13
body, 70, 78, 96, 103, 124, 131–32, 182n3, 185n15
Burt, E. S., 193n14

caritas, 8, 18–21, 179n22
chiasm, 70–71, 73, 138
Chrétien, Jean-Louis, 86
Christianity, 20, 55, 174n4, 191n4; Christian, 18, 20–21, 23, 55, 59, 172, 174n4, 180n5, 181n10, 189n5, 190–91n4, 192n10
citizen, 9, 14–15, 21, 58; citizenship, 3, 10, 17–18, 23
creation, 85, 89, 91, 93, 99, 109, 114–16, 119, 129, 141–43, 145–48, 150, 152–59, 160, 161–62, 186n17, 186n18, 192n9, 192n11
Crépon, Marc, 157–158, 180n7

Dastur, Françoise, 191n4
death, 3, 36, 46–48, 55, 67–68, 72–74, 77–78, 81, 83, 86, 91–92, 95, 97, 99, 107, 116–17, 124–25, 135, 144–45, 147–48, 155–56, 159, 179n4, 190n3, 190–91n4, 191n5
Deleuze, Gilles, 102, 137, 184n13

de Man, Paul, 154–55, 184n13
Derrida, Jacques, 2, 4, 10–11, 24, 27–28, 46, 52, 54–55, 57, 70, 72, 77–80, 82, 102, 106–107, 117, 149–50, 158, 170, 176n8, 177n13, 179–80n4, 180n7, 181n8–9, 183n4, 7, 186n18, 192n11, 194n2
Descartes, René, 103–105, 109, 190n2
difference, 3, 14–16, 22–23, 28, 78–79, 81, 93, 97, 101, 124, 132–33, 150–51, 173n2, 180n7, 188n4
distance, 6, 8, 17, 37, 47, 50, 70, 82–84, 121, 123–24, 127–30, 135, 154–55, 186n18
Doubrovsky, Serge, 185n15, 185–86n17
Dufourmantelle, Anne, 193–94n1

ego, 22, 28, 31, 104–105, 109–11, 132, 137, 143–44, 150, 190n2
egoism, 27, 33, 35, 47, 59, 83, 93, 101, 137
empathy, 129–33, 135, 149, 189n7–8
eros, 3, 19, 26–28, 34, 83, 94–95, 98–101, 103–104, 120–21, 146–48, 173n2
eternity, 50, 67–68, 82, 114, 125, 141, 148, 153, 181n8; eternal, 67–69, 82, 114, 148, 172
ethics, 4, 17, 23, 31–33, 36–38, 40–42, 44–49, 51, 54–56, 60–61, 64, 81, 84, 116, 134–35, 145–46, 148, 153, 162, 171, 176n5, 177n14, 180n7

Falque, Emmanuel, 39, 67–69, 81–82, 85, 124–25, 128, 135, 168, 175n12, 181n8, 188n1–2, 191n4
fidelity, 4–6, 23, 28, 33, 42, 51, 53–55, 57–61, 77–79, 81–83, 90, 94, 107–108, 110, 117, 119–21, 123–31, 135, 141–46, 148–49, 151–56, 158–59, 161–63, 165, 170, 172, 178n18, 187n21, 190n1, 4, 191n5, 192n10
finitude, 4–5, 63, 66–72, 74–75, 77, 81–85, 87, 123, 150, 156, 163, 172, 180n5, 7, 181n8, 191n4
Fitzpatrick, Melissa, 49, 179n24
foreign, 15, 38, 76–77, 100–101, 110–111, 130–32, 171, 184n10, 190n8; foreigner, 9–11, 14–15, 110, 150, 174n1, 184n10
Fos-Falque, Sabine, 182n3

gift, 6, 20, 28, 46, 48–51, 57, 74, 109–10, 117, 120, 122, 125–26, 129, 134–35, 139, 145, 150, 161, 163–64, 167, 177n14, 192n8
God, 8, 18–23, 28, 46, 52–55, 58, 66–68, 81, 83, 85, 143, 172, 174–75n9, 175n11, 178–79n22, 180n5, 181n8,10, 189n6, 190n2, 190–91n4, 192n10
Gödel, Kurt, 151
Gschwandtner, Christina M., 176n5

Heidegger, Martin, 7, 23–28, 47, 67–68, 83, 125, 188n1
Heraclitus, 24–25, 27, 148
hospitality, 4, 8–12, 16, 18, 23–26, 35–36, 100–101, 110–12, 134, 139, 145, 149, 171, 174n3, 184n12
hostility, 4, 8–12, 16, 18, 23, 26, 58, 101, 112, 139, 174n3

interpretation, 99–105, 107–108, 110–12, 114–15, 117, 119, 120, 129, 132–35, 160, 176n5, 182n4, 189n7, 190n1
ipseity, 8–11, 14–15, 18–20, 22–23, 33, 35–36, 64, 94, 99, 121, 183n4

Jullien, Stanislas, 180n7

justice, 11–14, 34, 38, 49, 51–58, 60–61, 74, 81, 127, 146, 163, 170–171, 175n1, 188n3, 192–93n12

Katz, Claire Elise, 178n22
Kearney, Richard, 11, 28, 70, 112, 128, 147–48, 184n12–13, 188n4
Kierkegaard, Søren, 53–54, 59, 168–69, 178n20, 22
Kristeva, Julia, 15, 184n13

lack(s), 13–14, 19, 44, 50, 63–69, 74–75, 80–81, 107, 153
Ladenson, Elizabeth, 182–83n4 184n8
language, 4–6, 10–11, 24–26, 28, 35, 42, 47, 56–57, 60, 77, 79–80, 83, 87, 91, 94, 101, 106–12, 114, 116–17, 120–21, 128–29, 134, 148–58, 171–72, 174n7, 175n2, 178n20, 181n10, 185–86n17, 187n19, 192n9, 193n12, 14
Levi, Primo, 177n11
Levinas, Emmanuel, 4, 31–41, 44, 46–51, 54–58, 60–61, 64, 71, 86, 93, 116, 126, 145, 146, 148–50, 152, 162, 170, 175n1–2,4, 175–76n5, 177n14, 178n22, 179n24, 3, 180n7, 184n13, 187n21, 190n2
Lewis, C. S., 177n10
limit(s), 5, 10, 63, 67–69, 77–78, 81–82, 85–87, 100, 127, 131, 139, 142, 156, 169–171, 192n10

Marcel, Gabriel, 123–24, 128, 131, 142–44, 146, 148 190n3–4, 191n5, 192n8
Marion, Jean-Luc, 163, 175–76n5
marriage, 95, 145–47
McEvoy, James, 19 174n7, 174n8
memory, 78, 97, 112–16, 147, 159–61, 163, 185n14–16, 187n19

Merleau–Ponty, Maurice, 69–71, 188n23, 4
Montaigne, Michel de, 2, 42–44, 46, 51–52, 142, 158, 169–70
mourning, 46, 48, 72, 78, 85, 116, 129, 147–48, 163, 180n7, 191n4–5
Münchberg, Katharina, 120
mutuality, 31, 50–51, 71, 178n18

Newmark, Kevin, 185n15, 186–87n19
Nietzsche, Friedrich, 6, 60, 179n23–24
Nygren, Anders, 18–20

Other, 1, 4–5, 10–11, 22, 27, 31–42, 46–58, 60–61, 64, 71, 75, 80, 90, 93, 95, 97–107, 109–12, 114–17, 120–21, 123, 125–27, 129–35, 139, 144–53, 156, 158–59, 161–62, 164, 167, 170–71, 175n4, 175–76n5, 177n14, 178n19, 179n3, 182n4, 184n12, 185–86n17, 186n18, 187n21, 188n1, 189n6, 190n8, 1–2, 191n4

Penrose, Roger, 151
phenomenology, 39, 82
philia, 8–9, 12–21, 23–24, 26–29, 36, 78, 93, 127, 172, 175n11; philos, 8–12, 16, 82, 174n1, 3, 194n2; philoi, 8–14, 16–17, 26
philosophia, 7–8, 23–29, 83, 172
philosophy, 4, 7, 18, 23–24, 27–28, 33, 135–39, 162, 172
philotes, 8–12, 16, 24–26, 172, 174n2–3
Plato, 75, 135, 172, 190n2, 192–93n12
polis, 8–9, 11–18, 20–21, 56, 101, 172
politics, 12, 18, 32, 52, 171; political, 3, 6, 12–13, 17, 20–21, 32–33, 56–58, 64, 77, 81, 163, 170–72, 194–95n2

preference, 33, 40, 42–44, 51–52, 59, 170
presence, 5, 23, 33–35, 37, 72, 74, 95, 99–100, 113, 117, 119, 123, 127–28, 184n13, 186n18
promise, 5, 35, 44–45, 50, 82, 86, 95, 126, 130, 135, 139, 141–45, 151, 153, 156–59, 161, 163, 167–68, 171–72
Proust, Marcel, 5, 89–90, 102, 104–105, 135, 137, 141, 153, 157, 160–61, 171, 182n4, 184n8, 13, 186n17, 19, 187n21

reciprocity, 9–11, 16, 23–24, 32–33, 36, 48–49, 71, 134, 148, 163
Ricœur, Paul, 5–6, 49–50, 110–11, 148, 178n17, 184n10, 12–13, 187n20
risk, 5, 8, 11, 15, 18, 29, 60, 106, 113, 127, 139, 161, 164, 167, 169, 172, 192n10

Same, 10–11, 27, 36, 64, 81, 89, 98, 101, 111, 120–21, 126, 182n4, 184n12
Sartre, Jean-Paul, 40, 177n9, 184n11
Schacter, Daniel L., 160
Scotus, John Duns, 39–40, 55, 176n6–7
secret, 6, 40, 42–43, 52, 54, 58, 60, 77, 78, 81, 85–86, 107, 143, 164, 167–69, 172, 190n1, 194n1, 194n2
Silesius, Angelus, 177n11
similarity, 93, 132–34, 149, 186n17
singularity, 2–3, 37–40, 42–43, 46–47, 51, 55–58, 61, 72–73, 80–81, 84, 86, 93, 101, 107, 115–16, 145, 153, 157–58, 161–62, 165, 167, 169, 171–72, 177n14, 186n17
social media, 1, 128, 167–69, 194n1

Socrates, 75–77, 102, 135–39, 193n12
solitude, 35, 48, 65, 71, 74–75, 89, 93–95, 97, 99, 106–107
Stein, Edith, 129–32, 189n7, 189–90n8
stranger(s), 8–15, 17–18, 21, 23, 26, 28, 34, 73, 84, 89, 93, 98, 105, 109–10, 120, 133, 139, 174n1, 184n10, 193n14

Tatranský, Tomáš, 49
temporality, 34, 49–50, 59, 67–68, 82, 108, 146–47, 156, 164, 181n8, 192n11; temporal, 25, 67–69, 82, 148, 156–57, 181n8–9
Thomas Aquinas, 8, 18–21, 23, 28, 53, 68, 143, 172, 174n7, 174n9, 190n4
Torrell, Jean-Pierre, 20
totality, 27–28, 32, 37–38, 42, 48, 81, 109, 116, 149, 168, 179n4
touch, 28, 70, 96, 128, 185n15, 188n4
transformation, 20, 66, 71–73, 75, 79–80, 85, 89, 105, 161–62, 181n8
translation, 4, 6, 19, 25, 27, 79–80, 82–83, 86, 90, 106–108, 111, 117–20, 122–23, 129, 133–35, 149–59, 161–62, 171, 181n10, 184–85n13, 186n17–18, 187n19, 21, 188n4, 191n5, 192n9–10
Treanor, Brian, 148–50

Udoff, Alan, 33
universal, 6, 23, 37–38, 42, 54, 56–58, 61, 81, 86–87, 107–108, 119–20, 152–53, 175–76n5, 178n20; universality, 55, 61; universalization, 57, 59, 81, 134
unknowable, 2, 5, 33, 42–44, 63, 77, 79, 83, 90, 98–99, 101, 105, 107, 115, 123, 129–30, 161–63, 165; unknowability, 76, 84, 100, 106, 121, 127, 162, 164
Verkerk, Willow, 179n23

virtue, 13–14, 17, 22, 32, 34, 40, 41, 45, 52, 56, 57, 63, 74, 78, 85, 93, 162–63

Weil, Simone, 83–84
White, Carolinne, 189n5
Willcutt, Zachary, 192n8

wonder, 136–37, 139, 142, 150
writing, 4–6, 7, 84, 90–91, 100, 105–12, 114, 117, 119, 120–21, 129, 170, 183n7, 184n8, 186n17, 186n18

xenos, 9–11

www.ingramcontent.com/pod-product-compliance
Lightning Source LLC
Chambersburg PA
CBHW020654230426
43665CB00008B/436